Help Your Child Succeed at School

Help Your Child Succeed at School

Hilary Wilce

First published in Great Britain in 2004 by
Piatkus Books Ltd
5 Windmill Street, London W1T 2JA
email: info@piatkus.co.uk

Reprinted 2004, 2007

A catalogue record for this book is available from the British Library

ISBN 0 7499 2491 8

Text design by Tim Lattimore
Edited by Carol Franklin

This book has been printed on paper manufactured with respect for the environment using wood from managed sustainable resources

Typeset by Palimpsest Book Production Limited, Polmont, Stirlingshire
Printed and bound in Denmark by
Nørhaven Paperback A/S, Viborg

Contents

Part Three: School-related issues – and how to deal with them

Acknowledgements

MANY FRIENDS, PARENTS and colleagues have contributed to this book – thanks to them all. Special thanks to Dr Mary Cameron, Corinne Julius, Jan Maulden, Hilary McKendrick and Jane Waller for reading the draft manuscript and making suggestions. And an enormous thank you to the many heads and teachers who have allowed me to visit their schools, quiz them about education and sit in on their lessons over the years. Much of this book has grown out of what I have seen in their classrooms.

The extract on pages 12–13 comes from *Handsworth Revolution: The Odyssey of a School*, by David Winkley, published by Giles de la Mare; the extract on page 34 comes from *Could Do Better, School Reports of the Great and Good*, edited by Catherine Hurley, published by Pocket Books; the extract on pages 162–3 comes from *Help Your Child to Succeed* by Bill Lucas and Alistair Smith, published by Network Educational Press Ltd; the extract on page 352 comes from *Creating Kids Who Can* by Jean Robb and Hilary Letts, published by Hodder & Stoughton. All extracts are reproduced with permission.

Introduction

THIS IS NOT a book about how to help your child come top of the class, win all the school's sporting trophies or be the most popular person in the playground. It's about much more important things than that. It's about how to help your child to be as happy and fulfilled at school as possible, to discover who they are and learn how to make the most of any opportunities that come their way.

Because this doesn't always happen. In fact, it very often doesn't happen. I have been visiting schools and writing about education for more than twenty years and have long been struck by how dramatically children's learning can blossom or falter according to the conditions we give them in which to grow. But the seed of this book was sown not in a school at all, but at the supper table of friends who were trying to decide which primary school to send their daughter to. Since they lived in a part of London where the schools differed hugely from each other, it was a crucial decision and I understood why they wanted to go over it, and then over it again (although long before the evening was over, I was badly wishing we could move on to something else!).

The next morning I travelled north, to sit in on a classroom of eight-year-olds and watch an award-winning teacher at work. All should have been well, but somehow it wasn't. Children came in late. They didn't have their rulers. Then they didn't have their pencils. Many were yawning and tired, while others seemed wriggling and restless. One stared blankly out of the window. Another picked at her nail polish and giggled with a friend. The well-prepared lesson had to be repeatedly interrupted for admonitions, and all this energetic teacher's many talents still failed to galvanise a class that somehow seemed both torpid and distracted. 'I'm sorry,' she said at breaktime, 'but Monday mornings are always a struggle. They just don't come in ready to learn. By about Wednesday we've usually managed to lick them back into shape.'

I thought back to my friends in London, and wondered if, by the time their daughter was eight, they would be putting as much thought and concentration into her schooling as they were at this moment. Would they be thinking about how to send her off to school in the best possible shape for learning? Or would they, like so many of us, believe that once they had packed her off to the school of their choice, their job was mainly over?

Yet research shows that what we do as parents to support our children as they go through school actually matters far more than the kind of school they go to, the quality of teachers in it or the lessons those teachers deliver. Research also shows that parents want to help – nearly three out of four parents surveyed recently in England said they wanted to be more involved in their children's education.

The important thing is to know how to go about it. Because with the right sort of help from us, children will find life in the classroom fun and rewarding. They will build good relationships with teachers and classmates, discover which ways of learning work best for them and learn how to bounce back from setbacks. They will have the kind of healthy bodies and alert minds that make for great learning, develop their learning 'muscles' and acquire good tactics for approaching tests and exams.

How can we help them do all that? After looking closely at the evidence, I've come to believe that it is all a question of knitting together the best of the old and the new into a pattern that's right for our times.

In the past, parents knew important things about raising children (they knew, for example, what science is now confirming, that eating fish is good for the brain). But in recent years much of that traditional wisdom has gone out of the window. Our children urgently need us to rediscover how to pay proper attention to them – without, of course, becoming the kind of neurotic helicopter parents who hover over their every move. We need to remember the benefits of a slower lifestyle, good meals, early bedtimes, regular routines and clear boundaries on behaviour.

But that doesn't mean returning to the bad old days when children were expected to be seen and not heard, and to do, unquestioningly, whatever adults told them. On the contrary, we now know so many new and exciting things about how children learn, and what kind of questioning, encouragement and talking best wakes up their brains. If we take time to understand these, and act on them, we will lay down rock-solid foundations on which our children will be able to build right through school and beyond – vital in today's fast-moving world where, all their lives, they are going to have to carry on acquiring new skills and knowledge.

This book aims to help parents in several ways.

- It explains how schools work, who's who in them, what they teach, and how children are expected to learn, so that parents understand the world their children are going off into each day, and can see how best to give support – after all, schools now are very different from how they used to be in 'our day', and secondary schools are very different places from primaries. It also explains what the very best schools are doing about some issues, so parents can know if there are areas where they might want to nudge their children's school to do better. And it explains how schools are ever-changing places, constantly adjusting to new teachers, new pupils and changes in the curriculum.
- It looks at research about learning, and about what teachers and other parents have to say about helping children through school, in order to explain the ways in which parents can support their children – and why these work.
- It takes a blow-by-blow look at some of the tough educational issues that face all parents – how to choose a school, what to say to your child about tests and exams, and how to keep a child on track in the switch to secondary school.
- It looks at how to tackle school problems, if they arise, and where to look for further advice and help.

It is also arranged in three broad sections, so readers can easily find what matters most to them.

- The first section covers the basics of how schools work, and how we can support our children as they go through the school system.
- The middle section deals with the important broad questions of how we can best help our children develop the brains and bodies they need to be great learners.
- The final section looks in more detail at individual issues such as homework, out-of-school learning and school problems.

The book can be read cover-to-cover, or kept to hand to be dipped into whenever a particular situation or dilemma arises.

In the course of my work, people often ask me if I'm a teacher. I'm not. But I think that much of the value of this book is that it is written by an outsider, with a reporter's eye for what actually goes on in the classroom, and how parents and teachers talk about it. As a result, it doesn't pretend that all schools are wonderful, or that all teachers are perfect. It knows full well the kind of problems that arise, and aims to help parents deal with schools as they actually are, not as we would all like them to be.

On the other hand I am a parent. My three children have been to a variety of schools both here and in the US. So I do know at first hand the kinds of things that come up. But I definitely haven't written this book because, as a parent, I've known the answers. On the contrary, I have made just about every mistake that it is possible for a parent of school-age children to make. I've jumped to wrong conclusions, pushed my children too hard or not hard enough, criticised them when what they needed was praise, handled meetings with their teachers badly and failed to take action when they needed my help. Now, as the last one comes towards the end of her school years, and it's far too late to be of any use to them, I feel I might be finally seeing what it takes to be a good school parent. If so, I hope some of it seeps on to the pages of this book where it will be useful to others.

And, finally, a quick word about definitions. School here means primary and secondary schools – this book looks at children moving on from nursery schools and other sorts of pre-schooling.

Parent here means anyone with care of a child – natural, step and foster parents, grandparents and carers. School means any kind of school – public or private, mainstream or specialist (unless specifically stated otherwise). The pronouns 'he' and 'she' are used in alternative chapters to describe a child. This book applies equally to boys and girls, except where specific gender issues are talked about.

Part One

You, your child and the school system

CHAPTER ONE

Laying the foundations of success at school

'Whether you believe you can do a thing or not, you are right.' – HENRY FORD

IF YOU HAVE picked up this book, you probably have a child at school. And the chances are that your child is doing all right there. Because, although problems with school do arise – and one of the purposes of this book is to help you deal with them if they do – most children go off to school fairly happily in the morning, and do more or less OK there once they arrive.

But this is a book about how children can enjoy school even more, and do even better. Because virtually all children have a huge, untapped potential to do that, and parents are the people who can make it happen.

Why parents, and not schools? Well, first and foremost it is parents who shape the attitudes of their children towards life and learning, and positive attitudes are beyond price when it comes to getting the most out of school.

In fact parental influence is increasingly emerging as the single, most crucial ingredient of school success. According to recent government research tracking the progress of 3,000 pre-schoolers, good parenting can make a staggering

10 per cent difference to a child's educational performance – far more of a difference than a school can make. And it doesn't matter what sort of background you come from, or how good your own education was. It's the involvement that counts.

Also, although we now know a huge and exciting amount about how to unlock any child's individual potential, frankly even the best school in the country can't always do it. All schools are constrained by time, resources and human fallibility – and teachers are a varied bunch, good, bad, indifferent, just like the rest of us. They have a curriculum to get through, and large numbers of children to deal with. Anyone who sits in on a lot of lessons quickly sees how compromise has to be the name of their game. They can't keep every pupil with them for every minute of the school day, and especially not if they themselves aren't world champions at keeping order, or have pupils in their class who don't want to learn. On the contrary, all teachers constantly sacrifice opportunities to help individual children in order to keep the whole class on track. In fact, many parents who sit in on classes are shocked to see how little direct teaching their children actually get in the course of a normal school day, once all the comings and goings, linings up, changing rooms, getting organised, sorting out problems, answering questions, dealing with interruptions and all the rest of it are gone through.

In addition, many teachers are dealing with increasingly difficult behaviour. And just one or two disruptive children in a class can drain off such serious amounts of time and energy that other pupils start to play up as well. Try as they might – and they do – teachers just can't offer the kind of tailor-made support and encouragement that every child needs if they are to reach as high as they are able.

But parents can. In fact, reseach done for the charity the Campaign for Learning has calculated that parents who take an active interest in their children's education can help them do as much as 25 per cent better than children whose parents aren't interested. And even if the research wasn't there to prove it, teachers know it in their bones. 'Show me a child who's doing really well at my school,' said one primary school head, 'and I'll show you a child with a home that's right there behind them.'

Parents can have an influence right through school. According to the Department for Education and Skills (DfES), children whose parents are very involved with their schooling progress between 15 and 17 per cent more in reading and maths between the ages of 11 and 16 than other children.

However, this absolutely DOES NOT mean that you have to turn your home into a second classroom. You don't have to become the kind of neurotic home-educator who plays Mozart to your newborn, and hauls your pre-schooler off around museums and galleries. You don't need to spend hours at your child's elbow as they do their homework, or shell out for a tutor every time a test looms up. In fact, if you do, it probably won't work. Parents like this often scratch their heads over why their copious investments of time and money haven't brought them the results they were counting on – only a resentful, dependent and burned-out child.

What you do have to do is tune up your parental antennae to the fact that everything that happens in your child's life, from waking up in the morning, to the bedroom light going off at night, feeds into how much they are going to get out of their school day. And become aware, too, how even the smallest things, and those things which appear to have nothing whatsoever to do with the classroom, can make a much bigger difference to learning than most of us thought.

This book will look at what those things are, and how they can be harnessed to help. It will explain what goes on in today's schools, so parents can understand more about the opportunities open to their children, and it will explore how children learn, so parents will see how they can back up what their children's teachers are doing.

But first of all, what exactly is school success? And how can we lay the foundations for getting it?

David Winkley, a wise and gifted former Birmingham school head teacher, whose ground-breaking ideas about children's potential now influence primary schools across Britain, observed at the end of his long career that the children who do best in school 'are those who are quietly determined. There's a point as they grow older when self-motivation becomes the main driving

> *force of progress; and underlying this is self-confidence, and a belief that, come what may, all hurdles will eventually be overcome.' Because of that, he said, he constantly told his pupils to believe in themselves, not to think others were better than they were and to look people in the eye when they spoke to them. And to smile. 'People like people who smile.'*

What is a successful child?

Successful children come in many forms. One mother's definition is, 'One who's comfortable in their own skin and able to socialise effectively'. In the classroom, truly successful children aren't those who come top in every test, but who:

- learn as quickly and well as they can
- have fun as they explore their different talents
- develop good relationships with other people as they do so.

And all three of these things are equally important, and reinforce one another, even though schools have traditionally only measured the first. After all, what's the point of being great at exams, if you can't relish life, or operate successfully in the wider world? So as parents we need at all times to encourage our children's:

- capacity to understand new things
- knowledge and enjoyment of the different facets of themselves
- ability to develop their social skills.

That way, they will steadily gain the confidence and self-belief they absolutely must have if they are to find their feet as successful and independent learners.

Acknowledging success

Success builds on success, especially if progress is recognised and praised. But this can be harder for parents to do than it seems. Sometimes we get so locked on to one particular school goal – moving on to a higher-level reading book, say, or achieving a certain level in a particular test – that the tiny, everyday steps of progress get overlooked. But the child who learns to spell a simple new word, or who manages to negotiate a dispute with a friend without falling out, is every bit as successful as the prodigy who wins a place at Oxford at fifteen. And if you, the child's parent, notice and acknowledge these achievements, it will encourage them like nothing else on this planet.

The different faces of success

Children come in all shapes and sizes, their talents are different and their journey through school will always be their own. As a result, success comes in many guises, and it is crucial that we as parents know this and don't try to force our children into one mould.

Which of the following students, for example – all of

whom I have come across in my life as an education reporter – would you say was the most successful?

- Matthew excelled from the moment he entered school, and was good at everything. He was quiet in lessons, but he got terrific test results, played the piano, and as he got older became an accomplished badminton and hockey player. In the early years of his teens, he spent a lot of time in the school art room, but later gave this up to turn towards the sciences. Both his parents were hospital consultants and it became clear he was heading in the same direction. He got almost all A grades in his GCSEs, and all A grades in his A levels, and won a place to study medicine at Cambridge.
- Carrie was a cheerful, popular girl who whispered and giggled her way through most lessons. She wasn't much interested in sport, or in any other school activities. In fact, she wasn't much interested in school at all, and increasingly her teachers overlooked her, even though she always did moderately well in exams. She was old for her age, and soon liked boys, make-up and going out. When she was sixteen, she half-heartedly wondered about going on to do A levels after her GCSEs, but then she discovered she was pregnant and dropped out to become a teenage mother.
- David was a nightmare at school. He was impulsive, uncoordinated and found it impossible to sit down and concentrate. At nine he still wasn't able to read, and was in trouble for swearing at the teachers and kicking other children. At fourteen he would still take all morning to read a basic primary school reading book, following the one-syllable words with his finger and

sounding them out as he read them. Other pupils accused him of being a bully. His writing was always atrocious, his understanding of things like science and maths rudimentary, and he left school without a single qualification.

On the face of it it seems so simple. Matthew is top of the tree, Carrie is unmemorable and David is a failure. However, life is never that simple, as their later histories show.

- Matthew wasn't actually as clever as he had always seemed. He had had to work like crazy at school to keep up his near-perfect results – and his parents always made sure that he put in the hours of homework he needed to do this. (Alongside also making him stick at his piano and sports practice.) When he said he was interested in art, they made it clear they did not think anything artistic could be a 'proper' job, and he came to see that in their view only medicine counted. When he got five A*s, four As and one B in his GCSEs, he knew they were disappointed with him for not getting all A*s. At Cambridge, among other fast-track students, he began to flounder and question what he was doing. He found the work hard, started to drink, came close to a nervous breakdown and ended up dropping out into what he describes as 'a two-year black hole', where he had to work through a lot of issues about who he really was and what he really wanted to do. He thought about art school, but eventually decided that he really did want to be a doctor, switched to another medical school, and resumed his studies.

- Carrie had her baby, and then quickly had another. She and her boyfriend split up, but Carrie lived near her parents, so she always had help. As a result, she was able to get a part-time job with a building firm where she began to develop an interest in the bookkeeping and accountancy side of the business. When her younger child went to school she set out to build her qualifications in this area at the local further education college, and has recently finished a two-year foundation degree course – the firm has supported her in this because it greatly values her cheerfulness, enterprise and efficiency. She says that no one in her family really cared about school, and it is only now she is older that she has found the motivation and discipline to study for herself. She says she is glad she had her children when she was young enough to enjoy them, and that she has always known she would go on to do something with her life because she has always known she had 'a good head on her shoulders'.
- David is now a young adult who lives at home and works as an assistant at a nearby garden centre. To his parents, it is still a miracle that he is able to hold down a job, since he was born with serious learning difficulties and when he first started school no one held out much hope for him or what he might be capable of. In fact he was never able to join an ordinary secondary school, but his parents moved heaven and earth to find him the right special school place, and once there he made more progress than anyone could have imagined. He left able to read and write basic English, and do some things on the computer. At work, he manages to help customers, and enjoys telling them to 'Have a good

day!' He has learned to control his temper, and with his ready smile has been accepted as part of the team by his workmates. He earns a wage, feels useful and enjoys his life. His story is one of true educational success, brought about by the unflagging love and support of his parents and teachers, and David's own resilience and persistence.

Multiply these stories many thousands of times over – a different story for every child who sets foot in a school – and what you get is a clear picture that success comes in many shapes and forms, is not always instant, and has every bit as much to do with personality, as with inherent brain power or the kind of school a child goes to.

It also has absolutely everything to do with how parents foster their children's sense of themselves. Matthew was born with a first-class mind, but was never helped to build the confidence he needed to stop his pushy parents shaping his life. Carrie's parents may not have rated school highly, but they soaked their daughter in the warmth, self-esteem and optimism that allowed her to build the life she wanted – in her own time. Life dealt David a very poor hand indeed, but the dogged persistence of his parents opened up the best possible learning opportunities for him – while the same dogged determination in himself allowed him to keep working away to make the progress he has.

Providing the bedrock of success

One thing all children must have to become good learners is a sense of security.

If you doubt it, imagine this. You are being told you

have to master a difficult new language, let's say Amharic, but the squiggles on the page are unlike anything you've ever seen before, and make no sense. In addition, you are being expected to do this while you are cold, hungry and frightened about what is going to happen to you when you go home at night. You might get shouted at. You might get beaten. You might not even have any home to go to. The only certainty is that no one is going to care a jot whether you have started to master your Amharic, or not. It's easy to see that what would be hard enough under good conditions, would be virtually impossible under more difficult ones.

Children must be fed and housed and clothed in order to learn. It seems so obvious, yet, shockingly, there may well be children in your child's school who are hungry, poorly clothed and unsure where they are going to be living from one week to the next. Children also need emotional security. Yet thousands go to school from violent, abusive and chaotic backgrounds, and many, many more arrive in the classroom from homes where smaller, but still insidious things – raised voices, unspoken tensions, unpredictable discipline – create such knots in their stomachs that they simply can't concentrate on learning.

As parents, we need to be constantly aware of the way that everything that happens in our home will have a direct and immediate impact on our children's day at school. A house full of life, laughter and caring adults will mean an untroubled child in the classroom, free to learn, but a house of secrets, uncertainties and sharp tongues, will mean the opposite. And this is true whatever a family's background or income. The deputy head of one of the country's most expensive prep schools once told me that the children who broke his heart were those pupils who were picked up every Saturday lunchtime in flashy, expensive cars, and delivered back in them again on Sunday evening, 'but without the emotional small change to get through the week'.

Of course, none of us can control everything that happens at home, but if difficulties and crises are dealt with as sensitively and openly as possible, with an acute awareness of the effect they might be having on young minds, they are unlikely to do much serious damage to the inner core of a child's security.

The four crucial ingredients of school success – and how to foster them

The best learners have four key qualities under their belts. And while, of course, all children have different temperaments, if we do our best to foster these traits we will be helping put in place the very bedrock of success. They are:

- a positive attitude
- persistence
- resilience
- good motivation.

A positive attitude

These are the children who set off for school in the morning believing that they are going to have a good day, learn something interesting and enjoy being with their friends – and sure enough they do!

This attitude towards school stems from a positive attitude they have learned at home, so as parents we need to practise talking to our children in positive ways. We need to:

- praise them for their achievements
- praise them for trying
- encourage them to see themselves as good and capable people.

At the same time, we probably need to work harder at guarding our tongues against those negative epithets that so easily slip out ('Which moron of a child left this rollerblade on the stairs?'). Children who come to believe that they are stupid, hopeless, useless, incompetent, forgetful or lazy won't ever be bouncing into the classroom determined to take on the world. Neither will those who feel they are being compared unfavourably to siblings or peers. Those who are praised, encouraged and made to believe they can be successful at the things they set their mind to, will.

Persistence

This dull and rather unsexy virtue is the glue that sticks everything else together. Just watch a group of toddlers trying to get to grips with their first Duplo set. Their hands are tiny, the pieces seem enormous, the studs won't stick into the holes and banging them against the floor doesn't seem to help. But they try and try and try again until – bingo! – two pieces finally click together to make something excitingly new and different. Imagine that same quality coming into play when a six-year-old is struggling with reading, or a fourteen-year-old is tackling algebra, and you get some idea how crucial this quality is going to be to any child going through school. Yet teachers say that more and more children are coming into their classrooms now wanting to give up on things the very instant they start to get difficult. 'They don't even try,' said one despairing teacher of six-year-olds. 'They just throw down their pencils and say "Miss. Can't do it".'

We need to foster 'grit' or 'stickability' in our children by making clear that mistakes are a normal part of learning, and that persistence pays off. Let them see that we, and other adults, often have to try and try again, to get something right. Praise them for keeping on trying, and if something is really going badly for them, help them deal with their frustration by thinking about ways of doing it differently, or taking a break and then getting back to it.

Resilience

Life isn't always easy, friendly and nice. Much as we ache to protect our children from all things unpleasant, we aren't going to be able to. Once they are out in the great, wide world of school, bad stuff will happen to them. They may have a teacher with a tongue like a whiplash, or come across a playground bully, or fall flat on their face at an important test or exam. What matters is not the setback – everyone has them – but how robustly they are able to deal with it.

We need to build up our children's confidence so that small blows won't knock them off their perch, and help them come to understand how difficult situations can arise. We need to tell them mistakes are an essential part of learning, and talk to them about how there are all kinds of people in the world, who behave in all kinds of different ways, and that problems that result from this are not always their own fault (although sometimes they can be). We need to show them how to look for ways to make a difficult situation better, and how, if nothing works, to learn to let go of the situation and move on in their lives.

Good motivation

Children learn best when they understand why they are doing something, and can see a good reason for mastering it. This doesn't, of course, exclude developing a love of learning for learning's sake, but the truth is that most of us are galvanised by self-interest more than anything else. The head of a large comprehensive school once told the story of 'wild Amy', who was a nightmare at school, and constantly being excluded from lessons. But in home economics she was an angel. 'Amy, I just don't understand,' she said eventually, 'why can you behave in this one lesson, and not in any others.' 'Because,' said Amy, 'I can see the point of this.'

This kind of understanding takes time to root and grow in younger children, but it pays enormous dividends later. Foster it by encouraging them to learn because it is fun and enjoyable, because it helps them to do and understand new things, and because it gives them a good feeling about themselves and their abilities. That way, as they get older, they will come to know how to work for themselves and their own goals, and not just for bribes, or to please other people.

A secondary school maths teacher, with a keen interest in the horses, once pointed out that although many of his former pupils had told him there was no way they could do maths, he often saw them in the betting shop working out complicated odds, at lightening speeds, in their heads. 'But you must realise,' he said solemnly, 'this isn't maths. How could it possibly be maths? They don't do maths. No, it's not maths – it's misplaced optimism.'

CHAPTER TWO

Parents and schools

'Children have never been very good at listening to their elders, but they have never failed to imitate them.' – JAMES BALDWIN

WE'VE LOOKED AT the attitudes children need in order to succeed in school, but what about our own? Our attitudes are just as important because how we view school and learning will do more than anything else to shape the frame of mind in which our children head off for the classroom each day.

However, before we begin . . .

I'm acutely aware, as I embark on this chapter, how it might feel to read it.

In the course of researching this book, I read many accounts of what parents should do to teach their children at home, how they should shape and guide their homework, and the ways in which they could stimulate their mental development. One book had pictures of happy, smiling families bicycling together along by the sea; another listed the alphabet of true success (A is for aspiration; B is for buckling down . . .). At the end I didn't know if I wanted to throw them, or myself, off a cliff. All seemed designed to stir up great swirls of guilt and failure in the average parent.

This book has a rather different message, and that is that although schools are a long way from perfect, just about all of them have a tremendous amount to offer those pupils who come through their doors in good spirits, ready and willing to make the most of it. However, to help them do that, we parents need to start with ourselves, and this is what this chapter looks at. But it is very important to realise that the things outlined below are ideals – ideas, if you like – to try and hang on to on the daily roller-coaster ride of family life. Every parent in the world knows how impossible it is to live up to high principles as life pitches and rushes past underneath. All we can do is try. And then, when we fail, pick ourselves up and try again.

Speak no evil of schools and teachers

If we see school as a positive experience, and learning as something that is enjoyable and worthwhile to do, our children will, by daily osmosis, absorb the same values. If, on the other hand, we denigrate teachers, and put down what we think happens in the classroom, our children will feel the same. Teachers say they can always tell which of their pupils come from homes where the 'all teachers are rubbish' attitude holds sway. 'I actually had an eight-year-old turn round and say to me, "You can't make me to do that, you're only a f***ing teacher!"' said one shocked primary school teacher I talked to.

But this positive attitude doesn't always come easily. Not all of us have had good experiences of school. Some of us find going into our child's school intimidating, and others of us start to feel like children again, the minute we sit down in front of a teacher. Sometimes it can become automatic to reach for a put-down, just as a cover for embarrassment or unease, but it is important to remember that a young child knows nothing of such complex adult emotions, and only hears the words that are spoken.

Then there are the times when we feel genuinely cross about something that has happened to our child at school, or have big questions to ask about the way things are being run there. At such times, too, it can be hard to hold our tongues.

But if we find things to praise, and keep quiet about the others, we will not only foster good attitudes in our children, but also do our bit towards supporting the school and helping build a positive classroom atmosphere in which all children – including our own – will find it easy to learn.

That doesn't mean being hypocritical. Children always know when their parents aren't telling the truth. It does mean:

- keeping some things back for adult-only discussion
- not gossiping carelessly with other parents in front of your children
- always trying to create the most positive atmosphere possible towards school and learning.

Avoid being an 'expert'!

Unless we are medically qualified ourselves, most of us don't take our children to the doctor thinking we know what the problem is, and what treatment should be given. But schools are different. We all went to one. We all think we know what they are like. We all probably have strong views on what they should teach, and how they should run. A bit of humility never comes amiss here. Bear in mind that schools are complicated places where money is usually tight, teachers are usually overstretched and learning is different from how it was in 'our day'. Striding around saying they should do this, and why on earth aren't they doing that, won't help your child, or anyone else. Neither will paying too much attention to other parents who are doing the same thing. If you have concerns about your child's schooling, or genuinely want to see changes to how a school runs, there are much better ways of getting something done about it than this – see Chapter 8, on home–school relations, and Chapter 20, on school problems, for how to take action in a way that ensures your views will be heard.

It's their schooldays, not yours

This is a hard one to remember when every parent around you is boasting about their child's prowess and progress. How much we all long to have a high-achieving child whose achievements we can broadcast to all and sundry! But ask yourself: is this for your child's sake, or your own?

Bear this in mind when it comes to all tests, exams and pieces of homework. There are far too many parents around who seem to think that every spelling test, homework story, science project and history essay done by their child is a direct reflection of their own abilities. As a result they hover over homework, prompting, suggesting and amending, until the work is done exactly as they would like. But doing your child's work for them won't help them one jot in the long run. Just the opposite. So cultivate a healthy distance.

Remember the American mother who, every time she saw her child bearing down on her waving a worksheet, would shake her head firmly and say 'Nuh-uh. Not me. I've done Third Grade. I'm not doing it again.'

Keep your focus on their health, happiness and personal learning development, rather than their achievements and all will be well.

The class of five-year-olds was growing beans on the windowsill. Every afternoon the children would tug their parents in to show them how much their plants had grown. But one plant soon started to outgrow the others, pushing out big, green leaves at a staggering rate. The class solemnly debated this mystery and decided it must be a mutant seed – until the teacher discovered that this particular plant's mother was sneaking into the classroom after school to give it a surreptitious daily dose of Growmore.

In the same vein, beware those prizes and trophies. As parents, it is so easy to get caught up in the day-to-day competitiveness of school life, but resolve now to stay one step back from this. Not all children can come top of the class. Not all can make the netball or soccer team. And not all can turn into accomplished musicians or skilled athletes.

Does this mean that those who don't are failures? Of course not. What happens in school does not invariably set the course for later life, and anyway children blossom at different rates. Although it can be hard to believe when your child is struggling with the first stages of school, a slow reader might well overtake his classmates three years down the road, while every secondary school can tell stories of average pupils who went on to get first-class degrees, or quiet ones who later took to the world by storm. Chris Martin of the globally successful band Coldplay recently took to the stage shouting: 'This is for school nerds everywhere!'

Remember – it wasn't always better in 'our day'

My children once went to a primary school where there was a running joke between the headmaster and his pupils. At every possible opportunity, in assemblies, and when announcing school concerts, he would say, 'Of course, when I was a lad . . .'. And right on cue the entire school would groan in boredom.

Although many things about schools are almost spookily unchanged (how *do* they get that smell of school dinners?), many others are completely different. All kinds of things that we might remember – blackboards, satchels, those little glass bottles of milk – have gone out of the window to be replaced by computer rooms, laptops, interactive whiteboards, self-defence classes, breakfast clubs . . . and so on.

So pause and think before you utter those dispiriting (to children) pronouncements about how much better things were in your day. Whenever I see my children's misplaced commas and apostrophes I long to rant and rail about how schools are not teaching children anything any more. But then I cast my mind back. My French teachers were appalling, my PE lessons excruciating and I never had a single science lesson until I was eleven. My apostrophes might be immaculate, but that's about the sum of it, whereas my children have a whole array of skills and talents that I could not have dreamed of wielding when I was their age.

And take in the wider picture . . .

Whatever kind of school your children go to, it will always be part of a bigger education system. And education is so much a political football, that news about exam results and school funding is always in the headlines.

Vow now that while your children are at school you will keep an intelligent eye on educational news, but not be too swung around by the extremes of it. Ignore those media pundits who claim that all education's problems would be solved if only children were reintroduced to Dickens, or had to learn Latin again. It is all much more complicated than that. And if headlines suddenly scream 'Half of all primary school leavers can't read!', don't take it as a sign that your child will grow up an illiterate yob – statistics can be spun to tell whatever story the headline writer intends. On the other hand, if there are persistent reports that, say, schools in some parts of the country are finding it harder and harder to recruit good science and maths teachers, that might well be something you want to file away in your mind, and ask probing questions about, when the time comes to start looking for a secondary school for your child.

Beware the school-gate gossip

Every day, when parents wait for their children to come out of school, they chat about school life. This happens at the railings of urban playgrounds, and in the tree-lined car parks of private schools. Much of this chat is friendly, supportive and useful. You can find out about the school meeting that your child didn't bring home the note about, and get to know the parents of your child's new friends.

But it can also be poisonous. Rumour and allegations can spread like wildfire. Suddenly, before you know it, it's a fact that in this teacher's class all the kids run riot, and that in the playground certain kids are ridiculed and picked on. Or you might find that the school doesn't stretch kids enough; or that it is hounding them through their test revision as if nothing else matters. Listen and note, but don't get too caught up in it – and try very hard not to fan the flames yourself. Serious problems do arise in schools, and if your child is the victim of one you will need to take action, but getting your information and your action plan, from the school-gate gossips is probably the worst possible way to go about it.

The pendulum swings . . .

Also remember that as your children go through the education system, the school climate will change. Guaranteed. Educational progress, if that is the right term for it, always swings from one extreme to another. As I write this, we are at the 'targets and testing' end of of the pendulum swing and the signs are growing of a swing back to a softer, more creative view of what should go on in schools. The curriculum will probably change every few years while your child is at school. Computers will be seen as the answer to all educational problems, then as the source of them. We will worry about girls' progress in schools; then, when the girls start to do better, we will worry about the boys.

For parents these swinging currents of educational fashion can be unsettling, but remember that the real core values of schooling change very little. As one comprehensive school head puts it: 'Everything useful we know about education, we already knew by 400 years BC.'

Keep a balance

Much of the above amounts to the single message – keep a balance. And you will do this if you:

- encourage your child to work hard, but don't pile on so much pressure that he feels stressed and overstretched
- praise and support him to the hilt, but also help him see the difference between doing a good job and a half-hearted one
- think about all the different parts of your child's life – school, health, fun, exercise and sleep – and how they fit together to make a balanced whole
- and if you are wondering whether you need to take action about something that is going on at school, try to balance rushing in with all guns blazing, against hanging back and doing nothing.

Bear in mind that schools are institutions, anxious to run smoothly and not always accommodating to big or wayward personalities. John Lennon's school report dubbed him, 'certainly on the road to failure', while the head of actor Richard Briers's school wrote: 'It would seem Briers thinks he is running the school and not me. If this attitude persists one of us will have to leave.'

If children do not shine like superstars at school, or constantly seem to get up the noses of those in authority, so what? If they have confidence, happiness and a grounded sense of self-belief, you can be sure that they are going to be good at learning, and good at life.

Make time for your child

Children's lives unfold slowly. Our adult lives are often hurried and rushed. These conflicting rhythms are some of the hardest things any busy parent has to manage. If we have dashed across town to be at the school gate in time for the end of school and still have the shopping to do, it can be almost impossible to slow down enough to dawdle home at the pace of a tired five-year-old. If we have some major crisis going on in our lives it can be excruciating to have to stand and listen to a 12-year-old's meandering account of school ('You know what? Mr So-and-So's soooo unfair. He always picks on Hannah. This afternoon, in double geography, all she said was . . .').

Hold in mind that without your time, children cannot – ever – do their best. Over and over again I have heard teachers talk movingly about the stress and strains they see in their young pupils stemming from their parents' busy lives, and the lack of time and attention that these parents can, as a result, give to them. It shows, they say, in tired, anxious, abstracted, jumpy, aggressive or switched-off children.

Your children need you to listen to them, reassure them, help them, love them and just simply be there for them. And you need time with them, too. Because only by being around them will children slowly let slip to you things that are happening in their lives. And only by properly paying attention to what they are telling you, will you understand enough of what they are really saying to stay in touch. And only by staying in touch, will you be able to help and guide them through their school days as much as you would want to. It is something that simply cannot be programmed, timetabled or rushed.

So ration your time as if it was the most precious resource on this earth. If you are at home, don't get so caught up with the endless chores (they really are endless; they go on until we die) that you feel you can't sit down on the stairs and explain about how the planets go round the sun, or listen to what happened in assembly this morning. If you are rushing in and out from work, try as hard as you possibly can to be available for your children to talk to you, even if it means that supper is later than it should be, and the laundry doesn't go on until midnight.

And practise asking about their day in ways that coaxes out answers. Don't say 'What happened in school today, then?', but ask easier questions for them to reply to, such as, 'What was the best thing that happened to you today?' or 'Which was your worst lesson?' or 'Who scored in football?'. Then listen carefully to the answers. This ordinary, everyday, low-key chatting time is one of the biggest single investments any parent can make in their child's education. Of course, it doesn't invariably produce results. Boys, in particular, can sometimes be a nightmare to get information from. One mother of boys says she has to get all her information 'from the parents of girls in the class'. Yet it is important to try. And it is also important to realise that this unstructured chatting is often the thing that most quickly goes out of the window the very minute life gets stressed.

In addition, make every possible effort to get to important school events, even if you have to kill yourself to do so. It matters to your child more than you can possibly know, however much they protest that they couldn't care less if you get there or not. One of the saddest sights at primary school concerts and assemblies is the pale and worried faces of children turning round, and round again, to see if their parents have arrived yet – and one of the happiest is the beaming smile and fervent waving when they do. And while older children would never dream of being so demonstrative, your show of support for them still matters every bit as much – on the inside, where no one but them can see it.

And finally . . .

Here's a confession. Just now, in the course of writing this chapter, my youngest child put her head round the door to ask me if I would test her on her biology revision. No,

I snapped, not now. Can't you see I'm in the middle of something. I'll do it later. She closed the door and crept away. And, of course, we never did do it later.

As I said at the beginning, all the things listed above are ideals to which we can aspire, but almost certainly won't attain. Does it matter? Well, perfect parents simply don't exist. And while there are plenty of things that you can do at home to give an extra boost to your child's learning, it is unlikely to be the end of the world if you don't do them. If you never take your children on improving outings, or play educational games with them after supper, or rope in Grandma to tell them stories of 'living history', this will not mean they are doomed to school mediocrity. If you sometimes scream and yell at them, and are at times irritable and inconsistent and contradictory, this will not mean they are too insecure to learn.

Because if you constantly love them, give them as much time as you can and thoughtfully try to do your best for them, most children will make a pretty good fist of the rest of it by themselves.

CHAPTER THREE

Everything you need to know about how schools work

'Education is the most powerful weapon you can use to change the world.' – NELSON MANDELA

WHAT FOLLOWS HERE is a brief nuts-and-bolts rundown of how the school system in England and Wales works. Scotland and Northern Ireland have their own independent systems, and these variations are outlined later in the chapter, along with the ways that Wales, too, is now starting to go its own way.

But, first of all, why bother with this, when most of us, as parents, are really only interested in our own child's school? Well, for one thing, education is a major political issue. Tony Blair's government, after all, swept to power, on a manifesto that announced 'education, education, education' as the lead issue of the day, and it is important for all of us parent voters to keep abreast of how education policy is being shaped and changed. But there are also, I believe, two crucial personal reasons for getting a grip on the bigger picture:

- knowing how things work helps us make more informed decisions about what will be best for our children
- grasping how an individual school fits into an overall education system gives us a much more realistic view of what we can reasonably expect of that school. We can see why it might not sometimes be able to offer some of the things that we want. And we can also see when it might be failing to offer the things that it ought to be providing. And with this knowledge comes power, because armed with it, we will be able to act much more effectively on behalf of our child.

However, you may know it all already. Or you may not be interested. And the same might be true of the next two chapters, about choosing a school and starting at school. If all this is old hat to you, skip them and move on.

In England children must, by law, be in school from the age of five to the age of sixteen, unless arrangements are made to educate them 'otherwise', which usually means at home. However, many schools and local education authorities expect children to start in the year they are five, which means summer-born children can find themselves starting school when they are only four and a little bit. More detail on this is given in Chapter 5. But many children join a school nursery class younger, and then continue on at school after sixteen.

It is commonly said that children spend 15,000 hours in school – a famous piece of educational research showing how much difference an individual school can make to a child's attainments was called exactly that – and during those hours in school they will undertake a momentous journey from being tiny people clinging around your knees to being independent young adults.

More than nine out of ten of them will do this in state-maintained schools, while the rest will do it in private schools.

The state-maintained school system

There are 25,000 maintained or voluntary-aided schools in England and Wales, educating more than eight million children. Most children will join an infants class in the term in which they turn five, although schools increasingly offer children places a term or two earlier. These are known in the trade as 'rising fives' – a label that always sounds like something a plumber might look for when mending your boiler. This is much younger than children in most other European countries. In Scandinavia, for example, formal schooling does not start until seven – and their children do just as well as ours, and in some areas they perform better.

Primary-age children

Pupils could be in an infant school from four to seven, before switching to a junior school from seven to eleven. Or they could be in a single primary school from four to eleven. In a few areas of the country, they might be in a first school from four to eight, followed by a middle school, from eight to thirteen. The differences tend to be largely historic, although there are educational arguments both for and against middle schools. Some say they offer good specialist support for children as they make the transition from older child to young teenager; others argue that they make for a fragmented school system and mean that pupils have to change schools too often.

It's not unknown for education authorities with middle schools to decide to reorganise their systems so watch out for any up-coming plans if you happen to live in one of these areas. And if you live near the boundary of two education authorities, bear in mind that what's across the border could be different from what you have on your doorstep, and might be worth checking out.

Quite a lot of primary schools are church schools, run and administered by the church. Although these get government funding and teach the same things as other primary schools, they can offer their own religious education syllabus and determine their own admissions policy. A voluntary-aided school will have a board of governors controlled by its church group. A voluntary-controlled school will not have a church majority on its board of governors, but its religious ethos will be guaranteed by a deed of trust or foundation document. The main difference between controlled schools and other primary schools is likely to be that their collective acts of worship will be clearly Anglican in character. There are also a few Jewish and Muslim schools. In all, about a third of all primary schools have some sort of religious character. Church schools tend to offer children a strong moral framework, and get good results. For these reasons they are very popular with parents and can be hard to get into. Some sort of evidence of church attendance may be needed to secure a place, which means that parents can find themselves brushing off their Sunday best as their child comes up to school age, although this varies, and no schools are allowed to interview would-be pupils about their religious commitment. Some church schools feel their main aim is to serve local communities – so it is perfectly possible, as I have done, to visit church primary schools where most of the pupils are Hindu and Muslim.

Secondary-age pupils

Pupils may go to one school from age eleven to sixteen, then switch to a sixth form college or further education college to continue their education, or to an eleven–eighteen school, where there will be no need to switch after GCSEs – although increasing numbers of pupils are opting for a change of scene at this point in their school career.

Most schools are community schools, or comprehensives, run by the local education authority and usually taking in children of all abilities, although in a few areas of the country, such as Berkshire and Kent, there are still selective grammar schools, which children have to pass the eleven-plus to get into. These schools take the top 15 per cent or so of students and have a strong academic focus. Arguments about grammar schools have raged for years. Some see them as the last bastions of academic excellence among state-run schools; others say the eleven-plus system inevitably slaps the label 'failure' on the majority of pupils in this age group. The hard evidence is actually mixed. Grammar schools are good at helping their younger pupils make fast progress, although that effect seems to slow down later. But non-grammar schools in grammar school areas suffer badly from the creaming off of the brightest children and don't get as healthy a range of exam results as a result. Some can spiral into decline as they find it harder and harder to attract good teachers and to motivate their pupils. This is one reason why pressure is sometimes put on local authorities to get rid of them – although there is also usually pressure from grammar school supporters to keep them. If you live in a grammar school area, and are interested in sending your child to one, it is always worth checking with the school in question, and your local education authority, to make sure there are no plans in the pipeline to change the system, or active local campaigns to get rid of grammars.

In recent years many people have come to believe that what the Prime Minister's one-time spokesman, Alistair Campbell, famously termed 'bog-standard comprehensives' – local, non-selective, mainstream secondary schools – have not been as successful as they should have been and different types of secondary school have mushroomed into being. The categories – which can overlap – include:

- **foundation schools**, where the governing body is the employer and admissions authority, and the buildings and land are owned by the governing body or a charitable trust
- **specialist schools**, which emphasise some particular part of the curriculum such as sport, science or languages. There are now more than 1,500 of these, falling into ten categories (sport, technology, language, business and enterprise, engineering, arts, mathematics, science, music and humanities, and schools with more than one specialism), and by 2006, nine out of ten secondary schools are expected to have applied for such specialist status
- **city technology colleges**, which are run as charitable

trusts, often have lots of whizz-bang technology and new buildings, and focus on preparing pupils for the world of work
- **beacon, or leading edge schools**, which have been deemed so good they have been given money to share their expertise with other schools
- **school federations or consortia**, where a number of schools join together to share facilities and expertise
- **city academies**, state-funded schools, built with both public and private funds, which have the freedom to vary their curriculum and the length of the school day, and pay teachers at different rates.

The thinking behind the evolution of these different types of schools is that if individual, excellent schools are encouraged to evolve, this will force those other schools that are resting on their laurels to get going on improving themselves in order to continue to attract students.

Unfortunately, it tends to be more complicated than this kind of free market thinking would suggest, with the fates of individual schools waxing and waning according to a whole raft of factors including the level of funding, the calibre of the head, any changes in the neighbourhood and in neighbouring schools, and the political climate.

However, what is absolutely certain is that no secondary school should ever be allowed to languish in the doldrums any more. The whole issue of 'school improvement' has become a huge educational industry over recent times, with books, research papers, workshops and conferences devoted to it, and all parents should know that everyone now understands a lot about what makes schools work well, and that because of this there is absolutely no reason for serious school problems to be blamed on outside factors, or left to drift untackled.

Any school can get better. Even the worst. I once visited a school just north of London, which had become such a sink comprehensive that parents had fled from it in droves, and it was touch-and-go whether it would actually be able to keep its doors open. Then a new head had been appointed, some extra funding had been scraped together, and the first thing he had done was to round up some volunteers and spend the summer painting and sprucing up the reception area and corridors. The second thing he had done was to spend money on the cloakrooms and toilets – if pupils and staff had to endure dirty and derelict facilities, he argued, what message did it give them about what the school thought they were worth? Lots of other things followed in quick succession: a revamped timetable, new teachers, pupils' work on the walls, a new discipline code and homework policy – so that by the time I visited what had been an educational disaster zone just eighteen months before had done a complete U-turn and was rapidly becoming one of the most popular schools in the area.

On the other hand, there is a huge body of educational research that underlines the fact that the single biggest thing shaping how pupils do in school – both primary and secondary – is still their family background. Poverty, in short, and the things that go with it, are not good news for doing well in school, and schools in poor areas have to work their socks off to get the kind of results that their equivalents in more affluent areas can pluck from their pupils with ease.

In recognition of this, a lot of money is now being poured into schools in the most disadvantaged areas, and parents living in large towns and cities may well be aware that their local schools have extra money to employ additional staff, tackle bad behaviour, offer mentors to support struggling pupils and encourage children to aim high.

But what all of this mainly means for parents is that secondary education in the UK is a lottery. If you are lucky, you will have a first-class school on your doorstep, and be able to get your child into it; if not, finding a good secondary school place might well be the biggest practical challenge you face during your child's school years.

Who runs the education system?

National education policy and funding for both primary and secondary schools is set by the government, and administered by the uncatchily-labelled Department for Education and Skills, or DfES. Local education authorities distribute this money, and run services to help schools do their jobs. They might, for example, provide educational psychologist services, or advisory teachers. However, their role has shrunk. More money now goes directly into schools, and some educational services are run by private companies. In a few areas, entire education services have been contracted out to private educational consultants, although the jury is still out about whether this brings improvement or not.

Who runs schools?

Maintained schools are, by law, run by their governing bodies, which consist of a mix of elected or nominated representatives. There will be the head, at least one teacher, some elected parent governors, political representatives from the local authority, and other members of the community, often people with a useful specialist knowledge or particular interest in the school. Governors hire and fire staff, decide how money is spent, exclude pupils when necessary, keep an eye on what is taught in school, and draw up school policies on things like bullying and equal opportunities. However, there aren't nearly enough good people able and willing to be school governors, and governing bodies vary in terms of how vigorous and effective they are.

Day-to-day management is the responsibility of the head, whose job is to have a vision for his or her school, and inspire staff, students and parents to work towards it. Less excitingly, heads have to manage their school's finances and respond to all the many choppings and changings that pour out from the government. Both of these are heavy tasks, and paperwork often threatens to overwhelm the vision thing. The influence of a school head cannot be emphasised too much. A good head will run a good school – and if the opposite isn't true, it is usually because of heroic efforts by other staff! Parents therefore need to keep an eye out for any changes. If you have a glowingly successful primary school near you, but its inspirational head is about to leave for pastures new, be aware that it might not be the same school under a different head – although it's also worth bearing in mind that there are many different ways of being an outstanding head.

Other management tasks in school, such as running subject areas or handling special needs education, will be delegated to individual teachers. And a good school will usually have a school council, or other forum, where pupils can contribute their views on how things should be run.

Who's who in schools?

All kinds of different adults now work in schools, and their widely varying roles can be confusing to new parents. Schools are run by heads, usually in conjunction with a group of senior staff known as the senior management team (SMT).

Individual teachers often wear a number of hats. At primary level, as well as having their own class (or, occasionally, instead of having their own class), teachers might have responsibility for a particular area such as literacy, special needs education or early learning. Or there might be peripatetic music teachers, or other specialists, who divide their time between a number of schools, and are only there for a day or so a week.

At secondary level, as well as classroom teaching, a teacher might be a form tutor or year tutor, and the deputy head, or head, of a subject department such as history or science. Or they may have responsibility for anything from careers counselling to running the sixth form. Bear this in mind, if a teacher doesn't always seem to have all the time in the world to chat with you – it isn't necessarily personal.

Schools may also be helping to train student teachers, or hosting visiting advisory teachers and inspectors, and are also likely to have quite a lot of parents and other volunteers around – for more on volunteering in school see Chapter 8.

Teachers also now have helpers known as learning support assistants (or sometimes teaching or classroom assistants), who work with them in the classroom, helping organise lessons and giving individual attention to children who need it. Many of these will have had some specialist training in things like teaching reading, or working with dyslexic children, and will be invaluable pairs of extra hands. In secondary schools there will also be a range of technical support offered by office workers, lab and computer technicians, and media centre staff.

All schools have lunchtime supervisors (formerly dinner ladies) as well as, possibly, helpers who supervise playgrounds at break and lunchtimes. They also have secretaries and administration staff. While last, but by no means least, comes the caretaker and his or her maintenance staff – crucial workers without which all schools would quickly grind to an insanitary halt.

Parents should know that all adults who work in schools now have to pass a police check into their background – although the tragic case of the murders committed by Soham school caretaker Ian Huntley highlighted the fact that there have been flaws in this system.

What do schools teach?

Less than twenty years ago, the answer to this question would have been: almost anything. Then, with great upheaval, the national curriculum was brought in, prescribing what children should be taught. This first document was a great steam engine of a thing: huge, heavy and hard to drive. Over the years, though, it has slimmed down and bedded in. Today's teachers are all trained in how to deliver it, and see it as a normal part of classroom life. 'In fact, I can't imagine how you'd do without it,' said one young primary teacher. 'It's annoying sometimes not to be more free, but at least you always know what you're supposed to be doing.'

Core subjects are maths, English and science. Then there are the compulsory foundation subjects: history, geography, design and technology, information technology, music, art and design, physical education, citizenship and sex education. All children get religious education, and older children, in secondary schools, get career education. Children once had to do a modern foreign language at secondary school, but this requirement has now been waived – although more primary school children are now doing a language. When pupils come to starting their two-year GCSE course, they have to continue with English, maths, science and information technology, but can choose their other exam subjects, although all students still get lessons in citizenship, physical education, religious education, careers education and sex education. At sixteen, students choose to do a range of different academic or vocational courses.

Tests and exams

The content of the national curriculum is divided into stages, at the end of which children are expected to have acquired certain knowledge and skills. They are then assessed on this by their teachers and by government tests often still known as SATs (standard attainment tests), although their proper name is end of Key Stage tests.

- **Key Stage 1.** This covers children aged five to seven. At the end of it children are tested on English and maths – although formal testing is now being downgraded in favour of teacher-based assessment.
- **Key Stage 2.** This covers children aged seven to eleven. At the end of this period they are tested in English and maths again, and also tested in science.
- **Key Stage 3.** This covers children aged eleven to fourteen. At the end of this they have the same three tests.
- **Key Stage 4.** This effectively ends at sixteen in GCSEs, GNVQs or other national qualifications.

For more detail about tests and exams turn to Chapter 13.

How schools are monitored

Schools that are wholly or mainly-state funded are inspected about once every six years by the Office for Standards in Education (Ofsted), a government department, independent from the DfES. Ofsted exists to improve the quality of education by inspecting, reporting and advising on how schools are running – although that is not how most teachers see it! If your child's teacher starts to look more harassed than usual, and to do slightly demented things like dusting the top of the classroom cupboards, you can be sure Ofsted is on its way. Be very kind to her. It is unnerving to have to operate under the eye of a team of inspectors going through a school with a fine toothcomb. During an inspection they will sit in on lessons, talk to pupils, look at results and interview parents. (Schools, having dreaded their arrival, are sometimes surprised to find how human inspectors are.) The team's final report will outline the school's strengths and weaknesses, and suggest ways in which it can improve. This is available to be read in the school, but a short digest of the main findings is also sent out to parents. The school then has to respond with an action plan that can also be made available to parents. In rare cases, if the inspectors feel a school is failing, they will introduce 'special measures' and demand urgent plans for improvement.

Teachers hate Ofsted inspections, not just for the obvious reasons, but also because it means they have to spend time on updating paperwork when they feel their focus should be on teaching and planning lessons. It is undoubtedly a bureaucratic and lumbering process. On the other hand, Ofsted reports are a useful way for parents to know what is going on in schools. Find them at the local library, ask for them at the school, or visit Ofsted's website: www.ofsted.com.

Scotland, Wales and Northern Ireland

To a greater or lesser extent, Scotland, Wales and Northern Ireland all have different education systems from England, run in different ways.

Scotland

Education has traditionally had a high profile in Scotland, with high standards and a highly regarded school system. It is run by the Scottish Executive Education Department, and the country has its own qualifications body and school inspectors. Schools do not follow a national curriculum, but broad guidelines set out by the government. Subjects are similar to those in the English national curriculum, but five broad skill areas are woven through them – communication, numeracy, problem-solving, information technology and working with others. Pupils take curriculum tests when their teachers think they are ready for them, and there are no league tables. Pupils in Scotland transfer to secondary schools at the age of twelve, not eleven. More info: www.scotland.gov.uk and www.ltscotland.org.uk/parentzone.

Northern Ireland

Compulsory education in Northern Ireland begins at the age of four, not five, and when it comes to secondary education the grammar school system prevails. Most schools have a religious affiliation, being either Protestant and Catholic, although efforts are being made to promote integration in schools. Education is run by the Department of Education for Northern Ireland, and the country has its own curriculum and qualifications body. The curriculum is set by this, and is similar to England's, with stages from age four to eight, eight to eleven, eleven to fourteen and fourteen to sixteen. For more info: www.deni.gov.uk.

Wales

Schools in Wales are covered by legislation passed in Parliament, but are increasingly going their own way under devolution, pioneering interesting experiments in what pupils study and how they are assessed. The main differences are that the Welsh language is a compulsory part of the curriculum – although only tested in Welsh-speaking schools – and tests have been abolished for seven-year-olds. Instead, children are assessed by their teachers. Tests for eleven and fourteen-year-olds may also be abandoned. Secondary school league tables have been abolished, and Wales is pioneering a broad, baccalaureate-style qualification for post-sixteen students. For more info: www.learning.wales.gov.uk.

Private schools

Only about 630,000 children go to independent schools in the UK. If it seems like more, it is because many prominent people have traditionally been educated in private – or, as we still like to call them, much to the confusion of many Americans – public schools.

However, this is changing. Increasing numbers of judges, cabinet ministers, barristers, bankers and lawyers are coming from state school backgrounds, and a public school education is no longer seen as such an automatic passport to success. Top universities are working to attract students from a wider range of backgrounds and employers are acutely aware that the world is becoming a more egalitarian place. 'I now go on red alert whenever I look at a curriculum vitae and see a school like Eton,' says one City employer, himself a public school product. 'I feel it's hard to know how much they've been handed on a plate, and how much they've done for themselves.'

Having said that, many parents choose private schools for very good reasons. It might be because of family tradition, or because classes are smaller – average pupil:teacher ratios are 1:10, compared to 1:17 in the maintained system – facilities better, and exam grades higher. It might be because they want a single-sex school, or a strongly religious one, or they feel that independent schools offer a better all-round educational experience, with plenty of sports, music and drama incorporated into the school day. Or it might be that they want their child to board.

Or it could be that they want a completely different educational experience for their children. Steiner schools, for example, focus on developing the whole child through spiritual, physical and moral learning alongside more traditional learning. The curriculum is more creative and rounded than in other schools, and teachers are freer to choose how they teach. There are thirty-one Steiner schools in the UK and Ireland. For more details visit: www.steinerwaldorf.org.uk.

Mainstream private schools are organised in two main ways. A child will either go to:

- a pre-prep school from three to seven, a prep school from seven to thirteen, then to an entirely separate school from thirteen to eighteen.

Or to:

- the junior department of a senior school from five to eleven, and then the senior school from eleven to eighteen.

However, it is increasingly common for children to move between state and independent schools. A child might go to a primary school for a time, then move over into a prep school. Or an older student might decide to do A levels at a sixth form college and move the other way at sixteen. Parents who cannot easily afford the heavy cost of private school education will make strategic decisions about when their money might be best spent. But this takes careful planning. Good private schools often have both long waiting lists and stringent selection procedures. In some areas, parents feel they have to put their child's name down at birth (or before!) and popular prep schools may screen children as young as three and four to see which ones seem the brightest and most alert when it comes to interacting with other children and handling simple problem-solving tasks.

Bursaries and scholarships can be available from individual schools to help talented children take up places.

Schools which belong to the Independent Schools Council (ISC) are inspected by the Independent Schools Inspectorate (ISI). Most are run as independent charities and trusts, by governors or trustees. Independent schools don't have to follow the national curriculum, although many of them choose to use at least some elements of it, or to follow its broad progression. Some prep schools, for example, will do the national curriculum Key Stage tests, while others won't.

Children leaving prep school take the Common Entrance exam at thirteen. This is marked by the individual schools the candidate is applying for, to see if they come up to the level demanded. GCSE and A level exams are national public exams, and are therefore taken by independent school pupils in exactly the same way as state school pupils.

Home schooling

Strange as it may seem to parents who think that one of the prime roles of school is to get the children out of the house during the day, growing numbers of children are being home educated. One estimate puts the number at 87,000; others put it higher. Parents have the legal right to educate their children at home. The law states that a parent's duty is to see that their child receives a suitable full-time education at school, 'or otherwise'. You do not have to ask permission, except in Scotland, although if you are withdrawing your child from school you need to write and inform the school what you are doing. Neither do you need to be a trained teacher or tutor. Parents sometimes choose home education when their child runs into difficulties at school, or because they feel that one-to-one tuition at home offers a better, more flexible education. Home-educated children do not have to follow the national curriculum, take tests and exams, or follow normal school hours, although sometimes local education authorities will ask for details of educational planning. If you are interested in home schooling, but wondering whether it is a good route forward, you might like to consider that:

- a quarter of home educators in the UK are teachers
- figures show that home-educated pupils perform above average on national literacy and numeracy tests
- Albert Einstein and Britney Spears were both home educated.

Enthusiastic home-schoolers also say their children have great social lives, but any parent considering home education will need to think not only about the educational side of things, but also how to encourage their child to mix with others. However, abundant help and advice is on offer. Good starting points are: Education Otherwise, 0870 730 0074, www.education-otherwise.org; Home Education Advisory Service, 01707 371854, www.heas.org.uk.

Flexi-schooling

More families are also asking to flexi-school, by having their children in school for a a few days a week, and educating them at home for the rest of the time. This idea is still in its absolute infancy, with only one or two heads even willing to consider it. Although the arrangement may be attractive to parents, schools tend to see only organisational problems and a loss of funding from not having full-time pupils on roll. Since the arrangement hinges on school and home working closely together, everything depends on finding an accommodating school and local education authority. However, interested parents can find out more about the possibilities from home–school organisations.

CHAPTER FOUR

Choosing a school

'A wise man makes his own decisions, an ignorant one follows the public opinion.' CHINESE PROVERB

ONCE UPON A time choosing your child's first school meant sending him off down the road to the nearest one to hand. Today it is different. Even if you are lucky enough to have a really good school on your doorstep, and no problem securing a place at it, you will probably take soundings about it among friends and neighbours, and at least consider the alternatives.

Why have things all changed so much?

- We know more than we used to about how one school can differ from another.
- We talk more about schools than we used to.
- We can theoretically choose to send our children to whichever school we like.

Alas, this choice is often only theoretical – limits on class sizes mean that popular schools are quickly oversubscribed, and if there is pressure on places, most schools give preference to children who live near the school, or who have siblings already there.

This can throw up some seriously frustrating situations. 'We live within half a mile of our local school, but we can't get a place there,' says one parent. 'The school has recently moved its junior section over from another site a mile away, but is still taking children from that old catchment area, so there's no room for us.'

Or, it can cause families to up sticks and move to a new house. A south London mother outlined the nightmare of looking for a good school place in an area where the best primary schools have queues around the block. 'We came to realise that it came down, quite literally, to how many steps your house is away from the playground. In the end we moved to be really close to the school we wanted, but we had to pay a lot more than we wanted for a not very nice house.'

Are such moves worth it? Plenty of people believe so, with estate agents reporting that in some areas the proximity to a particular school can put up to £100,000 on a house's value. But if you are thinking of making one, you need to do your research carefully and be very sure about what it will give you in terms of securing the school place you want. And you should probably aim to buy six months or more ahead of the start of the school year.

Before you start

Before you embark on any serious school searching, there are things to think about.

- **Know what matters to you**. Sit down for a couple of minutes and think about your child, about what kind of school you think would suit his character, and the kinds of things, in education, that matter to you. You may not know much about schools at this point, but that won't stop you knowing that you think creativity is important, or that you are sure your child must have a calm, orderly atmosphere in which to work well. This kind of 'blue sky' thinking can give you some very useful things to hang on to later, when your head starts to spin from league tables, school visits and other parents' opinions.

- **Think ahead**. Parents who leave choosing a school to the last minute can get caught out. Children start in school nursery classes at the age of three or four, and in reception classes before they are five. And, since it is often sensible to put your child's name down early, it is well worth starting to think about schools while you are still wheeling your child around in his buggy.
- **Geography**. Unless you are prepared to move, or devote part of your day – or the day of whoever is looking after your child – to the school run, only consider schools that you can easily get to. That might sound simple-minded, but it can be surprisingly tempting to start to look further and further afield. However, if a school journey seems long the first time you do it, it may well have burgeoned into a two-way, daily nightmare five years later – especially if the traffic has got worse by then, or the demands on your time have changed. Bear in mind that a huge amount of rush-hour congestion is directly due to the school run, and also that something like a difficult school run can be an enormous source of family stress and tension, making every day more scratchy and ill-tempered than it needs to be.
- **Assumptions**. The minute you start to think about

schools you will hear an awful lot about them from other parents, colleagues and the woman at the corner shop. They will tell you, as if it is written in stone, that X school is 'good', and Y school is 'awful'. Listen and learn, because this kind of street buzz is useful. But keep an open mind, as well, until you can see them for yourself. Schools can rarely be summed up quite so simply, and anyway it may be that the 'fantastic' school that everyone battles to get into, is actually heading into the doldrums of complacency, whereas the 'terrible' one may have a dynamic new head who is really starting to take it places.

Where to start

Once upon a time it was hard to find out anything about schools. Now so much information is available that it is positively daunting, especially if you are coming new to all the acronyms and jargon of education.

- **First step**. Find out school names and contact details from your local education authority – you'll find it in the phone book. Or check to see if the authority has a website. More and more do, and many are excellent sources of local information.
- **Prospectuses**. Ask schools to send you these and read them – with caution. A good one will give a thorough introduction to a school, including such things as how many pupils and teachers it has, the length of the school day and what its facilities are like. It will tell you if there is a nursery class, and give some indication of class sizes, and how its pupils do on national tests. It

will also undoubtedly start with some glowing outline of its aims and ethos – and this is where the caution comes in. All schools, these days, offer 'a happy learning environment' in which children 'strive for excellence', while at the same time developing into 'rounded and thoughtful individuals who care for each other and their community'. But fine words, as they say, butter no parsnips, and you will have to dig a bit deeper to find out if it's actually true.

- **Ofsted reports**. These will tell you more. You can find them at the school, or in the library, or online – www.ofsted.gov – and they will tell you what the school inspectors thought of the school the last time they visited. Ofsted inspections go into all aspects of school life, and point the way they think the school should move forward. If a report highlights problem areas, you will need to remember to ask the school what it has done about them since then.
- **Annual reports of the school governors**. These are things all school governing bodies have to issue. They outline up-to-date information about developments in a school, and you may well be pointed in this direction if you have a query about how problems are being tackled.
- **League table results**. These show how well pupils have done in the national tests in English, maths and science, which they take at seven, eleven and fourteen. They also now show the 'value added' by a school to its pupils' results. This is important because any school can do well with an intake of bright, well-motivated kids, but if a school is good at building on its pupils' abilities it will improve on its pupils' results at eleven, while a poor one lets them slip back. These results are

shown as a plus or minus of 100, and most schools come just a few points to either side. Local education authorities publish league tables for all their schools, and these allow you to compare different schools within an area, and also to look at how schools are doing against national averages. The tests taken at eleven, and the 'value added' score at this age, will tell you most about what a primary school can do for its pupils – at seven children haven't yet spent much time there – but all results need to be read carefully. A good school may have a dip because last year's eleven-year-olds weren't such a high-achieving group as previous years, or because it has more pupils with special needs in that year, than in the years before. Alternatively, a school might be getting impressive results – but only by dint of driving pupils through stultifying amounts of revision and practice. With all that in mind, a school with bright children would probably have more than 75 per cent of its eleven-year-olds gaining Level 4, the level expected for their age; if it has more than 10 per cent getting Level 3 or below, it's a sign there are lots of strugglers. At seven, most pupils should be on Level 2, with others on Level 3, and no huge imbalances between the boys and girls.

The visit

Don't ever think of putting your child into a school if you haven't seen round it. And that means seeing it when it is up and running, so that you get the chance to go into classes, and watch teachers and pupils at work. Most parents find, when making these visits, that it's easier to do it without your child in tow, if possible, to really concentrate on what they're seeing.

- **Open days**. Schools invite all interested parents in for exactly this purpose, and it is well worth going along to several of these in different schools, even if you are pretty sure of the school you want for your child. Comparisons are always useful, and it also takes time to get used to what you are being shown, and to know how to make sense of it.
- **Personal visits**. You arrange a visit with a school when you are seriously interested in placing your child there. These give you the chance to talk individually to the head and the teacher who will be teaching your child. Just as importantly, personal visits give teachers a chance to find out about you and your child, and to lay the foundations of what both sides no doubt hope will be a good future relationship.

What to look for on a visit

- **First impressions**. How does the school seem as you walk up to it? What is the reception area like? How noisy is it? What does it smell like? How welcoming does it feel?
- **The school building**. How does it feel to be in it? Is it light, bright and airy? Are the classrooms big or cramped? How does the school use its space? Is it clean and neat? What sort of things are on display? What are the loos like? (Very important, this. Clean, well-maintained toilets show a school cares for and respects its pupils.) Is the

school the kind of place you would like to spend your day in?

- **The children**. How are they behaving? And do they look happy? Are you seeing frowns, scowls and noisy, aggressive exchanges? Or do they look cheerful, busy and absorbed? How do they react to visitors? And behave towards their teachers?
- **In the classroom**. What does the atmosphere feel like? Do the pupils seem occupied and purposeful? Can they explain to you what they're doing (if they're old enough)? And also why they're doing it? Does the reception/early years class feel light and airy, with a warm atmosphere, plenty of adult help, and lots of opportunities for children to explore and play? And what does the school 'end-product' look like – the ten- and eleven-year-olds in Year 6? Are they the kind of children that you would like your child to turn into?
- **The head**. Is the head approachable, confident, organised and clear about the kind of school he or she is running? Are parents' questions welcomed? As the head walks around, does he or she know individual pupils and seem to have good relationship with them? And with their teachers? (And do you feel this is genuine, or a bit of a show? Heads these days know well what makes for great PR.)
- **Teachers**. How do they interact with pupils? Do they seem happy in their work? Can you hear raised voices from behind classroom doors? What do they have on their classroom walls? Who is on the teaching staff – all old blood, all new, or a good mixture of both?

Good teaching is at the heart of a good school.
A good teacher will:

- *speak calmly and clearly, without any sarcasm, put-downs or patronising tones*
- *praise and encourage pupils*
- *run lively, whole-class sessions, which engage all the pupils*
- *move around the classroom when children are doing individual or group work*
- *have good radar about what is going on everywhere in the classroom*
- *use a range of different teaching aides – posters, music, objects, computers*
- *question children carefully and listen thoughtfully to their responses*
- *run an organised and efficient classroom*
- *have work of all abilities pinned up on the walls, to encourage everyone*
- *seem confident about having observers in the classroom.*

- **Other staff**. Do the classroom assistants, office staff, cooks and playtime helpers look cheerful and purposeful? Does it feel like a nice place to work? Is there a good sense of community?
- **Pastoral care**. How does the behaviour policy work? Does it emphasise praise and encouragement more than punishments? What about bullying? How does

the anti-bullying policy work? Have any pupils been excluded recently? If so, what for? How is every child helped to feel important? What about equal opportunities? What support is available for children experiencing difficulties?

- **Special educational needs**. How well geared up is the school to help children who have difficulties with learning, behaviour, emotions or physical health? What would it do if your child showed signs of having a learning or behaviour difficulty? How many children are on the special needs register – the list of children who need some sort of extra support with their schooling – and is there a greater proportion of special needs children in the top classes than in the younger years? How many children are 'statemented', that is have a level of severe difficulty, and an official 'statement' of their needs?
- **General facilities**. What does the school have by way of a music room, computer suite, library, school hall and spaces where children can be taught in small groups, or one-to-one? If it lacks any of these, how does it manage without them?
- **Lunchtimes**. Who cooks the school meals, and what does a typical week's menu look like? What about table manners and healthy eating? Who supervises the dining hall? Are there rules about what children can bring in their packed lunches? Do children have ready access to water?
- **Out-of-doors**. Is there a good-sized playground, with markings and equipment to encourage active play? Are the younger children separated from the older ones? Who supervises the playground? Do they just watch

out for trouble, or get actively involved with teaching children games and activities? Are the children themselves involved in keeping the playground happy, through systems like playground monitors, or buddy benches, where children can go if they have no one to play with and then be invited by other children to join in? Are there any sports pitches? Or garden, or wildlife areas? And how are they used? And what is the attitude towards sport and physical activities? Are children encouraged to take exercise (without being dragooned into it in a way that might turn them off for life)?

- **Out-of-school activities**. What's on offer? Is there a breakfast club? How can children pursue their interest in sports, writing, art, science? Do they do any charity work, or anything that encourages them to think about people less fortunate than themselves?
- **Links with other primary schools**. Does the school have good links with neighbouring schools? Do schools join together for music, drama and sports events? Do you get the feeling that the school's sense of community extends beyond its own playground?
- **What secondary schools do they go on to?** Are these schools you would be happy for your child to go to in due course? Are there links with these schools? Do they use their sporting facilities, or go there to see plays and concerts?

Who will my child be mixing with?

Although we don't always admit it, this is one of the biggest things on our parental minds when we choose a school. We know that over the coming years friends and classmates will have an enormous influence on our children – how they speak, work, behave and learn – and we want them to find friends whose aims, ambitions and values are similar to those that we are working to instil in them. But when weighing up what schools call their 'intake' it's worth bearing the following in mind.

- You can't always judge by appearances. Some of the worst bullying my children ever came across was in exclusive private schools. When they were in a very mixed inner city primary school they had no such problems.
- Schools are places where children lay down the foundations of the adults they'll become. And it doesn't necessarily do them any favours to only expose them to a tiny sliver of society. All it means is that later, when they are disgorged out of the school system, they will have to scramble to acquire the kind of broader social skills and knowledge that others will have woven into their lives from the age of five onwards. I know children who were desolate when they moved to a quiet country school after the fizz and bubble of their big, multicultural city school and complained for a long time how boring it was when 'everyone was the same'.
- Don't put too much store by labels. Some parents, for example, worry about the effect of having the children of asylum seekers in a school. But, while it is true that to have lots of pupils struggling to learn English, or with social problems, will deplete a school's energies, some schools have found that such children can inject new vigour and commitment into the classroom. Exactly the same kind of drive that makes a family uproot itself

to travel across the world in search of a better life can sometimes translate itself directly into that family's children being far more determined and hard-working than their English-born peers.

- Children are different these days. They grow up quickly, and can be much more 'in your face'. In addition, words that used to be taboo, are now common currency. A school will, of course, ban them, but that doesn't mean they can always stop them shooting out of pupils' mouths in the playground. If your own children are still small, you may be taken aback by some of the behaviour of older pupils in a school, and think that they are rude, ill-disciplined louts. This may, of course, be true. But it also may not. Keep in mind the whole picture of what you are seeing, and make your final judgements on whether your overall impressions of a school are of politeness, consideration and respect.

After the visit

Go home, put your feet up – if you can – have a cup of tea, and let the impressions percolate down through your brain.

Go back to your first impressions and see if they square with what you saw later. If something is niggling at you, don't put it out of your mind. Face up to what it is, and if you feel you need more information go back to the school and put your questions, or ask around among other parents who might be able to shed some light on your worries.

Talk things over with your partner, and raise any issues of concern with each other. People can have very different takes on what kind of school they want for their child, so clear these things up at the start, rather than get into later recriminations ('If it had been up to me, he'd never have gone there in the first place . . .').

When you do finally make a decision, make sure to do everything the school requires of you in order to convert your interest into a solid application. One of the saddest stories I ever heard was of a disorganised mother who failed to get her daughter into the popular school of her choice, because she had thought a telephone confirmation was all it needed, and had never even noticed the form they sent her, let alone got round to filling it in and sending it back.

Private schools

Choosing a prep school

If you have always known you want your child to go to an independent school, the chances are you know how the system works, and quite probably know the school you want for your child.

Parents less familiar with private schools – and that's a lot since in many schools more than half the parents haven't been to a private school themselves – need to bear a couple of important things in mind:

- The long-term costs of paying school fees from age five to eighteen are enormous and growing. Children can and do swop between the two systems, but once in independent schooling they usually tend to stay until at least sixteen, and it can be embarrassing and difficult for a child to be pulled out of a school where he is perfectly happy because his parents can no longer afford the fees. At present, these can be anything from £1,000 to £6,500 a term per child, depending on whether you are paying for a day or boarding place and what sort of school it is, but they will almost certainly have gone up by the time this is printed. At the time of writing, fees in the independent sector are rising steeply – about 10 per cent a year. Indications are that this may drop back, but probably only to about 7 per cent a year.

- Independent schools differ greatly from each other, depending on their individual traditions and purposes. All schools like to present themselves as balanced, all-round institutions, but a school might in fact be highly academic, extremely sporty or quirkily individual. You need to be aware of this, find out what you can from the school and on the grapevine, and think carefully about whether it will suit your particular child.
- Not all private schools are geared up to deal with pupils with special educational needs, and some may ask a pupil to leave if these needs become apparent.
- Most independent schools belong to one of seven school associations, whose single voice is the Independent Schools Council (ISC). All ISC schools reach guaranteed standards, and are inspected every few years by the Independent Schools Inspectorate (ISI) under a framework agreed by Ofsted. However, there are more than a thousand private schools that do not belong to the ISC and are therefore not required to meet its specified education standards. Many of these schools are fine, but others have been criticised by the chief school inspector for things such as poor management, and failing to check into the background of teachers before

they start work. Ofsted inspectors have now started to inspect them, but it will be some time before reports are available for all schools, and even then they will be more rudimentary than a full inspection. If a school doesn't belong to the ISC, it may be worth asking why not.

- Pressure on places, particularly in city areas, can be enormous. One north London prep school has fathers phoning in from the hospital delivery room to put their newborn sons on to its waiting list. So find out how much of a stampede is there for the school you're interested in, how early you have to put your child's name down, how much of a deposit you will have to pay at this stage and whether this is a guarantee of a school place, or whether there are selection procedures to decide which children get offered a place at three, five or seven.

Making a selection

- Collect information from the ISC information service, which can give details of individual schools – www.iscis.uk.net – and also has advice on fee planning. Look at school websites and ask for prospectuses.
- About two-thirds of prep schools take the national Key Stage tests, and the results will be available from the schools themselves, as will any recent inspection reports. However, it's worth being aware that tests are not always marked externally and so marking criteria may vary from school to school. Schools should also be able to tell you how well they do at Common Entrance – that is, how successful their thirteen-year-olds are at

moving on to the schools of their choice. Or, how successful their children are at getting into selective secondary schools at eleven.

- National newspaper league tables will list the 'best' schools in your area, but bear in mind their criteria might be limited, and might also exclude perfectly good schools that just don't happen to fit into these.
- Open days can be quite a razzle, with music groups, art exhibitions and other facets of the school on full display. Facilities may be impressive, with shaved playing fields and spacious buildings. Then there is the appeal of well-scrubbed children, often decked out in uniforms with a whiff of the 1950s about them – certain to tug at the heart-strings of anxious parents looking to shield their children from the big, bad world. All these things may be eye-catching, but you must see the school in its everyday colours. The true heart of any school is in the relationships between the head, teachers and pupils, and you will only get a feeling for this by watching closely what goes on as you walk around a school during a working day, and by asking around among existing parents.

Boarding

Although only a tiny proportion of prep school pupils board full-time, increasing numbers take advantage of 'flexi-boarding' arrangements, which allow pupils to stay for the occasional night, or for a regular one or two nights a week, or full-time for several weeks if their parents are away. In fact, such arrangements can be a great attraction for busy parents who find it hard to get to school every day, or who are out a lot in the evenings, especially as children get into the pre-teen years and hate babysitters, but want to spend more and more time with their friends.

This may not be you now. But it may be in the future, so it makes sense to look at any boarding facilities, and get details of the possibilities on offer.

Most prep school boarding houses these days are bright, warm, colourful places, plastered with pop-star posters, and with just a small handful of children to each room. As a visiting parent, it should be easy to see at a glance why many pupils love staying overnight at school. In fact, if the boarding facilities don't feel completely homely, and if the teachers in charge of them don't seem warm, caring and approachable, something is wrong.

CHAPTER FIVE

Starting school

'All I really needed to know . . . I learned in kindergarten.' – ROBERT FULGHUM

THE DAY MY first child went to school I was asked to settle him in his nursery class, then leave and return after morning break. I can still remember how tightly he gripped my hand as we set out from home, and how big and looming the Victorian London primary school seemed to us both as we crossed the asphalt playground. Enormous children – nine-, ten- and eleven-year-olds – hurtled about, confident rulers of this alien kingdom.

The nursery class was a haven, with its bright wallpaper and smiling teacher. In many ways it was just like play-group, and my son was quickly absorbed with the sand and water. But as I crept out and walked away down the now-empty school corridor, I realised it wasn't like play-group at all. I smelled that distinctive gymshoe and paper smell of school, heard muffled voices from behind closed classroom doors, saw steel drums and drumsticks stacked at the back of the hall, and was acutely aware that he had entered a whole new world – his own world – that I would only ever be a small part of.

However, since my work has always taken me into

schools, I did at least have some inkling of what that world might be like. For many parents it is a mystery. They have never set foot in a school since their own schooldays ended, and the routine of the school day, and the rhythm of the school year, come as entirely new strands to be woven into the pattern of family life.

Getting ready for school

Getting ready for school starts at birth, if not before. The better the quality of what we, and anyone else looking after our children, puts in at this stage, the better our children will do when they skip off to school.

If we can manage to give them:

- security
- self-confidence
- the skills they need to cope with learning

then we will have given them something far more precious than all the treats, holidays, new outfits and presents in the world. We also need to encourage them to play, explore and use their imaginations, as these things are the most basic foundations of all learning.

> *Findings from a scheme that has been running in the US for twenty years, and has recently started in the UK, show clearly how good pre-school parenting affects a child's life at school. The scheme is called Parent As First Teacher, and helps*

parents to be aware of how their baby and toddler is developing, and what kind of activities they might enjoy at each stage of development. It encourages parents to read, talk and play with their children, and to be alert to signs of any possible problems – with hearing, for example – in order to have them checked out.

Parents who sign up to it (and in the US all kinds do, from university academics to teenage mums) get monthly visits from a trained visitor, although these are nothing formal, more like a friend popping in.

In one that I sat in on, in the south-east of England, the mum and her visitor chatted happily about twenty-one-month-old Adam's stair-climbing and football-kicking, his enjoyment of going to the library, and his growing independence.

Adam's mother said the visits gave her confidence that things were on track, helped her deal with any worries she had, and made her feel that her decision to stay at home with him during the day and go out to work at night, when her husband came home, was worth while.

It could not be more simple. Yet research shows that, at the end of the first year of school, children who have been in the programme do significantly better at maths and reading than their peers, and that their teachers feel that their social and language skills are also better. In addition, parents who have been through the programme are much more likely to come into school to talk to teachers about their children than those that haven't – something that is in itself important, since there is other educational research showing that parents who are involved with their child's schooling really help their child's school career.

Alas, our society doesn't yet properly understand or appreciate the enormous value that everyday, attentive parenting contributes to young children's development, and families suffer because of it. Parents who are struggling with financial or social problems get little support, while many high-earning parents in the UK feel trapped in a career culture that has the longest working hours in Europe.

But schools know exactly what its value is, because every day they see what happens when it is not put in. In a recent national survey, teachers reported that a staggering half of all children now start school unable to speak audibly and clearly, respond to simple instructions, recognise their names or count to five. And they also know that it is not only disadvantaged children who are like this. 'I had a child in my class last year who could barely speak English!' one commuter-belt pre-prep school teacher told me. 'I couldn't understand why until I discovered his parents were both working up in London, and he'd been brought up by a succession of Czech au pairs.'

A highly experienced nursery head, working in a mixed city area on the south coast of England, wrings her hands in despair about how children are now arriving at her school. 'They've been dumped for three years in front of the television, no one's really talked to them, so they don't know how to speak, they don't know how to listen, and they don't know how to play with each other. In the old days, children would be out playing in the street, watching and learning from older children. Today they are always in the house. Some don't even know how to hold cutlery. They've lived on pizzas and chips and never had a sit-down meal in their life. We now have to spend a whole year putting in those things which we used to be able to take for granted – that's a whole important year these children have to use just catching up.' Of course, she adds bleakly, some of them never do.

If we want our children to start off badly in school, here's how to go about it – give them poor-quality child-care, too many videos or too much television, a diet of convenience meals and parents who are too stressed-out or distracted to give them any attention.

If we want to do well by our children, here's how to do it: 'Talk to them,' says a primary school teacher. 'It's as simple as that. Talk to them all the time. It doesn't matter about what, but let them hear different words and tones of voice. When you do their buttons up, count the buttons; when you see things in different colours, point them out and tell them what the colour is called. Sing nursery rhymes to them. Read them books and talk to them about the pictures. Don't make a big deal of it, just make it something you do as a matter of course.'

Ironically, while schools are seeing children less and less well prepared for school, the amount of books, posters, videos, CDs and worksheets available to encourage pre-school learning are proliferating. These days it is impossible to walk through a big newsagents or toy store without being assaulted at every turn. Many are attractive and well produced, and as a result parents can find themselves forking out lots of money for them. But remember that resources like these are often marketed by playing on parental anxieties. They can be helpful – if they are introduced lightly, and a child finds them fun. But they can also be counter-productive, if a child feels that they come with a sense of nervous pressure to perform. Bear in mind that here in the UK we already start our children in school at a younger age than many of our European neighbours, and yet our children don't do noticeably better in the long run. Formal learning grows out of play, so introducing it too early just won't work. And resources like these can never, ever replace being involved in the everyday chat and happenings of family and friends, from which a child learns so much.

In the run-up to starting school

Starting school should feel like a natural and normal part of life. Don't build it up into a huge, great threshold. And don't ever wave it like a stick over your child's head in moments of exasperation – 'You won't be able to get away with that at school, you know!' – however great the temptation.

Children will find it helpful if they know how to:

- speak clearly and audibly
- listen (very important to start fostering this. A reception class teacher says, 'It's getting harder and harder to get children's full attention.')
- ask for help
- answer to their name
- remember and follow simple instructions
- say please and thank you
- be willing to have a go at things without needing constant help.

In practical terms, it will help if they can:

- dress and undress themselves – short-cuts like velcro fastenings and ties on elastic are useful here
- go to the toilet unaided and wash their hands afterwards – teachers absolutely hate those cries for help from behind the toilet door (also know to use the word 'toilet', even if it's not what you call it at home)
- use cutlery and comply with basic table manners – you would be amazed at some of the stomach-churning eating habits school staff have to deal with.

However, it is worth bearing in mind that the younger the child is when she starts school, the more challenging some of these things may be – if you have a summer-born child who starts school in September remind her teacher to make allowances for this.

Useful things to know before school starts

Your child's school will have given you introductory materials about the school, and about how your child will be settled her class. Make sure you are clear about:

- any uniform regulations or dress code
- what time children can arrive at school, and when the school day starts
- what they are allowed to bring in, or not
- what can be eaten and drunk at break
- how lunchtimes are organised, and what the school says about lunch box contents (also, remember the spoon for the yoghurt, and please, say meals supervisors, don't send the kind of plastic-wrapped snacks and drinks that are a struggle to open and end up splattered everywhere)
- the name of your child's teacher – it can be so depressing, say teachers, to know that you aren't even deemed worthy of the proper label!
- how the school wants you to notify it about illness, and by when – it costs schools a fortune to make phone calls chasing up absent children; this is money better spent on other things
- how the school communicates with parents – so you know what letters and newsletters to watch out for
- what happens about birthdays – if the tradition is to bring in buns or treats, you'll want to know so you child doesn't feel embarrassed at not having brought

anything in when it's her birthday; if the school hates whole birthday cakes, because of problems with slicing and distribution, you'll want to know that, too.

And some things to do

- Make sure your child has visited her new class and had a chance to look around the school. The unknown is always scarier than the known. (This is often something nursery schools will arrange, as well as getting early years teachers to come and visit the top class at nursery.)
- Time your journey to school, so you aren't taken by surprise on the first day.
- Label clothes, shoes and bags. Yes, it's boring. But with an indelible pen it needn't take long, your child's school will love you and it could save you a fortune. Or you could use iron-on labels. Schools are often piled high with lost property – 'Leather shoes, lovely new anoraks,' mourns one teacher. 'It breaks my heart to look at it.' You don't want those things to be your child's.

First days

'I cried all the way home,' said one mother. 'I felt as if I was missing something at the end of my arm. I thought I'd do so much, but all I did was mope around the house until it was time to go and get her.'

Very often starting school is traumatic – for parents. Children might be very happy to embark on their new adventure, but parents know it is the end of one era and the start of another. Even if this is the case for you, you will, of course, act in an entirely adult way, and try and hide how upset you are – at least until you've made it out through the school gate.

Some children find adjusting to school tricky. They find separation hard, and cry and cling. If this happens with your child:

- stay calm
- don't push her through the door and leave her, but be clear you are going, and don't drag out partings unnecessarily
- when you go, try not to think that her crying and wailing will go on all day. Remember what everyone who has ever spent time in an early years class like this knows – that it is quite astonishing how fast the distractions of the day take hold once the parting is done
- don't be embarrassed. Teachers have seen it all before and won't be judging either you or your child if these first days are fraught. This is also something worth bearing in mind if you feel a teacher seems off-hand, or uncaring, about your child's problems. She probably isn't. She just knows from experience they will soon be history.

Summer-born children

Children born in the summer months are young in their school year, and some can find starting school hard. Ten months is a lot of difference in development when you're only four or five. Your listening skills, language, hand-to-eye coordination and general understanding of the world may be less developed than your classmates, school will seem tiring and always having to struggle to keep up can be demoralising.

If you have a summer-born child make sure the teacher is aware of this, and ask about things like whether the younger children get extra teaching assistant help, and whether there is a good mix of different kinds of play and learning. Some education authorities allow parents to defer their child's entry to school until the term that the child turns five, but many don't offer that flexibility.

On school mornings . . .

The following will make for a better start to the day.

- **Leave enough time**. How much will depend whether your child is zippy or a dallier. But children who arrive in school from a frantic scramble of shoutings and rushings-arounds can be too jangled to settle into the day. And if they arrive late at school it can be upsetting for them, and annoying for the teacher and for other children who have settled down to work.
- **Turn off the TV**. Life will be calmer, and there will magically seem to be more time.
- **Have a good breakfast**. And good means good. A pop-tart or a slice of white-bread toast just won't do. Drinking is important, too, since dehydration goes straight to the brain, and dehydration headaches are very common among young children in overheated classrooms. (For more on eating and drinking, see Chapter 10.)
- **Be prepared**. Getting into a routine of checking you've

got everything you need – keep a school timetable and notepad in the kitchen to help you remember about things like gym kit. But vow you won't start falling into the trap of scurrying up to school every time something has been forgotten.

One mother I heard of drove to and from her son's school with forgotten bags, lunch boxes and games kit so often that the staffroom started a sweepstake on how many times a week she would be seen in school. They christened her Mrs Doormat, and got the school secretary to keep a tally. Then somehow, it seemed, word leaked back to her. She stopped doing it. 'And guess what?' said one of the teachers. 'It was like a miracle. Little Master Doormat suddenly found he could remember his own things.'

. . . and after school

Your child will be worn out from all the new sights, sounds and impressions of her new life. And this will be true even if she has been to some sort of pre-school and is used to lots of children. The new demands on her – to sit still, pay attention and concentrate will be taxing. Also, her blood sugar will probably be low.

- Take her something she can eat and drink straightaway, if she always seems fractious and difficult when you pick her up.

- Allow time for decompression and don't bombard her with questions. Which of us likes to have to account for our every moment the minute we are met? Things will emerge in their own time – a relaxed walk home from school can be a lovely opportunity for winding down and chatting, while a shared drink or meal at home will often loosen tongues.
- Check her bag for any papers or letters home from school, and turn out any old food wrappers and juice cartons.
- Make a time for reading, or doing any little bits of schoolwork. Routines don't have to be rigid, but they help to build good habits.
- Do all you can to make sure she gets to bed on time and has a good night's sleep (see Chapter 11).

CHAPTER SIX

What goes on in primary schools – and where you fit into the picture

'You tell me, and I forget. You teach me, and I remember. You involve me, and I learn.' – BENJAMIN FRANKLIN

GOOD PRIMARY SCHOOLS are magical places. A few years back I visited a school in one of the bleakest areas of the country I had ever been to. It was a poor, outer-city suburb in the north-west of England where shabby blocks of flats alternated with parades of boarded-up shops and patches of wasteland where cars had been torched. The school was ringed with unwelcoming razor-wire, and firmly locked against intruders. If you had walked past it, you would have shuddered to think what was inside.

Yet what was inside was another country. Colour and life seemed to burst from every corner. Walls were crammed with children's work and music was coming from a distant classroom. There was a corridor-full of notices about school trips and breakfast clubs and writing competitions, and the children in the classrooms were cheerful and busy. It was easy to believe the head when he said one of his biggest problems was to get pupils to go home at the end of the day.

See for yourself

Primary schools are whole little kingdoms, but once your child is settled in school, you will probably hear little about what goes on there. As Ted Wragg, emeritus professor of education at Exeter University, says: 'The head might have had a heart attack, the caretaker might have run off with the petty cash and the roof might have blown off the school hall, but when you ask them what happened today, they'll still say "nothing".'

How do you find out? If your school uses parent volunteers, and you can spare some time, put your name forward. Not so much for the school's sake, as your own. When my children were in school in America, the local director of education always said he had to have his 'regular elementary school fix' in order to remember why he was doing his job, but as a parent, it's not always easy to see what that fix is. We tend to go into schools for only two reasons: to attend set-piece events such as schools concerts or parents' evenings, when normal school life is on hold; or to sort out problems, when tension and worry might well cloud what we are seeing.

Spending some time around the building during a normal school day can give a real insight into your child's world. Even if you aren't directly helping in your child's class you'll be able to watch how children work, get to know some of the teachers, and generally feel more in touch than if your only contact is to rush in and out at the start and end of the day. You may even end up with a whole new career – countless classroom assistants and teachers have started out as volunteers.

Even if you are at work, or tied up looking after younger children, it is still worth making the effort to help out on the occasional school trip, or elsewhere. One artist mother I know went in to help with Christmas decorations, a caterer set up an after-school cookery club and a car mechanic father volunteered to give his son's class a talk on how cars work.

> *One mother took her new baby into her daughter's reception class. 'I was apprehensive, but she insisted – she said she wanted to use him for show-and-tell. And they loved it. She explained all about him, and how he fed and slept, and how we changed his nappy, and I held him up and let them see him and touch him. We both got lots of brownie points for that.'*

The class

The class will be your child's second family for a year. So make an effort to get to know who's in it. Probe lightly about who is friendly with whom, which children are the class clowns and which ones never keep quiet. Apart from anything else, this can be a good way past those 'What did you do today?' – 'Nothing' exchanges. 'Did so-and-so fall asleep in story time again today?' is much more likely to get a response than, 'Did you have a good day?' Make a very big effort, too, to get to know the teacher, as good relations here can be invaluable. But be tactful. Whatever you do don't try and hold her up first thing in the morning when she will be busy trying to get her show on the road. A moment or two's regular chat after school is a much better way forward. (And it probably will be a her. Only a sprinkling of primary school teachers are men, despite efforts to encourage them into the profession. Which is a pity. Not only do men balance out a school's atmosphere, but with growing numbers of children living in single-parent households, male role models are pitifully absent from many young children's lives – if you are a father with some free time, your child's school is likely to welcome you with cries of joy and beckoning arms.) There is more on how to build good relationships with teachers in Chapter 8.

Also, get to know any classroom assistants, who help the teacher, or any learning support helpers, who might be in the class supporting individual children, but who will also be involved with the group as a whole.

> *A top tip for keeping in contact with your child's class is to ask if you can pop in and see any class displays he has been talking about, or look at a piece of work he is particularly proud of. This is definitely what management gurus call a win:win situation. It will make your child feel important, it will make the teachers and helpers feel appreciated – and your little heart will burst with joy at the talents of your offspring!*

Sometimes parents get wind of the fact that one or two difficult children are disrupting a class. If that seems to be the case, always go in and share your worries with the school, urges one teacher of ten-year-olds. She had an autistic boy in her class who seriously disrupted classroom life by, among other things, constantly making aeroplane noises. She prepared herself for lots of parental complaints, 'but on the contrary, they were all completely nice, understanding and sympathetic about him! Yet it would have actually helped him, and helped the school, and helped the other children, if they had complained. That way everyone would have had to get on and decide what they were going to do about his schooling. As it was, they just let things drift.'

But don't go in with all guns blazing. Listen to the school's view of the situation, ask them what they think they can do about it and wait to see if it improves. With young children things can change from day to day. But if you see no improvement, go back. Time is too precious a commodity in education to be squandered and if you fear that is happening to your child, you have to try and get something done.

Some schools operate a class representative system, whereby one parent acts as the link person for the parents in that class, in order to pass on information or drum up support for school events. These little networks are a great mechanism for getting to know other parents of the children your own child will be going through school with, so it is worth either volunteering for the post or going along to any class parents' meetings. That way you will be able to get to know your own peer group, and build useful allies for the next half-dozen years.

How classrooms are organised

Your child's classroom will look busy, and quite possibly crowded. Although early years classes are always thirty or smaller (by law), classes of older children can be bigger. And even thirty is a lot of bodies to get into a classroom when you consider all the books, paper, worksheets, cupboards, computers and so on, that have to be in there as well. ('It's awful,' says one country teacher. 'I can't even find room for a nature table any more.') A good classroom will look organised, but also like a place where work is in progress. A seriously untidy one bodes ill, as does one where every piece of paper is carefully squirrelled away.

Chairs and tables may be arranged in clumps or horseshoes. At the top end of some primary schools you may occasionally even see the return of slam-top desks, arranged in rows all facing the front. Such sights do tend to gladden the heart of us parents. Ah good, we think, a bit of discipline, a bit of order, a bit of life as we used to know it. But think about it. How many of us in the adult world do our jobs totally alone? A good teacher will use all kinds of different teaching methods, so pupils might come and sit on the carpet for whole-class work, go back to their tables to work in pairs or groups, or be spread apart to work alone. That way they are learning a whole variety of skills – teamwork, cooperation, listening and speaking skills, concentration and the assimilation of different ideas.

Children's work will be on the walls, often beautifully mounted and presented. But a good classroom will always have other things as well. As one famous children's artist once asked, how can you be inspired and stimulated by only staring at your own work? Expect to see a variety of charts, posters and other things, and if you don't understand why something's up there, show an interest and ask.

Small schools and mixed-age classes

Some schools, particularly some rural village ones, have mixed-age classes where children from different year groups are taught together by one teacher. Usually this is to organise small numbers of pupils into sensibly sized groups, although a few, larger schools choose to do it as a matter of policy. Mixed-age classes take a lot of managing in order to ensure that all pupils have their different learning needs met. Also, teachers working in small schools can be seriously over-stretched, with several subject areas to manage on top of their classes. If your child is in such a school, relish what will most probably be a delightfully warm and well-behaved atmosphere, but remember, too, to keep a watchful eye on progress in the classroom.

What is taught in the classroom?

This is the point in most education pamphlets and on most education websites where people start talking about Key Stage 1 and Key Stage 2, and core subjects, and curriculum options. And the point at which most parents' eyes glaze over! It can be hard enough for those of us not used to school jargon to even know what is meant by the different year numbers that teachers so readily trot out (nail them by adding five – Year 3 + 5 = 8-year-olds; Year 6 + 5 = 11-year-olds).

But what you most need to know at any given point is what your child is learning that term, and where the teacher hopes he will be at the end of it. Many schools now provide parents with leaflets explaining this, and it is good to know the kind of ground your child is covering. That way you can be supportive, and make sure any input you make at home is pitched at approximately the right level. If your child is working in class on how light passes through prisms, for example, it might be good to draw his attention to the colours in a rainbow, or how a bedroom make-up mirror is focusing sunlight, but it won't be helpful to launch into an elaborate explanation of how light can be both wave and particle. If you don't get this sort of information from your school, or you want to know more about, say, the science curriculum in Year 4, you can look it up on the Department for Education and Skills' parents' website, www.parentcentre.gov.uk.

As an overview, it's worth trying to think about your child's primary school education as a kind of grid. Along the bottom come the subjects – English, maths, science, information technology, history, geography, music, physical education, art, religious education, citizenship, and personal, health and social education (PHSE) – that he will be doing in school. Down the side are the key skills that he will be developing as he does so – communication, number skills, information technology, working with others, improving own learning and performance, and problem solving. Everything your child does will fit into this matrix. For example, if he is making a poster, with two classmates, on the computer, this will fit into the subject column labelled information technology. But as he does it, he will also be developing his skills in communication, working with others, problem solving and improving his own learning. Likewise, if the class goes out to map the layout of the playground, the project might come under the subject geography, but will develop communication, number, working with others, improving learning and problem-solving skills. It's worth referring back to this when you find yourself wondering what the point is of something your children are doing, to see where it fits on this grid.

It's also worth knowing that schools are sometimes directed to emphasise this, or do more of that. Recently, for example, they have been told they must develop their pupils' speaking and listening by teaching them things like how to debate, how to adapt their conversation to different circumstances, the importance of gesture and tone, and how to listen more carefully. This has followed worries about children arriving in school with very poor basic communication skills.

The national curriculum is also supposed to promote children's spiritual, moral, social and cultural development, both via all the curriculum subjects, and through other things such as assemblies, circle times (when children in a class sit down together to talk about issues and feelings), PHSE lessons, and lessons in citizenship.

However, there are four core subjects that your child will spend most time on: maths, English, information technology and science, and – as things stand at the time of writing, although this may change – they will be assessed and tested on maths and English at age seven (Year 2), and at the age of eleven (Year 6) on maths, English and science.

How they teach it

Literacy and numeracy hours

Schools actually don't have to have these, but most use them to cover the ground in English and maths. A common pattern is to devote the morning to literacy and numeracy, and the afternoon to everything else, and you don't have to be a mathematical wizard to work out that that means that everything else gets pretty shoe-horned in, which is one of the things that makes some primary school teachers complain so bitterly about the constraints of the national curriculum.

Part of these hours are devoted to whole-class teaching. They will probably open with some sort of oral warm-up – spellings, say, or mental maths – move on into group or independent work and end with so-called plenaries, where everyone gets together to go over the ground covered.

This highly structured approach was introduced specifically to drive up standards, and in the first years after it started, attainment levels shot up, showing that many children had been performing far below their capabilities. But this improvement has now slowed, and there have been growing criticisms of how literacy hours, in particular, are over-regimented and fail to instil in children a love of books and reading. Philip Pullman, the best-selling children's author, has called them 'poisonous' for the way he feels they rob children of joy in literature and imagination.

The numeracy hour, on the other hand, has more fans. Like a lot of us, primary school teachers are often not quite as confident with numbers as words, and many have found following a carefully constructed numeracy programme a real help.

Numeracy hours teach primary school children maths in ways that can be fast and fun, with a big emphasis on mental arithmetic. 'I was amazed by it,' said one secondary school head of maths who sat in on a top class of primary school children. 'Snap, snap, snap. They had all the answers. I went back to my own school and said to the teachers in my department, "We've got to start expecting more of the kids when they come on up to us."'

Science

At primary school, children learn the basics of how to pose scientific questions, do research and experiments, and evaluate evidence. They learn about forces, lights and sounds, get an introduction to how human beings, animals and plants grow and develop, and look at things like the weather and natural habitats.

They might start off watching seeds grow (the trusty old bean seed in a glass jar lives on!), doing simple experiments with buzzers, batteries and wires, and mixing colours to see what happens. By the end of school, they could be doing quite sophisticated experiments with magnetism, or exploring a complex environmental theme.

Well-taught primary pupils can quickly turn into first-class scientific thinkers. In a school in the West Midlands, groups of seven-year-olds were were given the task of sorting a pile of farmyard models into sets of the same thing. The answer the teacher expected, and which most groups came up with, was sets of animals, of birds, and of people (the farmer and his wife). The answer one group came up with was one group of models that had the grass painted in around their feet, and one group that didn't – and they defended the logic of their answer rigorously against all critics.

Technology

I can remember when computers were very first introduced into primary schools. In fact I remember Gerald. Gerald was in my son's Year 1 class (that's Year 1 + 5 = six-year-olds), and was clumsy, disruptive and had failed to grasp even the rudiments of reading and writing. The school knew the family well, and was resignedly expecting Gerald to follow the same disastrous path through school as his older siblings. But I happened to be sitting with Gerald when he had his first-ever go on a computer and it was as if a light had been switched on behind his forehead. He was entranced. What's more, he could do it. By the end of that term, to the astonishment of his teacher, he was batting out stories and poems that were every bit as good as those of his classmates, and his behaviour had quietened down so much he hardly seemed the same boy.

Since then I have seen the same thing happen often to struggling adult learners. Told that they were no good at reading and writing, they had learned to avoid paper and pencils, and think of themselves as stupid. But left alone with a computer that did not judge them and was forgiving of their mistakes they quickly made extraordinary strides.

Not that computers are a panacea for all ills. Like every educational aide, their effectiveness always depends on how well they are used. What is certain, though, is that they will be central to our children's lives, and so it is crucial that they get comfortable and familiar with them at the earliest possible stage.

The number of computers in any one primary school varies a lot, as does how they are used, but all children now do some work on screen, and are introduced to researching on the Internet, as well as using computers for things like writing a school newspaper, linking up with a NASA space probe to Mars or e-mailing pupils in their partner school in Ghana.

Your child's school may well also be using interactive whiteboards, which are a kind of futuristic blackboard linked to a computer, and which replace the functions of a marker board, overhead projector, flipchart and TV. Teachers use an electronic pen to write on them, while facing the class, and many report that once they get used to using them, they can't imagine life without them.

If your child's school is very forward-looking, it may be that your child uses a laptop, or a little hand-held 'tablet' computer. Technology is galloping ahead in the classroom, so if your child's school seems badly behind the times in this area, ask what plans there are for improving things. Although, at home, of course, your job may also be to limit and monitor computer use (see Chapter 14).

Other subjects

Even within the national curriculum, schools have the freedom to organise their own timetable, and add any other subjects they think fit. Schools might cover foundation subjects in blocks, or link them up through a theme such as 'seasons'. A class teacher might teach every subject, or your child might be taken by Miss So-and-So or Mr Such-and-Such for other subjects where they have specialist knowledge. A few schools make bold experiments with their timetables – giving children Wednesday afternoons off, for sport and creative activities, for example – and often seem like very enjoyable places to be in as a result of it.

Setting and streaming

Here's some more educational jargon:

- *setting* means dividing up children according to their ability in certain subjects
- *streaming* means dividing up a year group for everything, according to ability.

Your child's primary school will almost certainly not stream children, but it might well divide them up by ability for some subjects as they get older – maths is a common one.

Parents can get very agitated by this, and fret that their

child is not in the top set, but you will do him no favours by insisting the school push him up if the result is that he is struggling to keep up in a group that is moving too fast for him. In contrast, being at the top of a second set can do wonders for a child's confidence and self-esteem, although obviously if he seems bored and switched-off, it may be that he has been wrongly placed and you should talk to his teacher about it.

Learning support

Primary schools have many pupils with particular difficulties. They might be dyslexic. Or have emotional and behavioural difficulties, or some physical impairment, such as, for example, being hearing impaired. Often they will have a statement of special needs, and get some sort of additional help in class, or some one-to-one tuition elsewhere.

Although they don't always like to admit it, parents often worry what having a 'different' child in a class will mean. But provided the placement is well supported and managed, so that classroom life runs smoothly, it can actually be a positive benefit. All the children in the class are likely to benefit from having additional help in the class, even if the helper is officially only there to help one child, and children can also learn important lessons about differences and disabilities from such a situation. For years, one of my daughters was in class with a boy who had been born without eyes. Not only was he blind, but as he also had two glass eyes, he was rather unsettling to look at. Yet it was touching to see how easily all the children accepted him, and how quickly they learned how to help him, and look out for him if the class ever went out somewhere where he couldn't navigate his own way around. And even now, thirteen years later, my daughter remembers him clearly, not as a blind boy, but as a former classmate who happened to be blind – he did her and all her classmates the great favour of teaching them, at a young age, that disability always has a human face.

School trips, assemblies, concerts, clubs and other stuff

You wouldn't believe what busy places primary schools can be. They might have a visiting poet come in, or an African dance troupe, or the Sadler's Wells Ballet. They lay on assemblies where each class gets a turn to stand up and make a presentation in front of the whole school and/or the parents. They collect for charities. They put on concerts. They run orchestras and recorder groups. They make sculptures and murals. They write newspapers, and make video diaries, and go on trips to theatres and museums (for which you will have to sign a permission slip, and for which you will almost certainly be asked for a 'voluntary contribution' to the cost). They also have to have, by law, a daily act of collective worship, although many schools interpret what this means quite widely, incorporating different faiths and religions.

During lunchtimes and before and after school they run breakfast clubs, and sports teams, and chess groups, and story clubs. As your child goes through school, keep an eye on the opportunities available and encourage him to think about joining in. If he'll only go to something if a friend goes, too, encourage the friend to join in as well. The more things that primary-age children can try out and experience, the more they will come to know about themselves and the world.

And remember that an awful lot of learning also goes on at breaks and in lunchtimes. Children learn about eating and playing together, about team games – and, very often, about the underlying savagery of human behaviour! Keep an ear out for what your child has to say about these times of day, because if any bullying or friendship problems should spring up, this is where they are likely to show themselves.

Monitoring your child's progress at school

It is very important that you keep close tabs on your child's progress at school. A London mother says, 'I thought my child was doing well at school. She was happy, her reports were good, yet when I asked a tutor to assess her to see if she was good enough to try for a selective secondary school he found she couldn't even do basic multiplication or division. We couldn't believe it! We felt so guilty, not having noticed.'

The truth is your child may have good teachers, but he may also have mediocre and poor ones. As school inspectors have recently pointed out, many lessons in primary schools just don't come up to scratch, partly because many teachers themselves suffered from an inadequate education when they were going through school.

So always keep a close watching brief on your child, throughout his school life. Scrutinise reports, look at his books, help him with any homework, ask him about what he's learning, and try to get a feel for things he enjoys doing and the things he is struggling with. Don't hesitate to get in touch with the school if you think there is a problem, and go back again – and again – if it is not getting sorted out. It is really important that a child doesn't miss out on any of the basic building blocks of learning at this early stage of schooling.

If he does have a year with a poor teacher there's probably not a great deal you can do about it, except make jolly sure that you stay on the case, and give him all the help and support you can at home, so he doesn't start to fall back. There is more about this in Chapters 9 and 12. If you are seriously worried, you should certainly make your views known to the head. There may be little the head can do about it in the short term, but it is important that the situation is aired, and it is also very important that your child and his classmates don't get another weak teacher next year.

Helping with the basics

Every parent is keen to see their child get a flying start by helping launch them into reading, writing and 'rithmatic. And since many primary school children now get regular homework, from a few minutes to half an hour's worth a night, there are plenty of opportunities to do this. The important thing is that anything you do should dovetail with and reinforce what is being taught at school, and should make your child feel learning is fun and pleasurable. It should certainly not pile on the pressure, or confuse him with conflicting approaches. So if you are in doubt about anything at all in this area, always speak to his teacher to make sure you are going about things in the best way possible.

Helping with reading

To help with reading, make sure you immerse your child in books, and reading of all kinds. Help him associate reading with pleasure by cuddling up for bedtime stories (yes, even when he can read for himself), and by introducing him to a wide range of different books, comics and magazines. Read stories in a lively way, with lots of expression, and talk about any book you're reading together, and what's happening in the story as you read it. Remember that little and often is the best pattern, and that joining a library, or going to a storytelling session, will extend his exposure to books and language.

To help him as he reads:

- praise things that are right
- allow him time to try out words he doesn't know
- help him break down and sound out unknown words
- look at word beginnings and endings
- read on in a sentence to get clues about an unknown word
- help him see patterns in words – sounds and spellings
- read for sense, as well as accuracy
- encourage him to talk to you about, and explain, what he is reading.

Helping with writing

Handwriting, spelling, punctuation and composing things – letters, stories – all come under this umbrella, although unlike the old days where the first three were practised for their own sake, schools these days stress to children the importance of them so that they can better communicate what they want to say. To help your child become a good writer encourage him to write all kinds of things at home – messages, shopping lists, instructions, stories. Let him see you writing, expose him to lots of different kinds of language, and give him interesting pens and pencils, and different types of paper to write with.

To help him as he writes:

- talk to him about what he wants to say
- talk with him about ways he could say it
- encourage him to read his work over to himself to see if it sounds right
- read his writing carefully and with enjoyment
- praise his efforts, and for trying
- don't expect total accuracy
- encourage an older child to look for and correct his own mistakes
- explain any basic rules you feel he should know (depending on age) but that are missing – capital letters at the beginning of sentences; where to put an apostrophe – but do it clearly and gently
- always focus more on what he's written than on how he's written it
- help him learn spellings by looking at letters and sounds, making up sentences and rhymes, and testing him.

Helping with maths

Maths is many parents' nightmare. 'It's by far and away what most parents are most worried about,' said a primary school teacher emphatically. 'I spend my parents' evenings teaching parents about how we teach it.'

The problem is that it is taught differently from how most of us learned it, the vocabulary is strange and many parents fear muddling their children up. For example, while we probably borrowed and paid back when we were doing subtraction, today's children exchange from column to column. They are also taught to do a lot of mental maths, and to understand the relationships between numbers rather than just work automatically through calculations.

Good primary schools will organise evenings where they explain the numeracy strategy to parents and encourage them to have a go at some modern maths. These events are usually fun, not at all scary (everyone's in the same boat) and really illuminating – go to one, if you get a chance. Or you can find out more on the numeracy section of the DfES parents' website, www.parentcentre.gov.uk.

To help your child with maths:

- use everyday life to help young children learn about money, shapes and numbers
- get him to explain to you any work he brings home from school
- read instructions very carefully together
- help him learn the multiplication tables he is doing in class
- create opportunites for him to tell the time, count money and think about 'sets' of things (six-packs of cola; a packet of four chicken breasts)
- find answers together if you are stumped, in a book or on a maths website
- don't hesitate to go and see his teacher if you think he is stuck on a problem that you can't help with. Maths

is one subject where it is really important to understand each stage before moving on.

> *'I was trying to help my daughter do some multiplications,' says one rattled mother, 'when she suddenly started screaming at me, "What are you doing! What are you doing! We don't do it like that! That's all wrong!" I've never dared go near her when she's doing maths ever since.'*

What about teaching my child at home?

Apart from help with homework and general encouragement for learning, there should be no reason to push your child to do more work at home. Personally I think, by and large, that teachers should be teachers, and parents should be parents, and if you have chosen a good primary school, your child will have plenty on his plate during the day, without needing more in the evening. And, anyway, so much of what we do with our children – shopping, cooking, driving, tidying, bath-time, reading, watching television – offers limitless opportunities for informal learning, without any need to embark on anything more formal. Encourage a climate of learning by:

- chatting to him and explaining things
- answering questions
- pointing things out to him
- reading to him

- showing an interest in what he's doing at school
- giving help if he asks for it
- letting him see you reading and learning.

There is a lot more about this in Chapter 9.

CHAPTER SEVEN

Moving up to secondary school

'Small children disturb your sleep, big children your life.'
– YIDDISH PROVERB

THIS IS NOT a chapter about secondary schools in general. It looks at the process of finding a secondary school, and then starting out there. This is for the very good reason that, of all the different stages of your child's education, this switch-over is probably one of the most important, and in many ways the one most strewn with pitfalls.

At this stage parents have to make important and difficult choices, while at the same time children are finding their own feet and developing independence – with some inevitable clashes along the way!

For a few children, starting secondary school can be the point where they start to veer off the rails and never get back. Many, many more find themselves in danger of losing momentum, developing a bit of an attitude and generally failing to build on the promise they showed at the end of their primary school days. Meanwhile parents are juggling like never before. They need to give their children space to grow and breathe, while also keeping tabs on what is happening in their lives, and making clear what they expect of them. It isn't always easy to steer the right path at this stage, but it is vital to try.

Choosing a secondary school

By the time your child reaches the last year of primary school, you will know a lot about the local opportunities available, and about the odds of your child winning a place at the school of your choice. And, if not, your school head should certainly be able to advise you on this, and answer any questions that arise. You can also get details of secondary schools from your local education authority.

In some parts of the UK, this is a hugely stressful time for both parents and children. Popular schools are almost always oversubscribed, and select their candidates according to a bewildering mixture of different things – academic performance, siblings at the school and how close you live to the school gate. As a result it may be far from clear whether or not your child will get into the school that you want them to go to. However, all schools have to publish their admission criteria, and it obviously makes sense to go over these with a fine-tooth comb in order to estimate what you think your chances might be.

It is a terrible indictment of our education system that things are too often this way but parents have to deal with how life is, and your prime task at this point is to keep a cool head, keep your anxieties to yourself, and be careful not to make your child feel that all will be lost if she fails to make it into the school you have decided would be best for her.

Just as in choosing a primary school, try and step back from the general gossip and hype, and find out for yourself exactly what schools are like. There is no point blindly joining in the stampede for the top local school, only to discover that it feels like the sort of place where your daughter wouldn't thrive. Likewise, you could be working yourself up into a state of horror at the thought of her having to go to a school that you've been told is no good, only to discover that you actually quite like it when you go there.

Assessing schools

- Visit them to see how they look and feel and take your child with you. She will have important insights. Remember not to be overly impressed by things such as banks of computers – which all schools now have.
- If a school seems scruffy and threadbare, ask yourself why. Is it because it has made a conscious decision to pour all its resources into teachers and teaching? Or because it is poorly run and managed? A quick test is to send your child off to the loo – a good indicator of how well a school looks after its children (the children's commissioner for Wales found that school toilets were one of the things children were most quick to complain to him about). One London mother who did just that got an instant, whispered report back, 'It was disgusting! There was no paper and yucky stuff on the walls!' That school was immediately off her list.
- What are your initial impressions of the head? He or she will be the person who single-handedly most shapes the atmosphere your child will be living in for the next five to seven years, so if you don't immediately warm to him or her, ask yourself why not, and whether the

reason is something that could matter to your child. (Although remember, too, that first impressions can be deceptive, so listen to what people say about him or her as well. I once met a head who seemed in every way so limp and feeble you couldn't imagine he could run a school at all. His handshake was not so much wet fish as disintegrating seaweed. Yet, on further acquaintance, it became clear that this unprepossessing manner hid a core of leadership steel, and that he was widely respected by his students and staff for his own particular brand of gentle integrity. In the same way, other heads are not brilliant speakers, or particularly adept at dealing with parents – but this does not necessarily mean they are not good with the young people in their care.)

- Look at the league tables to see a school's record for GCSEs – and also AS and A2 exams, if students go on to 18 – and look especially at how well the school is doing in 'adding value' to the levels of achievement that students come in with. This is crucial, because any school can get good results if its pupils are bright and motivated, but a school that manages to do well with a mixed bag of children deserves all credit. The chances are that such a school, although not topping the league tables, will have lively teachers, good management and a really caring atmosphere. However, always view league tables with caution. In London, where competition between high-flying schools is intense, one school apparently managed to streak ahead simply by being the formal exam centre where a pupil who was studying Hebrew at home took her GCSE – that one extra pass put it top of the tree, and it had even more parents than usual stampeding to its doors the next year.

- Read any recent Ofsted reports – find them on the Ofsted website – and ask what the school is doing to make improvements in any area where the inspectors were critical.
- Ask how a school keeps tabs on the academic progress of individual children. A good one will always monitor its pupils carefully and be alert to the first signs of slippage or other problems.
- Ask about the pastoral care system and how it works. In a bigger school, it is absolutely vital that your child will have someone – a form tutor, a house head – to whom she can easily go with any problems, and who will be your link with the school.
- Don't be shy about raising the question of behaviour, since this will be one of the most crucial factors in determining whether or not your pre-teen child settles happily in school, and how well she does there. But be realistic too. All secondary schools – yes, even the poshest in the land – have problems with bullying and cliques. All have stealing. All have children who drink too much and take drugs. Any school that denies this is lying. What you need to know is how the school sets out what it expects from its pupils, to what extent it succeeds in getting that standard of behaviour from them and how it deals with the problems that invariably do arise.

Want to know more about a secondary school you're interested in? Turn detective and watch how pupils behave on their way out of school at the end of the day. None will be angels, but a high level of screaming, yelling, spitting, swearing, pushing and shoving probably indicates that they are spilling out of a building where they haven't been made to feel all that good about themselves, and where they haven't either worked or played hard enough to have used up a useful amount of energy. Smiles, on the other hand, are a very good sign. (Although, be aware that geography, too, can play a part in these impressions. One Surrey school governor blesses the thin belt of woodland that separates her school from the town centre. 'It's done more for our reputation than any amount of good Ofsteds. They've finished their fags, and let off the worst of their steam, before anyone gets to see them.')

What if you don't get in?

Parents are supposed to be able to choose the school their children go to, but pressure on places means that simply isn't possible, so parents usually have to rank their preferences. About 96 per cent of children get into one of these ranked choices, and nine out of ten parents are, apparently, happy with the school that their child moves on to. However, at present, just over 1,000 pupils a year in

England and Wales find that they haven't got into any of their preferences, and a handful even find themselves still without a school place at the start of the school year.

Now, though, the system is currently being streamlined to try and prevent this, and to avoid the situation where some families are dithering over a clutch of offers, while others are left waiting to see if anything at all will come up. Under it, mandatory admissions forums will discuss the admissions criteria of all schools in an area, and schools will be able to object to the basis on which other schools are admitting pupils. Complaints will be heard by the schools adjudicator.

According to national figures, the most over-subscribed school in the country at the time of writing is a city technology college in south London, which has 2,000 children chasing 200 places. But other popular schools face similar pressure.

It is a horrible system for families at the rough end of it. Failing to get into a school, for whatever reason, can be devastating to a child, particularly if it is their first taste of disappointment, so it is important to put a positive spin on things, and have back-up plans in place, so you can reassure your child about other options if the master plan doesn't work out. This doesn't mean pretending that the whole process doesn't matter – children will know that's not true – but genuinely trying to keep things in perspective, and to hold on to a wider view.

'What I told him,' said one father, whose son failed to get into his school of choice, 'is that the world is a funny old place and sometimes life has to knock you back in one area, so it can build you up somewhere else. And I also told him that maybe it would turn out to be for the best that he was going to another school. I said it might open up windows for him that we hadn't even thought of.'

Anyone refused a place at a school can appeal to an independent panel, and about a third of secondary school appeals are successful. This can be a complicated and time-consuming business, so much so that a number of private agencies have sprung up offering to do it for you, for a fee – you'll find them the minute you look up 'school appeals' on the Internet.

Don't, whatever you do, allow yourself to be made to feel that forking out for a such a service is your only chance of success. Your local education authority should give you all the information you need about how to appeal, and more advice is available from the DfES' school admissions team, and from the charity, the Advisory Centre for Education, whose phones ring off the hook every spring with calls about appeals procedures.

In very general terms, you are most likely to succeed if you can either prove that the local education authority has messed up its procedures, or you can convince the appeals panel (usually made up of three, neutral outsiders) that the problems caused by the school accommodating an extra child will be less than the problems your child will have to endure going somewhere else. To help make your case, think hard about your child's needs, and about what the school she wants to go to has to offer, and try to see how the two can be linked up. If you have a highly musical child, for example, and the school in question has a music programme that stands head and shoulders above that of neighbouring schools, then get your child's music teacher to write a letter saying how much she would benefit from being able to be a part of that.

If you are unhappy about the way an appeal has been carried out, you can complain to the Local Government Ombudsman, but the wheels of such procedures grind slow, and this is unlikely to be of much practical help in your immediate quest to find your child a school place by September.

And bear in mind, too, that although the lottery of the secondary school admissions costs many families time and tears, at the end of the day most pupils settle down in a secondary school where they are happy. And even if the absolute worst comes to the worst, and you continue to be unhappy about the school where they are, there are two things to hang on to. One is that there is a great deal you can do at home to bolster and supplement inadequate school learning, whether that means employing a tutor, or mining the Internet for help. And the second is that, these days it is common for pupils to move schools again for sixth form so a less-than-ideal situation need never last beyond GCSE.

Choosing an independent school

All the signposts outlined above apply as much to independent schools as to state maintained ones. However, there are also differences. Independent schools have highly distinctive characters, so matching your child to the right school is crucial. Prep school heads, and parents who are a year or two ahead of you in the business of looking around schools, are some of the best sources for the low-down on what lies behind the glossy brochures, and impressive open days.

Also, if parents going round maintained schools sometimes have to be careful of not being too turned off by shabby facilities, parents visiting private schools have to be equally wary of not being too bowled over by their imposing campuses and grounds. Some schools have quite fabulous new sports halls, science labs and computer centres. Others have old buildings, which can give off an intimidating air of historical, cloistered learning. Whatever the buildings are like, try to focus on the students, the staff and the relationships between the two groups. And if you are looking at boarding facilities, make sure you get a chance to ask existing students what it is like to board there. Modern boarding should be relaxed, comfortable and not too rule-bound, and if the students say it is not like that, you need to know why.

Starting secondary school

The early secondary years are a time when many children start to switch off from learning. As adolescents, they have so many other things going on that school can easily become little more than the place to hang out with friends, kick a ball about at lunchtime, check out the gossip, eye up the opposite sex and make social arrangements.

This 'dip' in the first few years of secondary school is well known to people in education, and schools are trying to do something about it. But they can't do it alone, and parents really need to stay on top of what is happening at this stage, and do their best to create a home atmosphere, which supports and encourages a good start in the new school.

Of course, as always, this is harder than it sounds.

To start with, lots of other things may be going on at this stage of family life. Parents, just like children, evolve and change, and many parents who have stayed at home, or worked part-time when their children are little, see the move to secondary school as a natural point at which to return to full-time work. Families also quite often move in these middle years, because of redundancy, promotion or some other change. Other children might be growing up and becoming more demanding. And there may be issues of separation or divorce to be dealt with, that can be particularly loaded where young adolescents are concerned.

Also, that comfortable relationship that you may well have developed with your child's primary school is now lost. Your child is now off to somewhere new, quite possibly somewhere further away in another town or suburb, and most definitely not somewhere where you will be standing at the school gate every afternoon, or popping in for a quick word with her class teacher after school.

On the contrary, secondary schools can be deeply intimidating places to parents. You don't know the ropes. Teachers are always busy, and anyway you don't know who is who. If you do make an appointment to see someone, you probably don't even know which gate you're supposed to go in by, and then you have to walk past all those groups of sassy, giggling teenagers. Plus your child is almost certainly desperate for you to have nothing whatsoever to do with her new world, and will do everything in her power to make sure you know as little as possible about what is going on in it. The temptation to write off secondary school as something you're never properly going to get to grips with, and relish the increasing freedom to get on with your own life, is very great.

But while all parents have to loosen their grip at this stage – those that don't set up problems for themselves and their children later – it is important not to lose touch more than you have to. Try to:

- find out anything you can from your child – subtly, of course – about new classmates, teachers and school routines
- encourage her to ask new friends over, and seize chances to make telephone contact with their parents by checking out a social arrangement, or a sleepover. Your child will squirm with embarrassment, of course, and probably do her utmost to make it unecessary for you to pick up the phone, but think about how pleased the other parents may be that you have made this first approach
- eavesdrop like mad on any conversations taking place in the back of the car – all children believe that drivers are completely deaf
- go to any Year 7 parents' events laid on by the school or parents' association – and force yourself to go even if you feel shy about not knowing many people, or know that it will be hard to make the time to get there. These events don't come around again, and often offer you your only informal chance to put teachers' faces to their names, and see something of the school, especially as your first formal parents' evening is unlikely to be

until quite late on in the autumn term, or even halfway through the next one. However, be aware that you are unlikely to make as close friends with your children's friends' parents as you did at primary school.

Also, try to encourage your child to check out what new opportunities are available in her new school, and help her – as far as you can – to make it possible to take up any she is interested in. That old saying about only getting back what you put in really applies here, and pupils who don't show any enthusiasm for sports teams or school clubs when they start at a new school can find either that they become defined (or define themselves) as a non-joiner, or that when they do decide they want to get stuck into something, it is a lot harder to break into than it might have been a year or two before.

Life at home

At home, try and make family life run in harmony with the rhythm of the school day, and do everything you can to encourage your child to start taking responsibility for her own life and actions.

- **In the morning**. Allow enough time for a proper breakfast, for your child to get organised, and for her to get the bus, or train or walk to school without arriving late and in a rush.
- **In the evening**. Aim for a routine that establishes the habit of homework. Television, supper and homework immediately afterwards is a routine that many families find works well – it offers a break after the school day,

fuel for a hungry body and then homework got out of the way before it gets too late. There is more on this in Chapter 9.

- **Negotiate the ground rules**. Determine how much and when she uses the computer, phone or her mobile – today's technology offers infinite opportunities for time-wasting – and also, as she gets older, about how much she goes out in the evening, and when you expect her home.
- **Encourage her to get organised**. Help her think about putting out the kit she'll need in the morning, and keep on reminding her, until the habit begins to take hold. But if you don't remind her, and she doesn't remember, and misses PE and reaps a detention as a result, then so be it. Sometimes learning things the hard way is the only chance of making them stick. And be careful not to make too big an issue of her disorganisation. Too many families fall into the trap of developing an 'Oh, she's so awful, she never remembers a thing, she loses everything, I don't know what we are going to do with her' attitude towards their children's chaotic habits. And the children, bathing in this clear admiration for their monumental incompetence, simply grin and get worse.

Everybody else . . .

However you run things at home, you will very soon hear that 'everybody else' does things differently. Everybody else will be allowed to watch late films, go out in the week and attend dodgy-sounding all-night parties. Ignore this. It isn't – entirely – true. What is true is that you will almost certainly find that, as your child goes through school, she will have friends and classmates whose parents have very different values from your own, who give their children oceans of money or who don't seem to give a damn about where they are and what they are up to. And at some point you will probably curse such parents for making your own life more difficult than it needs to be. Because, almost certainly, at some point, you will find yourself having to put your foot down and say you don't care twopence what 'everyone else's' parents are letting them do. You are her parent, and you are not going to let her go off to Glastonbury on her own aged thirteen, or whatever else the issue happens to be. If you find it hard, try and bear in mind what teenagers can say when they haven't had these limits put in place for them.

> *'I really wish I could have done better at school,' a young London nanny once told me, with passionate regret. 'I could have done, I know I could, I wasn't stupid, but my parents never cared anything about where I was or what I was doing. And it's really hard to do it for yourself. You don't see the point. Not when you're fifteen and all you can think about is who's going out with who, and where you're going to go on a Saturday night.'*

Life at school

There isn't much that parents can do about what goes on at school, but it can be helpful to know the kind of measures good schools are now adopting (see below) to try and keep students on track as they find their feet at secondary school. That way you can raise questions about why your child's school isn't doing them, if that's the case.

- **Booster classes**. These classes are held in the summer holidays for pupils who haven't done as well in their Key Stage 2 tests as they might. There is no statistical evidence that these make much difference, but children who take them say that they feel more confident and competent as a result. For this reason alone, if your child should be offered them, try and take up the offer. The classes are small, informal and make learning more fun than it is at school. And learning problems are always best addressed early. Otherwise a small wobble in maths at age 11 can all too easily develop into a wave of non-comprehension by the time GCSEs come round.
- **Matching the 'join'**. Schools are increasingly running joint projects that continue from the last term of primary school into the first term of secondary school. Secondary school teachers are also going into primary schools to see how they can make their own lessons more lively. Traditionally, secondary schools have saved their most experienced teachers for the exam years, and lessons for eleven to thirteen-year-olds have often been dull affairs, but more thought is now being given to who teaches this age group, and how they do it.
- **Having their own spaces**. Many schools now allocate younger students their own place in a bigger school,

via special assemblies, common rooms, activity weekends and the strengthening of pastoral systems.

What all this means for parents is that while, in the bad old days, pupils often arrived at secondary school and sank without trace, these days it just shouldn't happen. Parents have every right to expect to see their children quickly adjusting to their new school, enjoying interesting lessons, and feeling confident, secure and engaged. If it isn't happening, you need to go and see someone and find out why. And don't be fobbed off with assurances that it is completely normal for children to take a term or two to find their feet at secondary school. Those first terms are far too important to be allowed to go by like that.

CHAPTER EIGHT

Building good home–school relations

'Alone we can do so little; together we can do so much.'
– HELEN KELLER

IN THE OLD days schools used to think a good parent was one who, as a head once put it, 'leaves me alone to get on with my job'. Those days are long gone. Right around the world, everyone in education now knows that if home and school cooperate the result is a powerful alliance, and that 'partnership' has to be the name of the game.

But some schools are much better at it than others. Teachers and parents vary, as do circumstances, and the reality is that the nature of your relationship with your child's school will almost certainly vary from year to year.

One mother describes her odyssey like this: 'I loved my daughter's infants teacher. She was warm and friendly and always had time to talk, and I felt I had a really good relationship with the school. Then my daughter moved into Class 1, and I didn't get on with her new teacher at all. It was an awful year! I didn't like how she ran her class, and my daughter was unhappy, and it seemed like I was always in the classroom complaining. I back-pedalled for a year or so after that – my daughter was doing all right, and she hated me coming in and making a fuss about anything – but then someone asked me to join the parents' association, so for her last few years at primary school I got very stuck into that, and that gave me a completely different view of things. I got to know the head and quite a few of the teachers really well, and I understood much more about how the school ran and what it was up against. And it was really easy to chat informally with people about anything that came up, once I'd got to know them. I missed that sort of contact when she went to secondary school, where you only had formal parents' evenings to go on, although I did get to know my daughter's tutor quite well at one point. It was when she was in Year 9, and she was going through a rebellious patch. Her tutor called me in to school to see her, and we ended up meeting every few weeks for the next term or so to try and sort her out. Which we did, more or less, in the end – or else she just grew out of it!'

The ideal

In an ideal world, parents would feel their child's school was friendly and accessible, and that the teachers there were interested in their views and concerns. Schools, in turn, would feel parents were supportive and helpful, encouraging their children to work well, and willing to back up the school on things like discipline, behaviour, homework and uniform. But many things get in the way of good home–school relations.

They include:

- **Practical problems**. Teachers may be too stretched to listen to parents; parents may be too busy to make time for school meetings; a school may be so short of staff and space that it is difficult for teachers and parents sit down quietly together and talk; and a poorly managed school may not have good home–school policies in place.
- **Teacher problems**. There are still teachers around who resent parents 'interfering' with school; there are those who feel intimidated by parents (if you are dealing with children most of the time, it can be surprisingly threatening to have to talk to unknown adults); and there are others who will not take parents' concerns seriously (another hazard of classroom life – you get very used to being the authority figure who knows what's what).
- **Parent problems**. There are anxious parents who fuss about every issue; parents who are scared of teachers (yes, we can all feel like children again when we step into a school!); parents who want to blame the school for everything; parents who are not interested; and the ultimate 'parents from hell', who are either violent and abusive, make malicious allegations against teachers, or threaten legal action at every turn. And the numbers of those are growing. Thirteen per cent of teachers say they have been confronted by an aggressive parent, and nearly 300 teachers a year are physically assaulted, according

to official health and safety figures, often by parents. Meanwhile the number of legal cases against schools, concerning everything from bullying to exam results, is mushrooming. You, of course, won't be a parent from hell, but it is worth bearing in mind that you might well be talking to a wary teacher who has suffered from them.

One head of a leading boys' independent school finds the ever-growing demands on his time from parents the bane of his life. Recent demands include having to adjudicate between two rival groups of parents over an out-of-school dispute, fielding phone calls at home at weekends from parents 'too busy' to call him in the week and being expected by a parent to drop everything to look for a pair of lost trainers.

Building a good relationship with your child's school

You will build a great relationship with your child's school if you:

- try to see things from the teacher's point of view as well as your own
- pass on praise
- keep a sense of proportion
- stay informed
- do what the school asks.

Try to see things from the teacher's point of view as well as your own

'Please,' said a teacher friend, 'please, please, can you write a chapter saying teachers are human too! So many parents think, like their children do, that we go back into the cupboard along with the overhead projector at the end of the day.' On any given day your child's teacher may be trying to do their relentless job while feeling tired, unwell or distracted by personal problems. Remember that their job *is* demanding – they are constantly squeezed by things such as bad behaviour and the pressure to raise standards. And hold in mind that their responsibilities are different from yours. Your job is to worry about your one child; they have to worry about thirty. So, for example, if you go in to complain that the behaviour of a boy in the class is giving your son sleepless nights, remember that the teacher has to think not only about your son's distress, but also how to better manage that bad behaviour while also meeting the needs of this difficult boy. If you go in to say your son needs to be more challenged in maths, the teacher has to work out how to do this, while still paying full attention to the struggling or average children in the class. It sounds obvious, but it is amazing just how myopic we can be when pursuing our own child's interests. And understandably so, since our job is to focus on our child. But it's worth realising this myopia is not helpful. It can cause a lot of ill-will. And being aware of the wider context of your child's problems does not mean you will be less assiduous in pursuing solutions to them; only that you will be able to talk them through with the class teacher in a more realistic and empathetic – and therefore, hopefully, more productive – way.

Pass on praise

Let your child's teacher know when something has gone right. If he has been excited by a lesson or really likes a particular subject – teachers need appreciation as much as the rest of us.

Keep a sense of proportion

Some parents get so anxious about their child's schooling, that they are in and out of school for every little thing. This is bad because:

- your child's teacher will resent the time you are taking up
- your child will come to expect you to solve every problem – and not learn to be independent and do it for himself
- your child may get embarrassed by your constant complaints
- if you cry wolf too often, no one will take any notice when there is something seriously wrong.

Other parents, on the other hand, let even major problems develop without getting involved or, worse still, push their children through the school gate in the morning and take no interest in school from then on. This is bad news because:

- the school won't know when a child has a problem or
- it will guess there is a problem, but not know what, or how serious it is
- unresolved problems tend to get bigger

- the child will feel that no one cares
- the child will get the message that school is something that doesn't matter
- the child will feel embarrassed if their parent doesn't do what the school asks – buy the right gym shoes, for example, or provide a packed lunch for a school outing.

As your child goes through school, try to develop antennae that tell you when a problem is fleeting, when it is small but needs watching and when it is serious. Learn to ask yourself, as one infants' teacher always does when pupils come running to her, 'Are you whingeing, telling a tale or is it serious?' Finding the right answer is a real art, and takes some working on, but it is possible. Name-calling in the playground, for instance, may mean nothing if it is merely a squabble between friends who are always falling out, then falling in again. However, if it goes on longer, and your child is clearly unhappy, it is obviously time for a quiet word with his teacher. And if something is going on in the playground that is making him cry and lose sleep at night, then that is definitely a situation that you will expect the school to help sort out – and also let you know how it has done so.

Stay informed

Read any newsletters your child's school sends out, and any letters from the head or the class teacher. Keep an eye on noticeboards in the school, and encourage your child to remember to hand over any pieces of paper he has been given to bring home. Again, it sounds obvious, but in schools' experience, most parents don't do it. This can make schools feel that trying to involve parents is not worth the time and effort. Or it means that it has to waste valuable time and effort phoning round about things like getting back permission slips for class trips.

And make use of any system that your school has for communicating with home. Reading and homework diaries are there as two-way communication channels, but they can't work unless you play your part. A little comment is all it takes to keep the lines open, while questions and queries should prompt a teacher to respond. But little is the word. Lengthy essays will not be appreciated.

Also, if your school has a website, log on to it from time to time to keep yourself up to date.

Do what the school asks

Schools require things of parents. They need them to get their children to school on time, pick them up on time and send them to school in a state fit to learn – which means looking to things like breakfast and bedtimes (see Chapters 10 and 11). They need them to comply with its policy on illness, and policies vary, so be sure you know what yours is. Some schools, for example, ask parents to keep their children at home if they have been vomiting the night before, to be sure the problem's over with.

If your child's school has rules about uniform, games kit, what children can bring to school, jewellery and haircuts, follow them – unless you have some violent objection to what is being asked, in which case take it up formally with the school. But don't feel that it somehow doesn't matter if your child doesn't have regulation shoes, or if he takes his mobile phone to school even if he's not supposed to. If every parent thought the same, the school's discipline policy would go out of the window.

Attend parents' evenings, show an interest in what is going on in class, try and send in dinner money promptly, and return permission slips and school outing money on time. Your school will thank you for it, and it it will also mean that, should you need to tackle a difficult issue, teachers will respect you as a parent who is sensible and supportive of your child in school.

How to raise an issue with a school

If something is bothering you, don't let it go, raise it with the school. Start with the class teacher concerned, if it is a primary school, or with your child's tutor, or an individual subject teacher, if it is a secondary school. But raise it tactfully, in a way that makes it clear you hope you can solve it together. You might say, 'I'm not sure if I've got the full picture here, but I'm worried that . . .' or 'I really felt I had to come in and talk to you about . . .' or 'I don't know if you've noticed this, too, but it seems to me . . .'. If you feel things are not getting resolved, or if you feel it is too difficult to go to the teacher immediately responsible for the problem, go to the head, in a primary school, or to your child's tutor, or to the department head in a secondary school, before moving on to the head.

A small issue

This can often be dealt with a casual word, but pick your time. The end of the day is generally better than the start, if you are trying to catch a primary school teacher –

although if there is an immediate problem – your son is upset, say, because he hasn't learned all last night's spellings – teachers will want to know before the school day gets going. And remember it's always good to keep your child's teacher up to speed with big events at home. If grandma has been rushed to hospital, a pet has died or you have split up with your partner, the teacher needs to know in order to deal sensitively with your child, and to be alert to any distress or problems.

Bigger issues

With these it can help to first put something in writing, then ask for an appointment. Outline your concerns, but be careful not to be too quick with any blame or accusations. You only have your child's version of events at this point and you need to know the full facts to make a judgement.

If you are nervous about going into school, make a note of the points you want to raise and take someone with you for support. If you feel very angry and worked up, breathe deeply and remind yourself that losing your temper is not going to help your child.

> *When dealing with a problem, try as hard as you can to be assertive, without being emotional. 'The most useful thing I've learned about being a school parent is this,' says one mother. 'If there's a problem, take a breath. Better still, sleep on it. And whatever you do, don't ever go rushing into school when you've got PMS.'*

Think also about what outcome you want from the meeting. For example, if the school promises to look into an issue, you may want to pin them down about how they plan to report back to you, and when. Will they write to you? And in a few days, or a week? Will you be able to have a follow-up meeting to discuss what has been done?

Try to be assertive without getting emotional – it's often hard when your own child is involved. Stick to what you want to sort out, and don't be fobbed off with lame excuses, or educational jargon. There is no shame in asking what, exactly, something means, if you don't understand it. After all, why should you?

At all times, hold your child's well-being at the front of your mind, and remind yourself that this, and only this, is what this meeting is all about.

The biggest problems

If things don't get sorted out then your recourse is to the school governing body, which is the formal, legal entity with responsibilities for running the school. You might start by talking informally to a parent governor. Later, you may need to put your complaint in writing. If you are still unsatisfied, you can write to the local education authority, outlining your concerns and asking them to do something.

Sometimes, sadly, problems never get sorted out, in which case you may have to think carefully about whether the answer is going to be for your child to move school.

School reports

Your child will have a school report at least once a year, and maybe once a term. Learn to read these carefully. They can be clear, or they can be full of jargon (and sometimes, regrettably, spelling and grammar mistakes). You need to note:

- where your child is doing well
- where he needs to improve
- how he is doing compared to his last report
- any general issues or problems.

> *A teacher says: 'If your child's school report reads, "He has wholly met his attainment targets and reached an acceptable level in Key Stage 2." You must go in and ask them what the hell they are talking about. We are the world's worst for talking in jargon.'*

If you don't understand anything in a report, you need to bring it up with his teacher, either at a parents' evening, or in a separate meeting. For example, if he's 'too easily distracted in class', you need to know more about where, why, and what you and the school working together can do about it. If his English isn't great, you need to know exactly what skills he needs to write better stories, and how he can work at acquiring those skills.

Go through the report with your child, praising his successes, and discussing – calmly – areas where he needs to improve. And discuss together what he can aim for in order to improve, and how he can go about it. Most children are used to target-setting at school, so will understand the process. Then stick to any schedule you work out. If he agrees, for example, to do half an hour's extra reading a week, make sure he does it – and, of course, give him lots of praise and encouragement when he does.

This close scrutiny of reports gets even more important at secondary school, where you can see whether your child is staying on track in his new school and what sort of progress he is making in separate subjects. If there is a clear problem in any area, if, for example, his work in biology or maths is well below his work in all other subjects, you must contact the subject teacher to see what can be done about this. And press for details. A vague, 'Well he just needs to put more into it' isn't enough.

Parents' evenings

Schools hold parents' evenings anything from once a term, to once a year, usually in the evening, but sometimes during the school day, and you should make every effort to get to them – although if you genuinely can't, most teachers will try to fit in a meeting with you at another time. In fact some schools have now abandoned traditional parents' evenings, in favour of a system of individual appointments with parents, at their convenience.

How they run varies. In primary schools parents usually only see the class teacher, and possibly the head. In secondary schools, your child will make appointments for you to see all his subject teachers – but be aware that children have plenty of tricks to avoid letting you meet us with those they don't want you to see ('Mr So-and-So didn't have any appointments left'). Insist that you must see the teachers you need to, which will include any teachers your child seems to clash with, or the teachers of any subject where he is not doing so well.

Time is always limited – in some schools they even use a bell system; when your five minutes is up you move on – so prepare your thoughts before you go, and take a paper and pencil in case there are things you want to take a note of. Read your child's report carefully, if you have one, and ask him if there is anything he wants you to raise. And think about what you want to know. And what you want the teacher to know. Are there things about how he is being taught that you don't understand? Or are there problems that are bothering you? And are there things you would like the school to do for your child?

However, if there are things you want to tell the teacher, remember to keep it brief or you could come away empty-handed. One experienced teacher gets through parents' evening by asking each set of parents, 'How do you think it's going then?' and then sitting back and listening to them talk. That way the teacher's input is minimal. But if you want to hear the views of your child's teacher, remember to button your lip and listen.

Don't expect to get much more than a thumbnail sketch of how your child is doing and try not to read too much into casual remarks. 'He's doing fine, but he does tend to talk a lot in class' doesn't mean your son is on the way to being a major troublemaker. It could just mean that he irritated that particular teacher one Monday morning when he had a hangover. On the other hand, if there is a pattern of comments that is repeated year-on-year, or by several different teachers, it will definitely point to an issue that needs addressing. And if you get the strong impression that no one knows too much about your child, that too, might ring alarm bells. Quiet, average children can all too easily get overlooked in schools, while disruptive and intrusive ones get more than their fair share of time and attention. ('If you find them all saying, "He's a lovely child," and not much else, you should definitely worry!' warns one primary teacher.)

And if anything comes up that needs more time, ask for an appointment to talk it through properly. The rush and hurry of parents' evening is no place for an in-depth discussion of difficult issues. Follow up anything that you want to pursue with a note or a telephone call in the next couple of days, and if a teacher has suggested anything useful, like earlier bedtimes, or making more use of the homework diary, talk to your child about it and start the new routine right away.

Ofsted

School inspectors are obliged to look at how well schools relate to their parents, and what parents' views are of a school. Read your school's last report to see what they found, and if you want to contribute your views when inspectors are next in school, you can fill in a questionnaire, write to them and attend an open meeting. Your school will circulate the details.

Parenting and other courses

Some schools run or promote parenting classes, to back up the work they are doing in school. A south London prep school, for example, which is following a programme to encourage children to develop responsibility and learn how to make good choices, encourages parents to enrol on a ten-week course, which teaches them how to follow the same techniques at home. Some schools send home information about local adult education parenting courses, or details of useful parenting websites.

Keep an eye out for such things and think about making use of them. Parenting is something we used to think we could pick up as we go along, but this isn't how we'd learn something new in the workplace, so why should home be any different? And there's lots of good expertise out there, so why not use it?

Other schools offer parents the chance to take lessons in class alongside students, or open up their computers for parents to brush up their IT skills. These are great opportunities, if you can take them. Apart from anything else, they will do a lot to help you keep in touch with your child's world, and it is always good for children see that learning is something their parents do, too.

Separated and divorced parents

Schools are obliged to supply information about a child's education to any natural parent who requests it, provided there is no court order limiting this right. This is true even if that parent is no longer living at home, or has no contact with the child.

This sometimes causes difficulties and disagreements, but if you are a separated or divorced parent you have a big responsibility to try and work something out with your former partner. You will need to talk through who will go to school events and parents' evenings, and whether you'll go separately or together. You will need to talk about the business of choosing a secondary school and, if your child is in a private school, who is going to pay the fees. If you don't do this, your child will definitely suffer. Child psychiatrists are very clear that children caught in the middle of marital conflict, who feel that they are the source of arguments and tension, can run into many serious problems, including getting turned off school altogether.

Home–school agreements

All state-maintained schools should have a written agreement in place, which outlines the school's aims and values and how it and parents will work together. It spells out the responsibilities of the school, and of parents, and what it expects of pupils. Parents are asked to sign it, but have no legal obligation to do so. These agreements can be a useful touchstone if things are going awry, but are not a lot of practical use to parents beyond that.

Getting involved in the school

If you can make the time, get involved. You'll know more about the school. You'll have more to talk to your children about. And you'll enjoy getting to know other children and parents – a United Nations-linked survey found that people rated volunteering the second-most pleasurable leisure activity of their lives. (And, no, the first one was dancing.)

The parent–teacher association

Most schools have a PTA, although it may be called something different, like The Friends of. . . . How active it is will vary from school to school, and even from year to year in the same school, but schools desperately need the support and fund-raising that parents can offer. In fact in far too many schools, tight budgets mean that PTA money sometimes has to be used for essential supplies such as books.

Most parents who get involved, love it. 'We always had such a lot of fun at primary school,' said one mother, whose husband traditionally played the dame in the PTA Christmas panto. 'He wore a wig and tights and rouge and everyone always fell about when he came on – until the year when our second child had just joined the reception class, and he jumped up from where he was sitting at the front and cried out, "Don't laugh at him! He's my daddy!" It brought the house down.'

Sometimes, though, new parents don't feel entirely welcome. Associations can look as if they are run by tight little cabals of friends who resent all newcomers. But any PTA must have new people to survive. So be proactive. Drum up other friends for support. Go to a meeting, or ring up the chairperson and ask what you can do to help. Proffer any skills you have – accounting, website-building, secretarial – or simply offer yourself as a willing foot soldier. And if you can't make a regular commitment, offer some time to help at events such as the school fair or Christmas bazaar.

PTAs also get involved in other things. Some run drop-in centres at their school; others organise informal evenings for parents to learn more about the curriculum. If nothing much is happening at your school, check the National Confederation of Parent Teacher Associations website (www.ncpta.org.uk) to see what's possible and get things going yourself.

On the other hand, PTA parents sometimes feel they are working their socks off raising money for their school, without getting much back from the school in return. As poet Robert Frost said, 'The world is full of willing people. Those willing to work, and those willing to let them.' If hard-working parents are starting to feel excluded or taken for granted, encourage the chairperson to talk to the head about it. Resentment is a very bad basis for good parent–teacher relations.

Governors

You could become a school governor at your child's school, or even another one, provided you are prepared to commit the time and take on the responsibility. Because, while being a school governor is fascinating and rewarding, you do need to be realistic about what it entails.

The country's 350,000 school governors in England and Wales come in all shapes and sizes, and they don't all arrive in post via the same route. Some are elected as parent, teacher or staff governors. If you want to be a parent governor, you may walk into the job, or you may have to stand in a low-key election against other parents. Usually this involves giving out a bit of background about yourself, and also saying why you would like to be a governor, and what you think you can do for the school.

Other governors are asked by the school to be co-opted on to the governing body, or nominated by the local education authority or, in the case of church-linked schools, by the church diocese.

Parents make very good school governors. They tend to be passionately interested in the issues, while also knowing about the day-to-day realities of school life. Plus they often have managerial, financial or other useful skills (common sense) to bring to the job.

You don't need to be an expert in education to be a governor, and they are in desperately short supply – about one in ten governorships in England is currently vacant; many more in London. If you were to put yourself forward, either by talking to your school, or by ringing up your local education authority, the chances are you would be welcomed with open arms.

A parent who was deputy chair of governors at her children's primary school through a stormy, political time, says the job was sometimes frustrating and stressful, but still rewarding. 'I managed to change some things and make them better for future children. And I learned so many transferable skills. I learned about negotiation, finance, consultation, delegation and how to run meetings. I also learned who to go to to get something done, if my children had a problem in school, which was really useful. And I made some terrific friends.'

Why would you want to do it?
Because governors have serious powers and influence over how a school runs. They can:

- help raise standards
- help children realise their full potential
- help develop a school's management team
- help identify where a school can improve, and help to make it better
- help improve a school's financial efficiency
- help engage more parents
- help create an environment that promotes learning
- help celebrate the success of school.

On the other hand, you must be aware of the work involved. A full governing body will probably only meet once or twice a term, but you will also sit on one or more of the various sub-committees, which deal with things like the curriculum, staffing and school buildings. You will have to read, or at least scan, a lot of papers entitled things like, *Consultation on draft regulations and guidance on School Governance Federation and Collaborations New Schools (General) (England) Regulations 2003* and get your head around the horrors of education jargon. And because school governors these days have responsibilities for things like making sure their school is meeting its targets, you will quickly become aware that, although the job is unpaid, it can often seem to be as burdensome as a paid one. Surveys show that, on average, governors spend about 180 hours a year on the job.

There are also circumstances when being a very involved parent might occasionally backfire on children. One school governor says her son definitely suffered because of campaigns she supported, which weren't popular with staff. 'He'd put his hand up, and his teacher would say things like, "Oh, no, we don't want to hear from you, clever clogs."'

But bear in mind:

- you don't have to sign up for ever. Governors are appointed for four years and plenty feel that once they have done this stint, they have made their contribution and it's time to move on
- these days there is a mass of advice, Internet help and training available. Also, if you do become a new governor, you may well be assigned a mentor who will, metaphorically speaking, hold your hand and shepherd you through those first confusing meetings
- being a school governor is a great way of developing your own skills, while also contributing to your child's educational environment
- governors take collective decisions. You, as an individual, will not be held legally accountable for them.

For more information contact the National Association of Governors and Managers (www.ngam.org.uk) or the National Governors' Council (www.ngc.org.uk).

Volunteering

If committee work is not for you, you could volunteer to help in school. These days, when schools have so many classroom assistants and support staff, fewer parents spend time in the classrooms washing paint pots and hearing children read. But there are still opportunities. In fact volunteers give a billion hours a year to supporting schools – work which, if it were charged at the average national wage, would be worth £10 billion per annum.

If you have artistic or sporting skills, think of offering those to the school. Or you could do something simple, but vital, like weeding the flowerbeds or picking up litter. Sometimes volunteers answer the phones, or work in the library, and you might be asked to hear children read – although maybe not in your own child's classroom. Schools have often learned the hard way that this is not always the best idea, and the charity Volunteer Reading Help will not place any parent in their own children's school.

If you are working with children you may be asked to have a criminal record check. This isn't compulsory for volunteers unless they are to have unsupervised access to children but many local education authorities now request it. It is tedious, but you won't have to pay for it.

As a volunteer in a classroom, you will need to be willing to fit in with what is going on there and be discreet about any information that comes your way during the course of helping out. It is not your job to report what you hear and see there all over the neighbourhood. And it's as well to be aware that you aren't going to change the world – research results conflict on whether or not school volunteers affect on how well children do in class, although some studies show definite improvements.

The charity Volunteer Reading Help found that 23 per cent of children helped by its volunteers for a year improved their reading age by two years. Eighty nine per cent of children had improved confidence about reading.

Part Two

Helping your child flourish at school

CHAPTER NINE

Learning to learn – better

'Vertical thinking is digging the hole deeper. Lateral thinking is digging it again elsewhere.' – EDWARD DE BONO

I BELIEVE THIS chapter is one of the most exciting in the book. It outlines some of the many new things we now know about how children can succeed at school – and shows us, as parents, what we can do to reinforce them.

Our amazing brains

In a nutshell, we know that everyone can learn, and everyone can learn to learn better. Our brains aren't just some finite lump of grey stuff, given to us at birth. They grow and change according to what we do with them. And this is especially true for children, whose brains are still plastic and malleable.

In fact the important thing is not the number of brain cells we have, but how well they connect with each other, and the more a brain is fed and stimulated, the stronger and more complex these connections grow. So, the more a child learns and thinks, the more powerful and effective her brain becomes, while a child who gets little mental stimulation will find learning anything an uphill struggle.

We also now know, too, that mood, behaviour and the 'stories' we tell ourselves about what we can and can't do, all have a direct effect on how well we learn. If we can help our children get those right, we will set them flying along the path to success.

How do we know this?

Our growing understanding of all this comes partly from new technology, which allows us to watch the nerve fibres in people's brains making connections as they think, and partly from an ever-increasing awareness that intelligence is so much more diffuse and multi-faceted than we once believed.

Intelligence floods every molecule of our being and is impossible to confine to that narrow band of learning we so love to test in school exams. And how we define it also depends on circumstances. To a bat, piloting itself around by ultrasonic sounds, human beings are blundering primitives in a world they completely fail to 'see', while to a Kalahari bushman, who has to know how to find water in the desert to survive, even a visiting Einstein would seem dumb.

And even within our own small world of Western culture, definitions of intelligence can be wildly off the mark. Is the child who comes top of the class necessarily the smartest kid in the room? Apparently not. Psychologists in the US have found that the best predictor of success in later life is not what children know, but how well developed their social skills are.

The eight, nine, ten intelligences . . . ?

Ever since the 1980s when American psychologist Howard Gardner revolutionised our perception of intelligence by saying it came in all sorts of guises, our thinking about brainpower widened. Gardner came up with eight intelligences. Others have since added more. It probably doesn't matter exactly how many, since these are simply ways of chopping a very complex whole into parts in order to help us understand the big picture. One list of intelligences might read:

- linguistic – you like words, stories, languages
- logical–mathematical – you like numbers, abstract thinking, problem-solving
- visual–spatial – you like pictures, colour, shapes
- physical – you like to use your body and hands
- musical – you like pitch, sounds, rhythms
- emotional – you enjoy thinking, reflecting and analysing yourself
- social – you like mixing, communicating, negotiating
- intuitive – you like feelings, values, self-knowledge.

As parents, we know at once that these ring true. We all have children who are good at this, and not so hot at that, and we've probably all had moments when we've felt exasperated that our children's schools seem quite unable to grasp the whole, miraculous picture of their abilities and talents. In fact the common grumble of us parents that our children are not being fully stretched at school may well be because we have this close-up, visceral knowledge of our children's many interwoven abilities, and see immediately when chunks of these are going unnoticed or unaddressed, while schools, which are judged on how well they deliver the national curriculum, have to focus mainly on the verbal and mathematical skills that matter most to them.

'This is all so stupid,' said a sixteen-year-old, stomping off to yet another GCSE exam. 'All it's about is how well you can remember stuff, and how fast you can write it down. It doesn't say anything about what you can really do.'

IQ tests

All of the above is not to say that IQ tests have gone out of the window. Many intelligence researchers believe that there is a factor of intelligence – known as g, or little g – which is inherited and measurable, and which makes up just over half of children's intelligence (or 80 per cent in adults, whose capacity to develop has slowed down). It is this factor that IQ tests measure. And in schools almost a million children a year sit IQ-type tests, often called 'cognitive ability tests', which are used:

- to separate pupils into different ability bands
- in the guise of what is still often called the 11-plus, to screen applicants to selective schools
- to help test for learning difficulties such as dyslexia.

Should I have my child's IQ tested?

Parents often wonder if they should have their children's IQ tested.

It can be helpful if it:

- reassures you there's nothing wrong
- gives your child a burst of confidence
- helps build up a picture of specific problems such as speech and language difficulties, or dyslexia, and can help make a case for extra help at school and time in exams (see Chapter 13).

But be aware that schools aren't always impressed with having a child's raw IQ score waved in their faces for no good reason, and may even turn stubborn if they feel they are being railroaded them into doing something, like moving a child up a set, that they don't feel is right. And be aware, too, that critics of such tests still argue forcefully that they offer nothing more than a snap-shot picture of the state of a small range of mental functions, on the particular day that the tests are taken. So always think carefully before taking your child to be tested. Ask yourself:

- why are you doing it?
- is it going to be worth the time and money?
- what do you hope will come out of it?
- are you sure your child won't feel freakish, or downcast about the results, in the process?

If you do want to go ahead and are willing to pay you can find a local chartered educational psychologist by contacting the British Psychological Society: www.bps.org.uk. But this will be expensive, and remember that even IQ's most fervent advocates now recognise that this only measures a fraction of our amazing brainpower.

Fostering our children's brainpower

There are numerous ways we can encourage our children's brains to develop and grow, as well as lots of ways we can help them to learn how to use them better. But to understand how this works, we need to understand what makes a good learner and how we can encourage our child to be one.

Good learners

Good learners must feel physically and emotionally secure, and be willing to have a go at things, and to get to that point a child needs certain basics. Bill Lucas and Alistair Smith, two of the UK's leading experts on learning, have pinpointed the following:

- feeling valued and loved
- having aspirations
- knowing it's safe to make mistakes
- understanding the child is an individual
- being able to take on everyday challenges
- experiencing an ability to be successful at things.

And to help create this positive environment, they say, parents need to:

- spend time with their children and listen to them
- establish routines for everyday things such as meals and bathtimes
- be consistent about rules
- let their children know they are loved for who they are, not what they do
- talk to their children about dreams and possibilities
- show them what they want them to do, not just explain – then criticise
- hold back on put-downs and criticisms
- use four positive comments to every one negative one
- help children to talk about their feelings
- share their own interests and enthusiasms with their children
- explain that it's all right to make mistakes
- help children to notice when they have improved on their skills and achievements.

Different learning styles

Parents also need to understand that not all children learn in the same way. Mary Tudor famously said that if they opened her up after her death they would find the word 'Calais' written on her heart. If you opened up a modern teacher, you would probably find the initials 'VAK' carved there instead.

These stand for the three main ways in which children take in information, and it is drummed into student teachers that everything they do must take account of these, in order to draw in every child in their classroom.

The styles are:

- visual – you take things in by seeing
- auditory – you take things in by hearing
- kinaesthetic – you take in things by doing.

And while no one is ever wholly one thing or another, most people have a preference, and some are very skewed indeed.

As a basic skills tutor I struggled and struggled to teach an adult learner some basic spellings. We wrote them out. We looked at them. We covered them over. We tried to remember how to write them out again. We put them into sentences. Nothing worked. The words flew out of his head just as soon as he had seen them. Until, that is, I heard him talking to someone on the phone and confidently spelling out his address, Hartland Road, Haitch-ay-rur-tee-el-ay-en-dee. And all at once it dawned on me that sounds meant more to him than things written down, and that if he tried to learn these new words by beating them out, so that the sound and the rhythm of them made a pattern in his head, then maybe they would stick. Which they did. And what's more, once he knew to how to do that, it was a routine he was able to repeat whenever he needed to commit a new spelling to his memory. He had learned how to learn – his own way.

Primary schools these days are much more aware that many of their 'naughty boys' are likely to be strongly kinaesthetic learners who need active, hands-on experiences and that whole-class mental maths sessions can suit auditory learners better than visual ones.

There are arguments about what proportion of the population falls into each category, but many researchers think that most people are mainly visual learners, with auditory learners making up the next biggest category and kinaesthetic learners coming last.

What kind of learner is your child?

Knowing the ways in which your own child learns can mean the difference between pushing on an open door, or a shut one. So watch how she responds to things and what she most enjoys doing. Does she talk herself through what she's doing, or need to get the feeling of writing a word down in order to come to know it? But remember – personality comes into it, too. A noisy, rushing-around boy isn't necessarily a hands-on learner; he could be a very active visual one. So pay close attention. And remember, too, that all children use all their senses to some degree or other, so when you try and teach them anything, always go for a variety of approaches.

Learning to learn at school

Here are some of the ways schools now encourage children use their brains better – all of which can be reinforced at home.

- **Study skills**. Teach children how to approach projects, how to be organised, how to manage their time and how to present their work. Older students learn how to do research, plan essays and revise for exams. These lessons may be woven into the school day, or taught as a separate subject.
- **Mind mapping®.** These spider-shaped diagrams (the ® means the phrase is a registered trademark), invented by learning guru Tony Buzan, offer a visual way of taking notes or thinking about a subject, using different branches to follow one area of thought. They help children get down lots of ideas on paper without using masses of words, and for some learners – especially visual ones – their twisting, pictorial nature mirrors the twists and leaps of the brain much better than linear notes.
- **Thinking skills**. These help children to ask good questions about things, to think creatively about ideas, to solve problems and make good judgements. Some schools teach them separately, others weave them through ordinary lessons. Games, discussions, debates and projects are all used to do this. One classic example is the famous six-hat exercise devised by Edward de Bono, one of the founders of the idea of thinking skills, which uses different-coloured hats to encourage students to approach a problem in many different ways. They wear a green hat when they think creatively, a red one for intuition, a black one for judgement and caution, and so on. Research shows that schools that teach science through a thinking skills approach at pre-GCSE level do significantly better at GCSE than others who don't. Pupils get on average 19 per cent more A*–C passes in

science, and also do better in maths and English, which seems to indicate that, once taught these skills, children are able to use them in all kinds of work. And you can tell how important they are by the fact that Cambridge University has just started to use a thinking skills test to spot its best applicants.

Why do we need thinking skills? Imagine this. Your child has to do a project on, say, Egyptian mummies. A decade ago this would have been simple. She would have gone to the library, taken out the two books they had on the subject and transcribed the most interesting bits from each. Today she is more likely to head for the Internet where a torrent of mummy-related information will pour out on to her screen. How is she to make sense of it? How will she tell the difference between the information on a site run by some mummy-obsessed weirdo holed up in the Rocky Mountains who think mummies are aliens come to take over the world, and the dusty, academic information available from the world's top museums? How will she decide which sites offer her good, reliable information, pitched at the right level of detail for the work she is doing? And how will she know, even from these, which information is most relevant and interesting to what she is trying to do?

- **Philosophy in schools**. 'How do I know what's real?' 'Where does time go when it's over?' Growing numbers of schools are using philosophy to challenge students, enhance their reasoning, to stimulate high-fliers, and to develop their speaking and debating skills. Some do it informally, maybe by adding a short session on to the end of circle time. Others do it with an after-school club, or in a specific lesson.
- **Brain breaks**. Draw a figure eight in the air with your finger, then draw it with the other hand; sing a song while energetically touching your right elbow to your left knee and vice versa; pat your head with one hand and rub your stomach with the other. If you walked in on a class doing Brain-gym® exercises you would think they had all gone bonkers. But these quick, cross-lateral exercises are believed to improve the coordination of all the different bits of the brain, release stress, and change the mental and physical alertness of learners. Teachers use them to get children ready for learning, and freshen them up when they are flagging.
- **Using music to learn**. Teachers use music to change pupils' moods, influence their thoughts and stimulate their ideas. They might use Bach as a background for teaching grammar, and Ravel or Debussy for loosening up the creative juices. Or they might raise classroom energies with an upbeat track like James Brown's *Feel Good*.
- **Circle time**. Schools use this 'on the carpet' time to raise self-esteem, develop emotional intelligence, build social skills and encourage problem-solving, often by discussing a hypothetical situation, or by encouraging pupils to explore how they feel about things.

Can music really help children to learn? The 'Mozart-effect' leapt into view ten years ago when a group of California scientists found that listening to a Mozart sonata improved children's reasoning abilities. Overnight, every classroom had its 'greatest classics' tapes, and every pregnant belly a Walkman clamped to it.

But the initial effect was only shown to last for ten to fifteen minutes, and when other scientists tried to reproduce the results they got only mixed results, so much of the initial hype came to seem misplaced.

However, the original researchers have since gone on to show that pre-school children who get involved with active music-making (via keyboard lessons) demonstrate improved reasoning, which lasts at least a day, while other studies have shown that Baroque music seems to harmonise the function of the brain and produce a state of calm, relaxed alertness. When postgraduates were asked to memorise a vocabulary list, for example, they did it best by listening to Handel's Water Music, *while also using visualisations of the words as they were read out.*

Music is known to help rats run through mazes more efficiently, to reduce the severity of epileptic fits and ameliorate the symptoms of Alzheimer's, all of which probably demonstrates what we all know instinctively: that music floods our responses and therefore inevitably influences our brain as it learns.

The brain-friendly school

Some schools now put all these things together to make a consciously 'brain-friendly' environment where children are strongly encouraged to feel that they can learn, and are then helped to do so effectively. This has a variety of names, such as Active or Accelerated Learning, and is likely to include:

- making the classroom feel very positive, upbeat and non-threatening (no one learns well when they are scared or intimidated), often with 'You Can Do It!'-type posters and slogans
- giving pupils crystal-clear explanations about a task to be done, how this connects to what has been done before and what will have been achieved at the end of it
- the teacher using visual, auditory and kinaesthetic ways of teaching
- lessons including a range of different activities, including things such as mind mapping®
- brain exercise breaks
- water available in the classroom
- brain-friendly snacks, such as fruit, being available
- music used to aid mood and concentration.

Occasionally a school will take up the outer shell of these ideas, without properly digesting the content, and then the whole thing degenerates into a few gimmicks – water, music – which are later dropped. However, when done properly, these ideas can be hugely impressive in practice.

I visited a small Midlands primary school where the enthusiasm for Accelerated Learning was palpable. One class was doing maths with Baroque music playing in the background, while in another room the deputy head was teaching his class of youngsters with verve and style. They discussed together a story they were going to write. Questions flew back and forth. The children began to make mind maps®. After a time they broke for a brain break – enthusiastic choruses of 'Did you ever, ever, ever in your long-legged life . . .', accompanied by mass touching of knees to opposite elbows and a great deal of laughter. The children were alert, happy and working well. Coming to the back of the room the teacher asked me if I could point out his 'special needs' pupils – those who found learning particularly difficult, and who in a normal classroom might well have been disruptive, day-dreaming or producing work with difficulty. Not one of the pupils answered such a description. I didn't have a clue. What I did know was that this was a classroom I would have loved my children to be in, and where I knew they would have learned well.

Learning to learn at home

What does all this mean at home? A thousand different things. For a start it means that every situation and conversation is full of possibilities for developing your child's complex intelligence. It would be easy to write a whole book on the subject, and people have – some of the best are listed at the end of this one, and if you are interested in these ideas, do make time to read them. You'll find them full of a wealth of possibilities and information.

But there are ground rules we all need to learn in order to help our child on their learning journey.

- **Do what comes naturally**. As parents, wisdom is often hard-wired into our systems, and we ignore it, or override it, at our peril. Every parent instinctively rocks a fretful baby, for example, and now it's known that there is a good reason for that. Regular rocking promotes the vestibular system within the brain, which is linked to balance and coordination. Rubbing, rocking and stroking newborn babies have all also been shown to improve learning, and it seems logical that overt gestures of love and caring must also help older children in the same way. So trust your instincts. Ignore the experts if you think they're wrong. Put aside anxiety and know that as a parent you have the wisdom to help your child.
- **Encourage young children to play and explore**. For them play is learning. Help them use all their five senses, and adopt the whole world as your classroom. Every situation has its potential for developing language, number and other abilities. Children can help sort the socks, grow flowers in the garden or sit on your lap and talk with you about the pictures when you are reading. Don't rush them into reading and writing. It isn't the best way for them to learn, and if they are not

ready it will only make you – and them – anxious. If they have been well prepared by having had lots of informal learning, they will make progress in leaps and bounds when they are ready.

> *In New York, the city that invented self-esteem, I once saw a big banner across the doorway of an elementary school. It read 'We Applaud Ourselves' and was surrounded by a appliquéd montage of clapping hands. But for what, I wondered? What had they done? The school had only got half of an important message. It understood that its children needed to feel good about themselves. It didn't understand they had to have something to feel good about.*

- **Be as positive as you know how**. No child – or young person – can ever have too much encouragement. Say well done, or point out that they did something well, or that they are getting better at something that they found difficult before. Praise them for trying, or for sticking at a tough task, or being thoughtful to their friends, or having the courage to admit they don't understand something, and help them deal with a mistake or a failure by trying to find something positive in the situation as well – 'You shouldn't have taken those chocolates without asking, but at least you owned up'. But don't devalue the currency by offering empty praise. If you praise what a child knows to be a careless scribble as if it were a Picasso, no one will come off well. You will look insincere, and your child will feel confused. To develop and grow, children need to feel good about themselves for a reason – and what's more, deep down, they know it.

- **Develop your skills as a coach and mentor**. Parents are often told they should be their children's first teacher, but this can sound as if we are all meant to sit down with our child and an early reading primer and a batch of multiplication flash cards. In fact, not that many parents do much by way of formally teaching their children (and those who do, often find it ends in tears). However, the informal feedback you give your child by giving her opportunities to see, hear and experience different things, talking to her about them, and helping her go over what she has seen, done or learned, is every bit as powerful as classroom-style learning. And learning a few simple techniques can help you make the most of these everyday opportunities:

  – practise asking open-ended questions – 'What do you think this picture tells us?', rather than 'Can you see how cross the girl looks in the picture?' – to encourage your child to voice her feelings and ideas
  – discipline yourself not to interrupt. It sounds easy, but in practice it can be very hard
  – learn reflective listening techniques, by which you make it clear you are listening to your child by making encouraging noises and repeating phrases and ideas back to her – 'So, you felt pretty angry when that happened, did you?' – without imposing your own agenda

– practise helping your child by hints and nudges – 'Does that word look at all like another one we've just seen?' – rather than giving formal instruction, or supplying answers
– use music creatively at home to set the mood – upbeat for energy, calming for bedtime, Baroque for brain-work
– help your child to set goals that are challenging, but achievable – 'I'm going to read this whole chapter by the end of the week' – and help her plan work and break learning tasks down into smaller, more manageable chunks if a task seems overwhelming ('Why not make a plan of what you want to write?')
– help your child to learn how to look over what she has to do (preview) and go over it once she's finished (review). This helps to lock in learning
– encourage her to focus on one thing at a time
– encourage her to ask questions, take them seriously and help her find answers ('I don't know, let's look it up')
– when you ask her questions, allow her time to think and answer; don't jump in over her thinking time
– talk to her as an equal, making it clear that her opinions and assessments of things are valid and interesting
– keep her motivated by encouraging her to see the big picture of what she is doing, by making her aware of the progress she is making and by talking with her about what she will get out of it
– encourage her independence – she must be able to make her own mistakes and solve her own problems in order to learn

- encourage her to try out different ways of learning things – using diagrams, drawing pictures, talking into a dictaphone, making up songs or raps or working with a friend
- help her to be able to recognise when she needs help, and to feel able to ask for it
- put in place the right physical conditions to help her brain and body learn. Which leads on to the very important next chapter . . .

How to make a mind map®. A child might be asked, for example, to think about writing an adventure story. In the middle of the paper (turned so the long side is at the bottom) she would draw a circle and write ADVENTURE STORY, then on branching lines going out from the centre, she might write character, plot, setting, and so on. In turn each of these branches will grow other branches. The setting – a wrecked ship – might grow branches saying things like creaking noises, broken floorboards, funny smell. Then each of these, in turn, might spawn further branches. Creaking noises, for example, could lead on to footsteps, a rusty door, the wind howling . . . If your child enjoys making these maps, and finds them helpful, it is well worth encouraging her to use them. The more she does, the better she'll get at them, and she will find them a powerful tool for learning. However, be aware that some children can get so absorbed by shading and enhancing their beautiful mind maps®, that they forget why they are doing them in the first place.

CHAPTER TEN

Top nutrition for success at school

'Never eat more than you can lift.' – MISS PIGGY

IT IS IMPOSSIBLE to overstate how important food and drink are for children's success in school. Put baldly: children simply can't be their happiest and do their best if their brains and bodies aren't properly fed. On the other hand, a well-nourished child will be alert, energetic and much more able to concentrate than one who isn't.

The really big problem for parents in this area is that there is a vast and growing gap between what most children now eat and drink, and what they need to eat and drink to do well in school. And, more worryingly, as this gap widens we are all increasingly coming to accept the results of it – lethargic, inattentive, volatile, impulsive, allergic and restless children – as the norm. Which means, in turn, that if we decide to go against the tide, first of all it's very hard, and secondly we quickly run into the danger of being seen as some kind of puritanical tofu-lover who has banished all fun and pleasure from the kitchen.

Yet there is good news here, as well. For one thing, we've all recently become much more aware of the importance of a good diet for children. When I started writing this book, it was quite hard to find useful information on the subject. By the time I finished, less than a year later, childhood obesity and other dietary problems were in all the headlines. Also, diet is one area where parents can have an absolutely enormous influence over children. And if we wield that influence thoughtfully, it will have a direct and immediate impact on our children's lives at school. Give them two weeks of genuinely healthy eating, say many nutritionists, and you will be absolutely amazed at the changes you will see.

So why don't we do it?

In fact there are now so many studies documenting how poor nutrition and dehydration affect children's health, well-being and ability to learn, that the puzzle is why we don't all act on it. It obviously isn't because we don't care. We teach our children not to run across busy roads, get them vaccinated, make sure they are properly clothed and shod, read them stories and encourage them to do their homework. Yet when it comes to eating and drinking, things often seem to go awry. This might be because we:

- don't fully realise how important these things are
- realise they are important, but don't know what to do about them
- realise they are important, but don't feel able to do anything about them
- feel pressurised by advertising
- feel cross that experts seem to hand out conflicting advice
- feel it's OK to do what everyone else does

- are scared to make our children different
- are scared of our children's displeasure
- are short of time or money
- don't want to make changes to our own lifestyle in order to set an example.

None of these pressures can be dismissed lightly. We poor parents are struggling against a tide of junk food ads, working the longest hours in Europe and living in a culture where food standards are often low. When the Consumers' Association asked a nutritionist to analyse food that a child aged seven to ten might eat, based on the claims and marketing messages carried on the products ('helps build healthy bones' and the like), she found a diet that would increase the risk of obesity, tooth decay, diabetes, cancer and heart disease. With the tide of society running so fiercely against us, it can be very difficult to take a stand.

Yet we really have to try. Because at any given moment our child is the direct product of what he has recently eaten and drunk. Varying levels of proteins and amino acids whizz around his brain and body, controlling both his mind and mood, and if those levels are not good he simply won't be able to seize the opportunities that come his way.

Water

We need to start with the most important of all – water. Without water, nothing works properly, including our brains, which become less efficient as the cells find it less easy to exchange their vital chemical messages. It's true for adults, and even more so for children whose skin area is greater in proportion to their size, and who are therefore much more efficient evaporation machines than adults are.

When children are thirsty their mental performance decreases by about 10 per cent. They are distracted, irritable and have poor concentration. Not surprisingly, a Leeds University survey found that school children who did best in class were those who drank up eight glasses of water a day.

In school, children probably need three or four glasses a day, and more if it is hot or they have been exercising. Yet they rarely get it. One paediatrician found that half of his young patients were going the whole school day without drinking anything – many schools still only have water available in taps in the toilets. And the result is not only a dehydrated child, but one who may not realise when he's thirsty because children who are constantly dehydrated tend to get desensitised to the symptoms of thirst and not know when they need a drink.

To get your child drinking more water

- First check to see if he is dehydrated by looking at his urine – pale, straw-coloured and inoffensive is good; darker, smellier stuff means trouble.
- Give him water to keep by his side when he is doing his homework, and encourage him to drink water before and after school.
- Make sure his school knows about the benefits of water and provides it, either via individual bottles or water coolers. You can get more details from the Water is Cool in School campaign: www.wateriscoolinschool.org.uk.

- If the school is reluctant, point out that eminent paediatricians have called current drinking water arrangements in schools 'barbaric', and drum up support from parents, governors, doctors and health officials.
- If the school does provide water, nag and prompt your child to drink it – point out that it's good for skin and sporting performance – and be sure to wash his water bottle well each night.
- If the school doesn't provide water, tuck a water bottle into his bag, tell him to sneak a drink when no one's looking – and say that if there's trouble you'll handle it.
- Remember water means water. Fizzy drinks, squashes and fruit juices just mean more chemicals and sugar.

Schools are often reluctant to introduce water to the classroom. 'I imagined it being knocked all over the place and an endless line of children trekking to the loo,' said one Year 3 teacher. 'But it has made such a difference to how they perform in the afternoons. It used to be impossible to get anything out of them after lunch, they always seemed half-asleep, but now they're so much more responsive – they seem like different children.'

Drinking more water can also be a first step towards a better diet. Interestingly, some parents have reported that their children stopped wanting to drink anything but water, once they got used to its clean, fresh taste in school – a testimony to how children's tastes do change when given the opportunity.

Food

What children need in order to be happy and successful learners is lots and lots of fruit and vegetables, plus protein, wholegrains and some 'good' fats. What they so often get is a diet loaded with salt, fat and sugar in the form of white bread, pizza, chips, chicken nuggets, burgers, crisps, sausages, biscuits, sweets and fizzy drinks. In fact, national nutrition surveys have shown that:

- one in five children aged four to eighteen eats no fruit and vegetables at all
- the foods most commonly eaten by 80 per cent of children are savoury snacks, biscuits, chocolate, white bread, chips and potatoes
- over the past fifty years, children's consumption of biscuits has risen fourfold, sweets by twenty-five times and soft drinks by thirty-four times
- more than £430 million a year is spent on crisps, sweets, fizzy drinks and cigarettes that children buy as they go to and from school
- the average child consumes fifteen glasses of soft, sweet drinks every week.

But, of course, they're not talking about our children. Or are they?

Do you really know what your child eats?

Some years ago, a magazine asked me to keep a food diary of what my children were eating. I thought their diet was pretty healthy, but written down, it didn't look a bit like that. When I ruthlessly made myself put down all the peripheral snacks and treats – cake and fizzy drinks at a friend's house, crisps after swimming, sweets shared out at school, a chocolate biscuit last thing at night – as well as the sausages and pizza we resorted to for supper when time was tight, it became clear that very often their daily food intake consisted of large doses of unhealthy stuff, with little more than an apple and a few peas holding the corner for fresh, wholesome produce.

At the time, I wasn't too concerned. Now I wonder why. Having learned so much more since then about what a diet like this does to a young brain and body, I would dearly love to be able to crawl back down the years in order to feed them again – properly.

What brains need

We all know about the health problems of bad diet. One in nine children is obese – the condition is rocketing and, as I write, the Government is debating what actions to take to try and curb this life-threatening explosion of flab – and Type II diabetes, once a disease of old men, is advancing among the under-sixteens. What we are less familiar with is the effect on mind and mood. Because brains need a whole range of essential nutrients to work properly and if they don't get them they simply can't function as they should.

'The brain is a metabolic powerhouse. It is only 2 per cent of our body mass but consumes 20 per cent of our available energy and to metabolise this energy requires a range of nutrients, vitamins, minerals and essential fatty acids. Anything that upsets this balance is likely to interfere with the brain's functioning,' says Bernard Gesch, senior research scientist at Oxford University's laboratory of physiology.

Brains need:

- foods that stop blood suger levels swinging about – wholegrains, beans, nuts, seeds, fruit and vegetables
- 'essential' fats (essential because we can't produce them; we have to get them from our diet), namely omega-3 fatty acids, especially those known as EPA and DHA, and omega-6 fatty acids, especially those known as GLA and AA, found in oily fish like salmon, mackerel, sardines and herring, eggs, meat, dairy produce, nuts and seeds
- phospholipids, found in eggs
- amino acids, found in lean meat, fish, dairy products, beans, lentils
- a range of vitamins and minerals, found in fruit, vegetables, nuts, seeds, lentils, beans and brown rice.

As you can see, the best sources of brain food are exactly the kind of foods that many children would shudder to see on the plate in front of them. Yet without them, all kinds of things happen. A deficiency of zinc (found in such things as nuts, grains, seafood and egg yolk), for example, has been linked to depression, eating disorders, hyperactivity, and a lack of motivation and concentration, while a deficiency of folic acid (found in such things as nuts and green vegetables) has been linked to anxiety. Low iron levels can lead to lethargy, poor concentration and delayed development – yet up to a quarter of toddlers are thought to be deficient in this mineral, as well as large numbers of teenage girls, many of whom are vegetarians and shun the red meat that would give them it, but who especially need to keep their iron levels up as their periods start.

On the other hand, too much of the wrong stuff also has a huge impact on children's brains.

- **Too much sugar.** This causes blood sugar levels to fluctuate, and use up a body's store of vitamins and minerals while providing few in return, fostering problems of poor attention and memory, and aggressive behaviour.

Researchers at the Massachusetts Institute of Technology have found that the more refined carbohydrates people eat – sugar, white bread, rice and pasta, and foods such as processed cereals – the lower their IQ, with the difference between lowest and highest sugar consumers being as much as twenty-five points. Conversely, British nutritionist Patrick Holford found that giving school children a high-strength vitamin pill led to a ten-point gain in their non-verbal IQ tests.

- **Toxins**. Even tiny amounts of pollutants have a powerful impact on the brain. Caffeine, found in colas and some energy drinks, is a brain toxin – in large amounts it is known to impair memory. Alcohol, which surprisingly young children are now consuming in alarming amounts, also impairs memory, as well as knocking out important vitamins. Then there is lead, often found in flakes of old paint, which children can ingest as dust and particles. If children have high levels of this in their bloodstream it not only prompts poor behaviour, but also lowers their IQ. This was a major reason why lead was banned in petrol.
- **Additives**. Within just two weeks of one identical five-year-old twin being given an additive-free diet he was calmer and more assertive than his brother and appeared to have jumped fifteen points in IQ. When the experiment was extended to his classmates, 57 per cent of parents said their children's behaviour improved. Parents know how children bounce off walls on a diet of brightly coloured sweets and other junk foods. However, the link between additives and poor behaviour is still scientifically disputed, especially by the food industry, which points out that all the additives it uses have been carefully tested. What hasn't been tested, though, is what potent combinations of these, ingested together, might be doing to our brains.

> *Schools that have cleaned out additives from their school lunches claim they can see at definite difference. A Worcestershire primary school removed twenty-seven E numbers from its pupils' diet after a teacher at the school had revolutionised her teenage son's behaviour by improving his diet. It reported that 38 per cent of parents noticed improvements in behaviour, 35 per cent said children were more cooperative, 30 per cent saw better concentration and 16 per cent said their children were sleeping better.*

Putting back the good stuff can dramatically change behaviour and alertness. One of the most recent studies to show this was carried out by an Oxford University researcher, Bernard Gesch, over eighteen months, among 230 young offenders. When a cocktail of thirty-five different vitamins, minerals and other fatty acids was added to their diets, there was a 37 per cent decrease in the most serious offences including violent behaviour, while incidents of anti-social behaviour of all kinds dropped by a third. Researchers point out that it is not yet possible to say which nutrient matters most. The human body is a complicated machine and probably needs all of them to work together. This is why it is unlikely there will ever be a simple pill, which we will be able to give our children to replace a balanced diet. But it is worth noting that the cocktail in this experiment was not a super-dose of anything – merely ensuring the prisoners' diets reached government standards.

Conflicting advice

Because this is such a complicated area, claims and counter-claims constantly vie with each other. The truth is that making links between nutrition and how the brain works is still such a new area of research, that we are like blind men feeling an elephant. One explores the trunk, one the ear and one the tail, and all come to differing conclusions about what sort of creature stands before them.

The real danger of this is that we can use it as a get-out to avoid tackling a difficult area. There's no point in worrying about it, we tell ourselves, when no one seems to know what they're talking about. Yet common sense dictates that a diet loaded with empty calories and over-refined foods is unlikely to be good for any of us, let alone growing children. And there is a now a very strong consensus on what is better. Almost without exception, nutritionists say a diet with lots of fruit and vegetables, wholemeal bread, brown rice and pasta, lentils, fish, eggs, some dairy products, and high-quality meat and chicken will keep a child healthy, especially if sugary, starchy, fatty processed foods are kept to a minimum at the same time.

Find out more

This is an area we should all know more about. For example, we are often told that children should eat five portions of fruit and vegetables a day, but, speaking personally, it is only recently that I fully realised just how substantial a portion is supposed to be – we are talking a packed half a cup of broccoli here, not two flabby slices of tomato and a fragment of lettuce in a sandwich. There are a number of books on nutrition listed at the back of this book, including Patrick Holford's *Optimum Nutrition for the Brain*, probably the most comprehensive account ever published of how food directly affects our mind and mood.

You might also want to research the different opinions on giving children vitamin pills and other supplements. Some dieticians think, for example, that a daily multivitamin, or fish oil capsule, can benefit all children; others say that a balanced diet should give a child everything he needs. This is quite a complicated area and one where parents have to work out for themselves what they think is best. And if you do decide, for example, that you want to give your child daily fish oil, try and find out all you can about the different types and dosages available. Don't just pick one off the shelf and hope for the best.

However, there is one thing that all dieticians agree on, and that is that supplements are supplements, and food comes first. Don't ever be tempted to think that by handing your child a daily vitamin tablet, you somehow need no longer bother about providing a good, balanced diet.

How to get them to eat better – the first steps

Even armed with all the nutritional knowledge in the world, it can be the Devil's own job to start feeding children foods they don't want to eat. 'I know all the theory,' said one despairing mother of a twelve-year-old. 'I cook. We don't eat junk. I constantly try and get her to eat good food, but she just refuses, and then the battles over it seem to be worse than the issue itself.'

Here are four basic steps you can take that should be helpful.

- **Honour family mealtimes**. 'Grab-and-graze' might be the commonest form of domestic eating now, but shared meals give eating a sense of importance and ceremony, and help oil family conversations. Children can be part of the team, laying the table or preparing vegetables, and it is sometimes surprising how quickly sulky girls and grumpy boys become pleasant and chatty as their stomachs fill up. If it isn't possible to do this often, at least make time to do it sometimes. And try getting everyone in the family involved in working out a weekly menu. It might take time and negotiation, but the pay-off can be that everyone feels involved with what's put on the table.
- **Be the adult**. Explain to children about how food works in their bodies and brains, and give your children the foods you want them to eat. Ask them to try the foods. If they don't like them, say 'fine', and resolve to offer them again at a later date. But at all costs avoid endless negotiations and power struggles about what is or isn't acceptable. Children can quickly become power-crazed despots at the dinner table, only willing to accept one brand of fish finger, or carrots cut on the diagonal rather than into rounds. That way madness lies. Be calm and patient. Set boundaries. Remind yourself it really, really matters. And keep trying. Children who protest vigorously about, say, wholewheat pasta one week, are often eating it without a second thought the next.
- **Set an example**. 'Both my girls are funny about food,' admitted one mother, 'and I know they've got it from me. I can tell you every calorie I've eaten since Monday.' Parents are children's first teachers, and one of the most basic lessons they teach is about how people fuel their

bodies. If you are a secret chocoholic, try and keep it secret. If you are dieting, don't go on and on about your lapses and successes in front of your child. Sit down to eat with them whenever you can, and let them see you eating fruit and vegetables, and all the other good stuff you want them to have in their diet.

- **Bother about breakfast**. This is the most important meal of the day. What child can learn if their tank is running on empty? Yet about one out of ten children regularly has no breakfast at all, and a survey by the Doctor–Patient Partnership found that a staggering one-in-four breakfasts on sweets and crisps on the way to school. At home, many eat only a bowl of sugary cereal, which will not give them the energy and nutrients they need. This is the prime reason so many schools now run breakfast clubs, with a notable effect on both learning and behaviour. Give your child a nourishing breakfast, with a good drink, and some protein and slow-release carbohydrates (brown toast and peanut butter; a boiled egg and soldiers; porridge with fruit and nuts), and you will be giving them a gift for the rest of the day, but to do this needs time and routine. Children often complain they can't eat breakfast because they haven't had enough time to wake up, or there is too much of a rush to get to school. If they really find it hard to eat first thing in the morning, give them a sandwich to eat at break. But make very sure they aren't going through to lunchtime with only a tuck shop bag of crisps to sustain them.

There are now many good books around on children's eating. Avoid the ones that suggest you craft individual, smiley-face vegetable platters for your children, and look for those based on common sense. Some are listed at the end of the book.

Improving your child's diet

Here are some tips for improving your child's diet:

- don't buy things you don't want them to eat – if they aren't in the house they can't have them
- fill up the fruit bowl
- don't use sweets and chocolate for bribery and rewards
- swop from white to brown when it comes to rice, bread and pasta
- buy 'healthy' eggs, high in omega-3, thanks to how the hens are fed
- make some small-step changes – substitute plain biscuits for chocolate digestives, unsalted nuts for crisps, peanut butter for jam on toast and bread, home-made chicken skewers for chicken nuggets, and vegetable sticks with humous as an after-school snack instead of cakes and buns
- talk to them about good foods, and why they are so important, and about bad foods, too. Some nutritionists tut-tut at this. They feel we shouldn't use the 'b' word in connection with food for fear of fads and phobias. But the fact of the matter is that many foods these days are, quite simply, bad for us, and we do our children no favours if we hide that fact from them.

Some years ago a report was splashed all over the newspapers saying health inspectors had found traces of urine and faeces in many of the soft-whip ice-creams sold from ice-cream vans. The sellers, it seemed, were not washing their hands after going to the bathroom. One mother was distraught. Every fine day she took her seven- and five-year-old to the local park after school, and in the summer treated them to an ice-cream as they set off for home. What was she going to do now? Her children would expect the ice-creams, but she couldn't bring herself to buy them any more. Nor was there a local shop where she could buy them a hygienically wrapped substitute. But there would be hell to pay if they got nothing! In the end she did the only thing possible, and explained the situation to them. Euugh! they said. Gross! And that was the end of that. They have never, she says, asked for an ice-cream from an ice-cream van again.

Packed school lunches

Millions of children take their own lunch to school, but teachers report that what is in these lunch boxes is often hair-raising. Neon-coloured soft drinks and salty snacks abound, and even children who bring carrot sticks and brown bread sandwiches, usually have crisps and chocolate as well.

As parents it is easy to understand why. We like to think of our child opening up their lunch box with pleasure, and the temptation is to want to balance the good stuff with a treat or two. But think how many hundreds of chocolate bars and packets of crisps that amounts to in the course of a school year – and about the eating habits that are being set up in a young child.

Try tipping the balance further. Add in more good stuff – red pepper slices, cherry tomatoes, celery chunks – and substitute low-fat crisps for the regular kind. Better still, go for healthy alternatives – nuts and raisins, or a handful of dried apricots (the dark brown ones, rather than the sulphur-treated bright orange). And add some imagination to the standard sandwich. Try pitta bread stuffed with humous, or a pot of home-made pasta salad. And, of course, pure fruit juice or water to drink, rather than chemical-laden squashes and colas.

However, be aware, too, that friends and classmates can be tyrants about lunch boxes, as about other things. One mother reports her children being teased about 'smelly' humous and 'bitty' (granary) bread. If that is happening, tell the school so they can keep an eye on things and chat with your child about why teasing happens, and possible ways of standing up to it – see Chapter 17. But don't make them suffer unnecessarily. Perhaps substitute tuna for humous, and wholemeal bread for granary, to make life easier for them. And getting together with other parents to plan for a mass outbreak of healthy lunch boxes can also help change the atmosphere.

What a healthy lunch box might look like:

- *tuna and cucumber sandwich on wholemeal bread*
- *cherry tomatoes*
- *carrot sticks*
- *plain yoghurt with raisins*
- *apple or banana*
- *diluted fruit juice or water.*

School lunches

It may be that your child has a school lunch, in which case it is impossible to have much control over what they eat. You can, as one dinner lady observed, lead a boy to the salad bar, but you can't make him eat. And by and large school lunches are not what most of us would wish. Or to put it more bluntly, as chef Jamie Oliver did recently, 'they are rubbish'. (He's now working on a television programme, training school cooks to serve up healthy, delicious, economical food.)

Schools must follow government nutrition guidelines, but these are not strigent. Budgets are low and private caterers need to turn a profit, so ingredients are as cheap as possible – meals are are typically turned out for under 50p a head.

Here is what a school sausage is made from, as told to the Guardian, by a manufacturer: 50 per cent meat, of which 30 per cent is pork fat with a bit of jowl, and 20 per cent is mechanically-recovered chicken meat, water, rusk, soya, soya concentrate, hyrolised protein, modified flour, dried onion, sugar, dextrose, phosphates, preservatives E221 sodium sulphite, flavour enhancer, spices, garlic flavouring, antioxidant E300, colouring E128. The casing is made from collagen from cow hide.

However, schools do now have the freedom to spend their catering budget as they wish, and increasing numbers are working to find good caterers, or preparing fresh meals at school.

The day's menu for one award-winning primary school in Nottingham recently read as follows: lasagne, macaroni cheese, fresh bread, broccoli and carrots, followed by fresh fruit and yoghurt. The catering manager said: 'The meat, which I buy from a local farm shop, travels no more than 15 or 20 miles from farm to slaughter. I know the farmers' names, and my head has joked that I know the animals by name, too. Milk, vegetables and potatoes also come from local producers.' Yet this school charges no more for its meals than other schools in the county.

Some secondary schools are going down other routes, using vending cards to give parents control over what their children can purchase. If you don't want them buying chips, burgers and chocolate, the card can have a block put on it for such things, and parents can also get print-outs of their child's weekly purchases, to see what they are, or aren't, eating – important if you have a teenage girl who has decided it's fashionable not to eat, or a boy who bunks off to the kebab shop in town most lunchtimes.

If you are worried about the standard of your child's school food, raise it with the school, or with the school's governing body (which is required to monitor the quality of what is provided and ensure a healthy diet), pointing out that more and more schools are now raising their game in this area.

One primary school head says: 'The children don't ask me what they are having for lunch any more. They ask me what shape they are having. They have learned they can't tell the difference on the basis of texture or taste.'

Healthy schools

All government-maintained schools are supposed to be 'healthy schools' by 2004, which means, in essence, they should be paying attention to food, water, exercise, and children's emotional and psychological health. They should also be trying to iron out contradictory policies like telling children about healthy eating in the classroom, then running a tuck shop, which sells nothing but crisps and chocolate.

However, what it means in practice varies. One school in the Medway Towns is typical of schools that have taken their responsibility for their pupils' health seriously. It brought in the following changes as it turned itself into a healthy school: lessons on nutrition, a healthy tuck shop, improved school lunches, voluntary no-chocolate days, quiet areas in the playground, a breakfast club, 'playground buddies' to stop bullying, water coolers all over the school, and a chance to discuss emotional and personal issues in classroom circle times. Staff, children and parents all say they notice a big difference in how the school runs now.

If your child's school isn't as healthy as it could be, it is worth asking why not, and what its plans for improvement are.

Advertisements

In an average Saturday morning's viewing, children will see sixty-four food commercials, according to the charity Sustain, which campaigns for better food, and 95 per cent of all advertisements aimed at children are for foods high in salt, fat and sugar. In 2000 the Food Commission, another food charity, revealed that for every healthy product targeted at children, there were ten 'nutritional disasters' – and this was in a survey that *excluded* sweets, soft drinks and crisps!

And the influence of the food companies is everywhere. Having a cola vending machine can net a secondary school up to £40,000 a year in much-needed extra revenue, while 'healthy food' classroom materials are often sponsored by food companies. Some companies place products directly in schools, for children to try; others link their unhealthy products to a more healthy outcome – buy more of our chocolate, they say, and you will be buying more sports equipment for schools.

At the time of writing, the question of curbing advertising to children is under discussion but no firm proposals have yet been made. Government plans only extend as far as educating pupils more in the classroom about how the power of persuasion works. So what is a parent to do? The only possible thing is to be aware of the dimensions of the problem, curb your child's exposure to it as much as you possibly can, and keep talking and talking about good food, and why it matters, and about bad advertisements, and why they mustn't be allowed to work.

And finally . . .

I am acutely aware, as I write, how dreary and puritanical this might all sound. Humous and brown rice. Celery and dried fruit. And who in heavens has time to fiddle around making home-made pasta salad for a child to take to school?

But if you really want your child to succeed at school, good nutrition is just not negotiable. This may mean spending more money on good food, even if it involves trimming expenses in other areas. It may mean having to stretch a very tight budget around the cheapest possible wholesome meals your imagination can devise – lentil soup here we come! It will certainly mean more time and effort. Buying and chopping vegetables for a stir-fry is not nearly as easy as slinging a pizza into the microwave. And it will also probably mean that, to the outside world, your family will sometimes look faddy and peculiar.

So be it. After all, aiming for good nutrition doesn't mean

you will never eat hamburgers or ice-cream again. If a family's diet is basically healthy, there will always be room for treats and diversions. And think of the big picture. Every day that you feed your child a good and varied diet, you are filling his brain and body with all the micro-nutrients he needs to be smart, happy and energetic, and to get the most out of life. And every day that you don't, you are not.

CHAPTER ELEVEN

Exercise and sleep

The best six doctors anywhere
And no one can deny it
Are sunshine, water, rest, and air
Exercise and diet.

TRADITIONAL NURSERY RHYME

MY CHILDREN HAVE been educated in both state primary schools and private preparatory schools, and for a long time I puzzled over the difference between these two groups of pupils. As far as I could see, it wasn't that private school children were noticeably cleverer than those in state schools, or better behaved, or better taught, but there was still some niggling, indefinable difference about them that I just couldn't put my finger on.

Then, one rainy day in north London, I found out what it was.

I was visiting a primary school to look at its new fitness programme. The school was a looming Victorian building with only a cramped asphalt playground. The neighbourhood was poor and its children came from a rainbow of different backgrounds. Yet the ten- and eleven-year-olds who had been gathered together to talk to me were – and there's only one word for it – glowing. They glowed with health, and pride, and confidence. Their school had decided to inject massive extra amounts of physical activity into the school day. The teachers organised games at break and lunchtimes, set up dance lessons, opened up after-school sports clubs and took PE lessons very seriously. They had also started school sports teams, and these teams were starting to do well in local leagues. They had scraped together enough money to buy smart team tracksuits, embroidered with the school's logo, and the children were bursting to talk about their successes in netball, football and cross-country running, and to show off this new kit.

Looking at these children, I realised that this was the difference.

Many private schools, with their long school days, run vigorous programmes of sport and exercise. Their pupils tend to be fit and healthy. And from this stems a whole glow of differences – bright eyes, quick responses, a clear skin, shiny hair and a tendency, at least among younger children, to skip and run about the place, rather than slouch and amble.

Also, private schools have never fought shy of team games and competition, and the benefits they can bring (if handled sensitively) in terms of confidence and social skills, whereas many maintained schools have little to do with them.

In fact PE and games have a lamentable recent history in state schools. A long-ago dispute between teachers and the government knocked many after-school sporting activities out of the ring, while at the same time some schools gave up team games because they worried what competition would mean for those pupils who were losers rather than winners. Then school playing fields started to be sold off, and the national curriculum put a squeeze on what else could be crammed into the school day. As a result, the provision of school PE and games is now often half-hearted, and sometimes downright pitiful.

This means that, more than ever, it is up to us, as parents, to take the lead in encouraging our children to keep fit. But why should we bother?

Children and exercise

Children must have exercise, not just to stay healthy, but to be good learners. As we've seen earlier, children's brains are not inert lumps of grey matter, but active webs of cells and connections, which grow and change according to what we do to them, and exercise plays a critical part in stimulating and energising these. Researchers have found exercise gives children:

- improved brain function
- higher energy/concentration levels
- better self-esteem
- better behaviour.

It is no coincidence that, in the corporate world, go-ahead companies know that providing their employees with gyms and fitness trainers pays for itself many times over.

And there are many other benefits, too. Children who get good, regular exercise will have:

- improved physical strength, stamina and flexibility
- a lowered risk of future health problems such as cancer and heart disease

- longer life expectancy
- better social skills
- more likelihood of keeping active as adults.

Put all these things together and you have a powerful engine for maximising potential. Because a well-exercised child will not only have a brain that's working better, but will also feel good about herself, which will make her feel positive and optimistic about any learning she has to tackle, which will in turn make her able to do well at that learning, which will in turn stimulate her brain, and improve her confidence, and make her work better.

And there is plenty of evidence that raising children's activity levels improves behaviour and learning in a clear and quantifiable way. Links have been found in studies conducted in Hong Kong, Australia, Scotland and the US, as well as in the UK. One English south coast primary school found that bad behaviour incidents dropped by 95 per cent, and tests results in maths, reading and writing climbed steadily every year after they rolled their sleeves up and devised ways to get their pupils moving.

In California a recent statewide study of nearly a million children, aged ten, twelve and fourteen matched test scores against fitness levels and found a 'distinct' correlation. The fitter the children, the higher their scores. This was particularly true in maths, and also, for reasons yet to be explored, for girls.

How much exercise?

The simplest answer is a lot. Babies and toddlers are constantly on the go. Movement and exploration are natural conditions for young things, so it seems absurd, as children grow up, that we start talking about how many minutes of exercise they should have in a day. All children ought to lead active lives that incorporate masses of everyday activity along with sessions of more structured and vigorous exercise. But it doesn't happen. Today's school children all too quickly subside into the back seat of the car, or on to the sofa. Which is why such guidelines are now thought to be necessary. For example:

- The UK's Health Development Agency specifies an hour of moderate exercise a day (where you get warmer and your heart rate goes up a little); half an hour for children who take little exercise. And twice a week, it says, children should take exercise that enhances and maintains muscular strength, flexibility and bone mass.
- The American Heart Association suggests that all children aged two and over should have thirty minutes of moderate exercise a day, plus a further thirty minutes of vigorous exercise three or four days a week.

But they don't get this

Very few children get as much exercise as this. In fact:

- nearly half of all girls and a third of all boys don't get even the thirty minutes a day minimum
- nearly a third of London schools do no competitive sport

- a secondary head has found that most of his eleven-year-olds can't run 200 metres without stopping.

Not in school . . .

The national curriculum says schools should aim for two hours' good quality PE and sporting activity a week. This is way under even the minimum recommendations for basic health and well-being, but even worse is the fact that many schools don't get anywhere near that. Primary schools spend about half the time on PE that they used to spend five years ago, while only a third of secondary school children get two hours of sport a week, compared with 46 per cent in 1994. And even then, some sports lessons contain about as much sport as a school sausage contains meat. Researchers have found that some PE lessons involve hardly any moving about, while anyone who has watched, say, a teenage girls' games class in progress will know what huge amounts of time can be taken up with changing, looking for lost kit, ambling to the sports field, arguing with the teacher about missing kit, not listening to instructions, not listening to repeated instructions, picking teams, arguing about teams and so on. If the pupils in such lessons get even fifteen minutes of sustained exercise, they are probably doing well.

Nor at home . . .

According to Exeter University researchers, half of all girls aged ten to sixteen and a third of boys don't get even the equivalent of a ten-minute brisk walk a day. And according to a poll commissioned by the British Heart Foundation, 18 per cent of parents never encourage their children to take exercise.

When they are little, we take our children to the park, or playground, and often sign them up for activities such as toddler gymnastics, but this tends to peter out when they go to school. What can be done to revive it?

Look to ourselves

One of the greatest influences on children's activity levels is how active their parents are – and 40 per cent of us take no exercise at all. Of course it's hard to find time for swimming or aerobic classes when looking after children, running a home and most probably doing another job as well. But you can still talk about fitness with your child, explaining why it matters, and pointing out that jobs such as carrying laundry up and downstairs, washing the car, or putting the shopping away are all ways in which you keep active. If your child sees you doing some sort of sport, or class, then so much the better. We also need to think hard about the things that stop our children getting exercise, and whether there is anything we can do about them.

How to get them moving

The school run

The simplest way to include exercise in a child's day is to have them walk or cycle to and from school. Eighty per cent of children live within a kilometre of their school – an easy fifteen minutes' walk – so you wouldn't think it would be too hard for them, as they get older, to do this.

But few do, as congestion caused by cars on the school

run clearly demonstrates. A trip in Cambridgeshire that takes seventy minutes in the school morning rush hour, takes only fifty-five minutes in holiday time. In fact, between the mid-1980s and the mid-1990s the number of children being driven to school nearly doubled – and the Government is now looking into measures such as tolls to tackle this.

We drive our children because:

- we drop them off on our way to work
- we feel it is too far for them to walk
- we are too worried about traffic, bullies and child molesters to let them go alone.

Efforts are being made to find safer ways for children to get to school, such as introducing bike routes, and starting up walking buses, where adults escort groups of fluorescent jacket-clad children to and from school.

If these are available in your area, think hard about the benefits your child will get from taking them up. Think hard, too, about any risks that you are worried about, and weigh them up against the benefits of going to school alone. Because it isn't only a question of exercise. As child psychologists have pointed out, children experience things differently when they are on their own, and learn faster when they have to rely on themselves. They gain confidence, get experience in weighing up risks and develop a greater sense of initiative. Without such opportunities, said one psychologist, 'their sense of identity is harder to establish, self-esteem is harder to build up and social adjustment – finding out how to operate in the world and belong to a wider society – is harder to achieve.'

Opportunities for learning and experience can also be lost. One teacher asked his class to write a story about walking to school in the rain. He envisioned exciting scripts about splashing through puddles and hearing rain drum on umbrellas. But they looked at him blankly. Walking to school was something few of them did, and the idea that the words 'walking' and 'rain' could be linked together in a sentence was quite beyond their ken.

Ask yourself:

- could you make time to walk to school in the morning?
- could you get out of the habit of reaching for the car keys whenever it is cold or wet?
- is there an older child your own child could walk safely to school with, or a group of children who could always go together?
- is there the possibility of compromise – maybe walking your child across the busy main road and letting her go on alone from there, or taking the car half way to school and walking the rest of the way?

Ask yourself, too, if there are practical things that would help. Could your school set up a walking bus? Find details on: www.livingstreets.com or www.walkingbus.com. If your child's school lacks a safe place to lock up bicycles, or a crossing scheme would improve the situation, get stuck in and campaign for it. Children's needs will never be met unless adults kick up a fuss on their behalf.

Of course, it may not be possible to ditch the school run, in which case you will have to look elsewhere for exercise.

Exercise at home

Each minute gives you infinite power to make your child more active. You can:

- hide the TV remote – getting up to change the channel uses three calories
- ask her to fetch and carry things around the house
- get her to tidy her room and make her bed
- encourage her to help in the garden
- ask her to take rubbish out to the dustbin
- pay her to clean the car.

There are things you can do together, such as:

- learn line dancing or aerobics from a video
- play back garden soccer, badminton, rounders or tag
- go for a family walk
- go swimming
- take up skipping – brilliant exercise for everyone!

Serious investments of either time or money can also help cement a commitment to fitness. You could:

- buy a dog – and walk it
- invest in a large-size trampoline, or a basketball hoop, or a soccer goal, for the garden
- join a health club as a family
- go on a fitness holiday
- commit to a charity challenge, such as a walk or a bike ride.

Exercise away from home

Relatively few children these days are allowed to play freely in the street, or in the fields near their home, but if you are lucky enough to live in a quiet cul-de-sac, or near a playground you can see from your window, or anywhere else where children can go out to play, make the absolute most of it. This kind of free-floating activity not only gets children on to their feet and out of the house, but also teaches them a whole mass of social skills such as negotiation and cooperation. Younger children watch older children to see how things are done; older ones push out their boundaries as they come to feel more capable and competent.

In most areas there are youth sports clubs, after-school clubs and holiday schemes. Check out your sports centre, or ask your council for details. And think laterally. If you have a child who hates football don't write him off as non-sporty. He may love martial arts, or rowing, or ballroom dancing. One boy who wasn't good at team games, and whose confidence was plummeting as a result, got moving, and his confidence back, when his parents bought him a punch bag for his room and encouraged his interest in boxing. A girl might loathe rounders and netball, but love taking a dance class, or doing yoga.

Your job as a parent is to:

- be willing to find ways to pay, and offer transport
- make sure she has the right clothing and footwear
- encourage her to stick at it for long enough to give it a proper chance
- let her try something else, if that really isn't working – exercise must be fun and enjoyable.

To motivate your child

It can take great grit and effort to get a couch potato moving, but it is worth it, and it does get easier. Fit and active children don't like sitting around unless they're really tired; they are glad to be moving. Start in small steps, and remember to make sure you're providing a diet that gives plenty of stamina and energy.

> *One parent says, 'My mother was passionate about fresh air. She always used to push my brother and I out to play in the garden. We hated going, but once we were out it somehow seemed all right. Now I do exactly the same with my children. I can't bear to see them lolling about, so I turn off the television and drive them out. They say that I'm cruel, but they always come back in with pinker cheeks and better tempers.'*

Also tell your child that if she gets fit she will:

- feel great!
- stay in good shape
- have stronger bones and muscles, and more flexible joints
- feel more confident in herself
- learn more easily.

Sport at school

Some schools provide fantastic sports programmes, and their number should be increasing rapidly now that £1 billion of government money is being ploughed into school sports. How can you tell if your child's school is among them?

Well, the best of them have usually thought long and hard about what they are doing, and have made sure that lots of different things come together to make them an active school. These might include, at primary level:

- playgrounds zoned for different activities
- a range of good play equipment
- support staff who start games, and encourage active play at lunchtime and break times
- after-school clubs in things like dance, soccer or gymnastics
- lively sports teams
- lessons that emphasise the benefits of being fit
- nutritious lunches and snacks available.

At secondary level, look for:

- good facilities – playing fields and sports halls
- a range of sports and other physical activities on offer
- keen and enthusiastic specialist staff
- after-school activities
- policies designed to include all students, even reluctant ones
- teams playing in local leagues
- regular coaching sessions.

If your feel your school isn't doing enough, ask the head or the governors what their future plans are.

If the answer is that they don't have the time or the resources to do anything more in this area, ask them to look at the growing evidence that physical activity improves children's test results, attendance and concentration.

Sleep

Good learners need activity. And they need rest. And most children don't get enough of either.

A recent survey found that up to two-thirds of children weren't getting the sleep they needed, and could have missed up to 4,500 hours by their seventh birthday. It found that one-in-eight children sleep less than the amount recommended for adults, with the figure rising to a quarter among children whose parents both work.

Admittedly, this was research commissioned by a bed manufacturer, which might have had its own agenda, but the findings are confirmed by teachers who report that many children come to school yawning and tired, and often fall asleep in the classroom.

The research also showed that bedtimes stories were falling out of favour – one in ten of the 500 parents surveyed said they never read them. Instead, children reported falling asleep in front of the television, a computer game or a video.

Yet sleep deprivation can harm neurological development, and contribute to problems at school – sleep-deprived children are physically unable to pay attention for any sustained time. They are often twitchy and inattentive as their bodies try to stimulate themselves into wakefulness.

Children are born needing varying amounts of sleep – some three-day-old babies sleep twice as much as others – so hard and fast guidelines are not especially helpful, but as a parent you will know your own child's pattern. Especially if you remember to bear in mind that young children tend to get hyperactive when they're tired, and that lots of rushing around at bedtime doesn't signal unused energy. In fact, it's just the opposite.

Be sure to:

- think about your child's needs, not your own. Even if you've come in late from work and want to spend time with her, your child needs to sleep
- harden your heart against pleas that 'everyone else' is allowed to stay up later, or watch this or that on television
- beware of 'bedtime creep', when bedtime gets a little later each week.

To develop calm, workable bedtimes:

- set a time for bed and stick to it
- switch off the television or computer an hour before
- keep to a wind-down bedtime routine, with calm activities such as a bath or a book
- read bedtime stories
- offer a warm, milky drink
- remove any mobile phone (no texting under the covers)
- video television programmes for watching later
- don't let her have a television, computer or Gameboy in her room

- if she does, have an absolute rule about when it must be switched off, and check she sticks to it.

Part Three

School-related Issues – and how to deal with them

CHAPTER TWELVE

Homework

'Perhaps the most valuable result of all education is the ability to make yourself do the thing you have to do, when it ought to be done, whether you like it or not.' – ALDOUS HUXLEY

HOMEWORK CAN CAUSE tears, tantrums and a huge sense of failure – and that's just among parents!

Of all the many issues that school throws up, this is the one that often generates the most family stress. It can be a daily source of anxiety, and sometimes an all-out battleground. When the charity Parentline Plus surveyed parents about their concerns it came a close second-runner to bullying as the thing they were most worried about, and more than half of 1,200 parents of children aged ten to sixteen surveyed for the BBC said they felt out of their depth when attempting to help with homework.

Why does it get like this?

There are lots of understandable reasons. Homework is the only part of their children's schoolwork that most parents see on a regular basis, so it inevitably comes to loom large. It is also the only school-related area that they feel directly responsible for – if it isn't done well, or on time, this reflects badly on home.

And there's another thing, too. Harassed parents, strapped for time, can latch on to homework as the one area in their children's lives that they intend to keep on top of. 'When I was working in London and not getting home until after seven,' says one mother, a publishing director, with children at the top end of primary school, 'I knew everything was on the slide, but I made it a point of pride that homework came first. No matter what else needed to be done, I would sit down with them until homework was over. But it completely backfired on me. They began to refuse to do it, and I would insist, and they'd play up, and I'd be tired, and we'd end up having a huge fight about it. In the end I realised I needed to back off. They felt resentful that the only thing I seemed to care about was their homework. It was much better when I just chatted to them, and got on with supper, and didn't worry about it so much any more.'

Homework is very important, but not for the reasons most parents might think.

Putting homework in perspective

For example, it is actually unclear what effect, if any, regular homework has on how well children do in school.

'You know Alison?' my youngest child once said, 'well, she does *tons* of homework. She does, like, *hours and hours* every night.'

Alas for Alison, these efforts may well make little difference to her future. In fact, there is no clear evidence that regular homework does anything at all to help primary children do any better at school, and studies from the US show that children actually get better results when they do homework-type tasks in class than when they do them at home. This is something to hold in mind if homework is becoming a bigger issue in your house than it ought to be, or if it is threatening to cut out other activities like sports practice or seeing friends.

For older children things are a little different. The National Foundation for Educational Research says that two to two-and-a-half hours of homework a night can boost achievement for eleven- to fourteen-year-olds, but doing more than that has no effect. So dutiful pupils like Alison are probably doing themselves no favours, and it isn't hard to see why. Children who labour excessively over homework often fail to see the wood for the trees. They might be working long, but not smart. They may be toiling to please the teacher, or their parents, rather than themselves. They can mistake quantity for quality, put too much effort into things that don't merit it, and spend hours trying to memorise every last fact about something, without necessarily understanding the subject in question.

What homework is about

In order to be balanced and clear-sighted about it, parents need to be very clear what homework is about, and why it is important.

Homework is about:

- reinforcing and extending what children learn in school
- encouraging them to become independent learners

- helping to promote their self-discipline and time-management skills.

And many educators believe that the last two are much more important than the first. In the world our children are growing up in, knowledge will be constantly changing and expanding. They desperately need to acquire the skills that will help them to harness and manage it. This means knowing where to find out about something, how to evaluate what they've found out and then how to apply it. It also means learning how to work independently, and how to make the best use of the time available.

This means that while a parent might be worrying themselves sick about not being able to help with writing a story, or about their child getting their maths homework wrong, much of the real value of the work comes from the actual business of sitting down and tackling it, as well as learning where to find help, if needed, and what can be done to improve things, if it all goes wrong.

What homework is not about

There are many things homework is not about. These include:

- parents showing off to their children about how much they know
- children pleasing their teachers and parents
- children getting gold stars and top marks
- parents getting ditto
- children producing copied-out pieces of work without a mistake or crossing-out in sight.

Bear these in mind and remember, too, that there is always life beyond homework, – the world will not end if your seven-year-old is too tired after swimming to sit down with his reading book, or if your fifteen-year-old gets a detention for not handing in his physics homework – it might be just what he needs to make him pull his socks up.

Homework needn't be a burden. One mother remembers how her younger child watched jealously as she and her husband helped their older child with her work. The little girl came to associate homework with getting lots of attention and was ecstatic when she finally got given her own twenty minutes of reading homework. Another parent says: 'I've always loved those afternoons, especially in the winter, when we sit down with a cup of tea and a biscuit and look at what he has to do. It's the only time he actually chats to me, so even if he doesn't need me, I still sit there and write a letter or something. I like having the excuse to stop rushing around and just sit quietly with him.'

How much homework?

There are government guidelines on this. Children aged five to seven should do about an hour a week – which might sound a lot, but isn't really when you consider that it is just ten minutes or so of reading, or perhaps playing a maths or word game, an evening.

Seven to eleven-year-olds should expect about two-and-a-half hours a week – half-an-hour a night – of reading, writing, doing a worksheet or finding something out.

When children move on to secondary school, they can expect about forty-five to ninety minutes a day, going up to one to two hours a day when they hit their teens.

None of these amounts are set in stone, but if your child perpetually seems to have either no homework, or hours and hours of it, this is not right, and you need to find out what's going on. Talk with him to find out what he is supposed to be doing, and then with the school if you feel the load is wrong. On the other hand, don't get too worried by minor flunctuations. This is perfectly normal, and almost inevitable once your child goes to secondary school and has homework in lots of subjects. And remember that not all homework is reading and writing. Some homework consists of playing a maths game, or interviewing someone in the family about something, or watching a particular television programme.

Homework policies

A good school will always have a carefully thought-out approach to homework, which it will explain clearly to parents. A good homework policy is one where, according to school inspectors:

- homework is appropriate to the age of the pupil, and increases gradually over time
- feedback is clear and prompt

- rewards and sanctions are clear and consistent
- there is extra guidance and support for those who need it
- parents and teachers work in partnership.

Home–school dialogue

One of the supposed benefits of homework, especially at primary school, is that it allows parents to get more involved in their children's learning, and gives schools and parents an opportunity to work more closely together. Often, it has to be said, this works better on paper than in real life. Homework planners, diaries and online communications are all used by schools to keep in touch with home, yet teachers report that many parents don't even seem to know they exist, while parents, in turn, complain that they get no response to remarks they've written in them. Do your bit to keep in touch with your child's teacher with a brief note – not an essay – about any progress and problems, and expect the teacher to keep in touch with you in return.

You should make your child's teacher aware if a piece of work has seemed too hard, if your child does not seem to know some important skill or technique, or if instructions have seemed muddled and ambiguous. It's also nice for a teacher if you can give good news too, pointing out when your child has enjoyed something, or has seemed to grasp something particularly well. If you don't feel you're getting enough feedback, you should talk to the school about this. They are supposed to keep in touch with parents over homework.

How can parents best help with homework?

There are three crucial basics that help children get into the homework habit.

1 **Creating expectations**. The biggest single help any parent can give their child is to make it clear, right from the start of school, that they believe that homework matters, and that they expect him to do it – unless there is a good reason why he can't. And to make it clear, too, that they see learning as an enjoyable and worthwhile part of life, not just a grinding chore that has to be got through before the good stuff starts up again.

   This doesn't mean parents always have to understand all the work their child is doing, or make a big song and dance about getting it done, but it does mean:

2 **Showing an interest**. By asking about it, knowing how it fits in with what the child is learning, commenting on it, signing homework diaries, listening to explanations and generally engaging with what a child is doing ('You know that work you were doing on climate change the other day? Well I heard on the radio today that robins are now laying their eggs seventeen days earlier then they were twenty-five years ago . . .').

3 **Providing a good environment for homework**. This means having enough of an after-school routine to help a child develop the homework habit, with a quiet and well-lit place to work and the right equipment.

The homework-friendly home is likely to have:

- books, including basic reference books such as a good dictionary and atlas

- paper, pens, pencils and other useful stationery
- materials and opportunities for creative projects
- adults who make learning part of their own lives – looking things up on the Internet; doing crosswords; taking evening classes; studying for extra qualifications
- good conversations – where everyone has a chance to talk and listen
- an atmosphere of praise and encouragement
- the feeling that it's OK to make mistakes
- lots of casual learning via moment-to-moment things such as telling the time, making shopping lists, discussing a new word or working out the price of something
- opportunities to do sports and other out-of-school activities.

When should homework be done?

Some children like to get it out of the way as soon as they get in; others prefer to do it later, maybe after they've eaten. It really doesn't matter when. The important thing is that they get on with it when they say they are going to, not keep putting it off until it is too late. And also make sure that they aren't working right up until bedtime – sleep experts suggest at least an hour of wind-down time is needed at the end of the evening for a busy brain to turn off.

> *Getting started can be one of the biggest problems. It can help to give a countdown. One mother uses an egg-timer. When she turns it over, it is a sign to her eleven-year-old that he has ten minutes to start thinking about his work and if he hasn't started by the time it runs out, he forfeits half-an-hour of television the next night.*

Where should homework be done?

Younger children usually need supervision and prefer company. Reading can be done cuddled up on a sofa; written work at a kitchen or dining room table. Older children tend to retreat to their rooms, which is fine provided you are sure they are getting on with their work, and not doing the 101 other things that can easily claim their attention once they are there.

Distractions

Modern life isn't good for quiet concentration. The distractions are multiple and include:

- **Television**. A great way of relaxing, but insidious in the way it eats up children's time and attention. Set times when they can watch it – either before their homework, or after – and be firm about turning it off at other times. Don't let children do their homework in front of it, however much they might protest that they can still concentrate. Maybe they can, but the probability is that they can't.

- **Music**. There is some evidence to show that certain kinds of music aid concentration. Whether that is true of the pounding hip-hop or wailing grunge much favoured by teen students is debatable. However, be realistic. What you can do about this is probably limited. You can – and probably should – encourage young children to work in a quiet atmosphere, but later on you are unlikely to have much of a say over what happens. However, if you feel it is a real problem, try negotiating a compromise – music turned off for some kinds of homework, for example, or played much more quietly, so it isn't so intrusive.
- **Computers**. These are great servants, but poor masters. If you have a child who says he is researching something on the Internet, make sure that he actually is, and not heading off down some more interesting and possibly suspect route – by way of the web's multiple branches. Make sure, too, he isn't wasting time with mindless mouse-clicking. If need be, help him find the most relevant sites, and, if you feel that he is still surfing aimlessly through this ocean of information, set him some limits for this task. 'Why don't you aim to find out ten really good facts in the next twenty minutes?' Many teachers do this when they set computer assignments. If not, and your child has problems, it is worth raising this with the school.
- **Mobile phones**. These don't mix with homework, and it is well worth trying to set a rule that they are turned off – or turned in – at homework time. Constant calls and texts will distract all but the most motivated students, and even if they protest that all these are

urgent communications about the homework in question, this is unlikely to be true. Of course, sometimes it does help to phone a friend about a piece of work, in which case different rules apply.

- **Video games**. These are mesmeric, and another big time-waster. Limit them in the same way you limit other distractions, and check that (if your child has a games console in their room) this isn't being used during homework time.

How to give hands-on help

When your child is young you will probably want to sit down with him and help him with what he has to do. But right from the beginning, allow him to do as much as he can himself, only prompting or explaining when he needs it. Try and develop a really good feel for this. It takes time, but it really is worth it. For example, don't be afraid of long silences as he thinks about a question or a problem – one of the biggest mistakes we amateur teachers make is always jumping in to supply an answer – but learn to know the difference between this and having him stare vacantly into space while he waits for you to help him. And make yourself as familiar as you can with how the school is teaching things. For example, in maths we parents tend to want to hammer home the mechanical how-tos of things like dividing and multiplying, whereas teachers know that it is vital children understand what they are doing, and why, before they move on. Schools very often hold parents evenings when they explain their approach to curriculum subjects, and these are always interesting. Go if you possibly can.

As he gets older, still ask him what he has to do, and discuss with him how he might go about it ('That's interesting. Have you thought about how you're going to look it up on the Internet?'). Use opportunities to extend his learning, by pointing out other associated things he might be interested in ('You know, there was something about that in the paper this morning. I'll find it for you.'), and suggest study techniques, like planning a story or essay before writing it, or breaking down a big task into more manageable sections. Try and make sure he's working productively. For example, researching something doesn't mean copying great wodges of text from books or websites without thinking about what it means.

But at the same time slowly step back, only getting involved if he is obviously stuck or specifically asks for help. Be around if you can, maybe by cooking supper while he works at the kitchen table – the occasional encouraging comment, or help with a spelling can do a lot to keep him at it – and if you do sit down to help him, make full use the kind of coaching skills outlined in Chapter 9, to nudge him towards thinking and learning for himself.

If you are worried that you are over-involved ask yourself the following question after each session with him: has my child learned something new from this? If the only honest answer is: yes, he has learned that if he plays his cards right, some other sucker will do all his work for him, then that is a big clue to you to back-pedal.

Two final points. First, if it helps to visit a library, or a museum, or to see a particular film, or to go to a relevant place, try and make it happen. Apart from anything else, it will show your child how much you respect and value his learning. And second, if he is totally stumped, support him by explaining that no teacher worth their salt will mind about homework not being done, provided a pupil has genuinely tried – then write an explanatory note to school.

What if I can't help?

Don't panic. You're not alone. Lots of us, when faced with a maths worksheet or list of French verbs feel totally inept. We also know that teaching methods have changed since we were at school, although we probably don't know exactly how. We may be baffled by new terminology, or not able to make sense of a school's instructions. In fact, a third of parents polled by MORI said they were worried about helping with homework and getting it wrong. But there is endless help out there if we look.

The Government, which is dead keen on getting parents more involved with their children's learning, has produced a number of general booklets about homework help. You may well get one of them from your school, or you can look at them on the Parent Centre website at: www.parent centre.gov.uk. And if you want to know more about, say, how seven-year-olds are learning maths, or what topics are being covered in Key Stage 2 science, you will also find that on the website. There's also homework help on the *Guardian*'s education site: www.learn.co.uk, and you will find plenty of subject-specific help if you go looking. For example, Leicestershire county council has a great Maths website, with lots of explanations and help for parents: www.leics.gov.uk. Good starting points for searches are Channel 4's *Homework High*: www.homeworkhigh.com and HomeWork Elephant, which has over 5,000 homework links: www.homeworkelephant.co.uk. Keep a note of other sites you think are good, and the things they are good for. And be aware that some homework sites make teachers available to answer queries – very useful sometimes, although the turn-around time on an answer can be slow, and again, your job as a parent is to make sure that your child does not start to use such a service as a crutch, rather than an aid.

You can also buy helpful curriculum guides from leading newsagents, as well as specialist books, some of the best of which are listed at the back of this book.

However, searching for information on the web, or reading up on the national curriculum takes time, so if you know that there is something you need to know, try and do some spadework before sitting down with your child. Otherwise it will just be the blind leading the blind. Also, try not to be too downcast by the chipper lists of homework tips that you will stumble upon. Remember it is far more normal for a harassed parent to yell, 'Well just try, will you!' over their shoulder while simultaneously feeding the cat and answering the phone, than it is for a calmly prepared one to sit down with a child and say, 'Oh, good, long division again. We loved doing that last week didn't we?'

Homework problems

- **If your child says he can't do his homework**. Try sitting down and going through it with him; helping him find help – in a book or via the computer; breaking it down into smaller chunks; or helping him draft a list of questions to ask his teacher. Explain that a good teacher will never mind being asked for more help, provided they can see you've tried.

- **If your child is taking too long over his homework**. Watch and see why; check whether there are distractions that are ruining concentration; make sure he is not wasting time on things like elaborate presentation; talk to him about not everything needing to be perfect; go and talk to the teacher about the problem and together find the best way forward – the work may be too hard, or your child may be misunderstanding what is expected.
- **If your child seems to have little or no homework**. Ask why; check that any work set is actually being done; check that any work being done is being done properly; encourage him to see that a little more time spent on things is likely to bring better results; talk to the teacher if you think not enough work is being set, or if it seems too easy.
- **If your child refuses to do his homework**. Think about why. Is he tired, scared or anxious? Try to make it manageable by getting him to work for short periods, then taking a break; explain that routine work like this is part of everybody's life; praise his efforts; encourage him to see the benefits of doing homework; talk to his teacher.
- **If your child gets poor marks for his homework**. Look over it with him; talk about the importance of checking his work; ask him what he thinks the problem is, and what he thinks he could do to improve; talk over projects with him before he starts; make sure he has understood any assignment; encourage him to think and plan his work, not just rush in; think about whether he needs to change his study habits; talk to his teacher.

You will help with homework if you:

- *are around and available*
- *expect homework to be done*
- *encourage a homework routine*
- *show an interest*
- *help where appropriate*
- *praise and encourage*
- *foster a good home climate for learning.*

You will hinder with homework if you:

- *aren't around*
- *never show an interest*
- *don't provide a calm working environment*
- *see homework as a chore*
- *let it become a battleground*
- *pile on the pressure*
- *supply answers or copy out work for him.*

Homework clubs and study centres

Not all children can go straight home after school, and as they get older not all children want to. Over recent years the Government has spent more than £200 million on homework clubs and study centres, with the prime aim of helping children who do not have a quiet place at home to study. These clubs, which may be at school, or at a nearby library or community centre, usually offer a snack, homework resources and study support, and are a boon to many children and parents. In well-run ones, children like the warmth, the structure and the sense of help and support, while parents like the way the clubs get homework done and dusted immediately after school, leaving the home free of arguments, and plenty of time to relax. This, incidentally, is the same model as that followed by many prep schools, who keep day children at school for supper and homework before their parents pick them up in the early evening.

And finally . . .

. . . don't, as a general rule, bribe. Children need to learn to do their work, for the rewards of the work alone. You will do them no favours by getting them to always expect external rewards. To the best of your abilities, praise, encourage, and be firm, patient and persistent. Homework is a very useful discipline when tackled sensibly, and good habits learned now will last a lifetime.

CHAPTER THIRTEEN

Tests and exams

'It is a miracle that curiosity survives formal education.'
– ALBERT EINSTEIN

LIKE DEATH AND taxes, exams and tests are always with us. Like it or not, they will come around regularly in your child's school life – English school children are the most tested in the world – and your job in this area is to take a long, cool look at what they are all about, and then decide, right from the outset, that you will help her approach them in the most positive and sensible way possible. Of course, as so often with things to do with school, this is so much easier said than done.

Attitudes are everything

As ever, your own attitude is vital, because your child will take all her most important – if subconscious – cues from how you approach the tests and exams in her life. This means not only in what you say directly to her about them, but also in:

- how you talk about them with her teachers and with other parents

- the choice of words you make when discussing them
- your tone of voice and body language – it's no good telling your child 'it's only a test' if your expression is telling her a completely different story
- how you approach challenges in your own life.

If tests make you nervous, and you see them as horrible hurdles looming ahead for your child, then so will she. If your child becomes aware that how she performs in them is crucial not only for herself, but somehow for you as well, then she will become anxious about whether she can live up to your expectations.

Equally, if you show no interest in them, or denigrate them as stupid or unimportant – even if you do this with the very best intention of trying to keep them in perspective for her – she may well take you at your word and not bother to try to do her best.

And if you misjudge the level of support you think she needs, and either cram her with tutoring when it really isn't needed or, equally, fail to spot when just a little bit of extra help in a particular area would do wonders for her, then she probably also won't be able to do the best that she is capable of. But to make these sorts of judgements, you have to know three things very well. They are:

- your own child
- your child's school, and the attitude the school takes towards tests and exams
- what the tests she is facing are all about.

Your own child

No one, but no one, knows your child like you do, and this knowledge can be vital when it comes to tests and exams. It is no good a teacher dismissing her exam fears with an airy wave of her hand, if you know they are tying her stomach in knots at night. If that's the case, your job is to make the teacher understand how much you both need to bolster and reassure her. On the other hand, if your child seems cavalier and uncaring about them, you may need to nudge her towards taking them more seriously – and share your concerns with her teacher and ask what she can do.

If, of course, she seems perfectly balanced and happy about the whole business, you need to do nothing at all – except enjoy it.

The school's attitude to tests and exams

In the same way, you need to get a feel for how your child's school views tests and exams, so as to know if there is anything you should be doing to even up the balance. A good primary school, for example, almost certainly won't make a major hoo-hah about any of the tests its pupils take, even though it will prepare pupils for them. A less confident one, on the other hand, might spend excessive amounts of time getting pupils to revise and take practice papers. It has even been known for schools to bring in therapists to deal with pupils' pre-test stress. The reason for this is that schools and teachers are judged on the results just as pupils are, but it certainly doesn't make for relaxed and confident children. If that seems to be the case, there is probably little you can do about it except make your concerns known to the school. But your job at home will be to dampen down the exam fever by pointing out things such as how many things exams DON'T test, and how much more there is to life than school tests.

Exam fever is also a well-known hallmark of some high-flying schools. Thirteen-year-olds feel it if their prep schools pile on the pressure over Common Entrance. And at secondary level, both state and private schools can be exam factories. When you come across a school with dazzling GCSE and A level results, always check carefully – via visits, questions and word-of-mouth gossip – that these are not being achieved at the expense of other important things.

Today's tests and exams

We've looked already at what a political football education can be. This is even more true of tests and exams. Governments know that parents care desperately that their children should be able to go to good schools where they can do well, and they also know that they need to be able to prove to them that things are getting better.

This has led to a whole battery of new tests and exams. The current English school child takes a staggering 105 tests and exams in her lifetime – a situation that costs £200 million a year, and which one professor of education has called 'utterly grotesque'. It has led, too, to a massive growth in public interest in exam results, to claims and counter-claims of cheating, dumbing down and of results being rigged. And the picture has been further complicated by the growing tendency for parents and students to query exam results and get them changed, and for older students to retake exam modules to get better grades. Exams and tests are certainly not the innocent, low-key things they probably were in your day.

Not surprisingly, this is leading to a backlash. So much so, in fact, that by the time you read this, some of the tests and exams outlined below may have already been abandoned or modified. As I write, there is growing support for doing away with the earliest tests and assessments – a poll of parents in south London found nearly 80 per cent of them thought tests at age seven were too stressful – and, at the other end of the system, drawing together all the different exams students can take in the years between fourteen and nineteen into a single, baccalaureate-style system. Some schools are already experimenting along these lines, and Wales has already scrapped all tests for seven-year-olds.

Whatever the changes, though, remember this: the kinds of tests and exams that students face won't change very much. And the basic principles of how you, as a parent, should approach them won't change at all.

Why exams are useful . . .

It is worth remembering that tests are there for a reason, and that a school life devoid of them would bring problems of its own. Those of us who can remember the days when primary children could go through school without a single test or assessment know how easy it was for a child to slip through the net. My son was still struggling to read when he was almost eight, and no one either noticed or cared. That would be unlikely to happen today, and even if it did, I, as a parent, would have the concrete evidence of his test results to wave in the face of an inattentive school instead of – as happened at the time – being dismissed as a pushy parent wanting to hot-house her child. National test results also give useful information to parents choosing a school for their child.

Tests are used to:

- assess children's progress through school
- monitor how those schools themselves are doing
- identify children's abilities
- diagnose what a child has or hasn't learned (very important, this one).

And why exams are not useful

However, the wise parent also holds in mind the pitfalls and limitations of tests.

First of all, test results don't show a great deal much beyond how well your child did in that particular test, that day. Schools these days often consciously or unconsciously 'teach to the test', giving their pupils lots of practice in the things they need to know in order to do well in them. But one exam reform group has pointed out that a quarter of pupils who do well in the tests they take at the end of primary school, fail to do as well in the same tests a year later, because they are no longer being 'drilled' in them. Other researchers have also pointed out that repeated testing tends to widen the gap between high and low achievers – high achievers get a huge boost to their confidence and self-belief every time a test comes round, while low achievers get increasingly demoralised by their poor performance and go into a downward spiral.

Always remember that tests are things designed by

humans, taken by humans and marked by humans. Inevitably, they are riddled with human errors. Papers get lost. Mistakes are made in how questions are phrased. And what they test is limited and arbitrary. Primary school children are quizzed on their literacy, numeracy and science knowledge, but not on all the other important things that make them who they are – their leadership skills, sporting abilities, sense of humour, imagination and empathy for other people. In fact school inspectors are increasingly worried about how much important work in subjects such as music, art, PE and geography is being squeezed out of the primary school day by teachers focusing so much on the test-based subjects of reading, writing and maths. And while primary school pupils are formally assessed at seven and eleven, there is no divine authority that says it should be so. It is just a pretty rough-and-ready system that educational bureaucrats have knocked up to try and keep tabs on what is happening in schools.

Likewise, as soon as you have a test, someone, somewhere will try to cheat on it. Because league table results matter so much to primary schools, for example, some teachers bend the rules as far as conscience allows them. They might, for example, raise an eyebrow at an answer a child has filled in, or cough significantly at a child's elbow. Some teachers and heads have even sunk to outright cheating, and a few have landed up in court as a result.

All this is by way of saying tests and exams have their uses, but parents must never, ever let them rule their children's lives, or give them any more importance than they deserve.

Tests at primary school

- **At five**. In line with our current love of testing, a five-year-old entering school is now assessed on a massive form with thirteen areas of performance (disposition and attitudes, writing, calculating, physical development etc.), each of which has nine levels. A child is rated on where she is with things like counting, recognising simple words, speaking clearly and listening well. Teachers then use these baseline results to measure how much progress children are making over the next two years in school. But these assessments are informal, children often don't know they're doing them and parents should never dream of trying to cram or coach their children for them. Nothing hangs on the results.
- **At seven**. At the end of Year 2, which is the end of the national curriculum Key Stage 1, she will be assessed on where she has got to in her educational progress, and what will be the best goals and expectations for her as she goes on into junior school. Her teacher will assess her on maths, English and science, as an unobtrusive part of the school day, while tests may cover reading, writing, spelling and maths, although such tests are currently being back-pedalled for this age group, and are likely be phased out altogether before long. SATs tests are printed in a booklet, and children are usually given chances to practise the kind of questions they will ask before they take them for real. Most schools keep things low key, and the hardest part for many children is sitting still, remembering to read the instructions and working for the time it takes. Tests are taken over several days in the summer term, adding up to less than three hours in total. Results are usually

sent home with a child's report at the end of the year, and are reported as national curriculum 'levels'. Your school may well send home a leaflet explaining what these mean – the thing to bear in mind is that each level is wide, and reflects a big spread of ability, that children of this age develop at different rates, and that a specific problem, such as dyslexia, or having a language other than English, will hold a child's results down.

- **At eleven**. At the end of Year 6, the end of primary school, she takes what are known as the end of Key Stage 2 tests. These cover English, maths and science, and, like the Key Stage 1 tests, are divided into teacher assessment and tests. The tests cover reading, writing (including handwriting), spelling, maths, mental arithmetic and science. They take place over a number of set days in the middle of May, and most children are expected to reach level 4.

Although these end of Key Stage 2 tests are primarily designed to give a thumbnail sketch of where each child is at with their learning, they have come to mean much, much more than this. In some areas the levels pupils achieve at primary schools are the main thing that determines which sets or streams they are placed in at secondary school. In addition, they provide data for the annual primary school league tables. The result is that everyone gets rather tense about them. The Government, which has set targets for how well children should do at this stage, pours money into holiday and weekend revision classes, teachers narrow their Year 6 teaching to push their children up to the highest levels possible, and parents panic, and sometimes even hire in tutors – one big national tutoring agency says that its biggest boom area in recent years has been, not A level, or even GCSE work, but coaching eleven-year-olds for these tests.

In-between tests

Primary schools can give pupils other optional tests, at other points in their primary school years, and many do, but you may well not know about it. This is partly because many schools have found that parents get more wound up about tests than their children. 'Tell parents,' said one primary school teacher, aghast. 'Good God no! Half the time, even the children themselves don't realise they're doing them. We do them just to help us know where we are.'

Eleven-plus and other selective tests

If you live in an area where there are still grammar schools, or if you are hoping your child might transfer to a selective private school, your child will take further tests – probably in the autumn term before she is due to start secondary school. Selective schools set their own admission procedures, within guidelines set by the Government. They use tests of verbal and non-verbal reasoning, as well as testing other things such as maths, English comprehension and essay writing. Most also interview candidates, and may look at a portfolio of work.

There can be feverish competition for selective school places, and if this is the route you decide to go down, decide, too, that you will shield your child as best you can from the heat of this. It makes sense to ensure that she knows what she's in for and has practised doing the kinds of tests she will have to take. It may be that her primary or prep school will do this for you. If not, you might want to consider a sensible amount of tutoring, or getting hold of some practice papers yourself – the target school should be able to advise you where to look – and helping her work through them.

But be careful. Too much high-pressure tutoring can turn a child off learning. And you will be doing your child no favours if you push and shove her into a high-flying school only to find she loses confidence as she struggles to find her feet there.

Try not to get caught up in the parental stampede for 'good' school places. Think what will be right for your child. And if you do put her in for a selective school place always make sure that you talk positively with her about other options, so she won't feel all doors have slammed shut if she fails.

You and the primary school tests

Tests and exams don't have much to do with real education, but children have to do them. End of Key Stage tests are compulsory for all children in school (although those who are ill or absent on the day are marked as such and don't have to take them on another day). So, how do we help them do their best?

> *'Tests and exams are not what real education is about at all,' says one educational campaigner, 'but as soon as they're there, we all want our children to do well in them. So what we have to tell them is that it's a game – a game that adults insist children play while they're at school, and if they want to do well at this game they are going to have to play by the rules. But we also need to stress to them that it is only a game, and nothing much to do with the real business of learning.'*

Obviously, first and foremost, comes praise and reassurance. Lots and lots of it. Focus on what she can do, and offer encouragement for anything she is struggling with. And you might want to give her some support, maybe by sitting down with her and running through some test questions on the computer (try www.gridlock.com or www.bbc.schools.co.uk/revisewise) or in a good revision book. You can find them in major newsagents and bookshops.

If you think your child needs some extra help in any area:

- talk to her teacher and get some advice
- talk to your child about what you are going to do together, and how you think it would be helpful
- listen to her suggestions – and objections – and be flexible enough to act on them in a way that takes them into account

- encourage her to try learning in different ways – writing things out, underlining things in colours, repeating things, doing them on the computer, even singing them or making up silly rhymes – so she comes to understand which ways work best for her
- help her to be organised in what she's learning. Have all the right stuff to hand, be clear in your mind what you plan to tackle, go over what you're going to do together before you start and review it together when you've finished. (These preview and review 'brackets' are a very, very powerful trick for all learning. Sometimes it's known as PDQ – plan, do, quiz yourself.)
- get her to repeat instructions back to you, so you can be sure she's understood fully what she is supposed to be doing
- don't overload her with too much work – little and often is better than loads and loads occasionally.

Use word tricks to help children learn. For example:

- *to remember how to spell 'said' – Sally Ann is dead*
- *to remember how to spell 'rhythm', remember – rhythm helps your two hips move*
- *to remember how to spell 'potassium': think – one tea, two sugars*
- *to remember the order of the colours of the rainbow, remember: Richard of York gave battle in vain (red, orange, yellow, green, blue, indigo, violet).*

Tests at secondary school

The national curriculum tests march relentlessly on into secondary school.

- **At fourteen**. Your child will take the end of Key Stage 3 tests. These are on the same pattern as previous ones, but more wide-ranging and detailed. Teachers assess pupils on the whole range of subjects – English, maths, science, history, geography, a modern language, design and technology, information technology, art, music and PE. The tests cover English, which includes reading, writing and studying a Shakespeare play, maths, mental arithmetic and science. They are taken over several set days in May and add up to about seven to eight hours of tests. After that pupils get to choose some of the subjects they choose to pursue, and also which educational paths they want to go down.

- **Coursework**. As your child moves through school she will have individual study projects to do, and by the time she hits GCSE and beyond, these will count towards her final exams. Parents often feel confused about how much they should or shouldn't help with these, but the rule of thumb is that while it is OK to discuss things with your child, make suggestions, guide them to sources and read through anything they've done, the actual work should be her own. Having said that, many, many pieces of coursework clearly show an adult hand. It is your decision what you do about that, but bear in mind what spoon-feeding might do to a child's long-term motivation and learning. Ask yourself, at the end of any session helping your child: has she actually learned something from this? Or have I just done everything for her?

You and secondary school tests

This is the time when it gets harder and harder to help your child in anything but a background role. And rightly so. She needs to develop her own learning muscles. And she will only be able to do this if you step away and let her.

Also, to be frank, most of us aren't well equipped to offer help in anything except one or two areas that we might know something about. It is one thing to sit down and work together on sums or handwriting, quite another to get your head around German translation or human genetics.

Study and revision skills

The trick at this stage is to begin to step back from the nitty-gritty of her work – unless, of course, she specifically asks for help – while also keeping an unobtrusive eye on how she's doing, and helping her foster in herself the skills she will absolutely have to have as the educational stakes get higher.

You may be able to find out more about these study skills by asking her what she has learned about them in school. There is also a plethora of books on the subject, plus lots of terrific websites – individual universities and colleges have some of the best. But some of the basics are:

- **Time management**. Keep an eye on how your teenager is using her time. If she is struggling to use it well, help her break it down into smaller chunks with manageable goals and in-built rewards. Two 40-minute periods of concentrated revision, with a break in between, for example, might earn a phone call to a friend, or the television programme recorded earlier. One problem many students struggle with is getting started. See if you can help by suggesting routines to break down the procrastination barriers. Lists and rituals can be helpful (setting a clock, filling a glass of water), as can stripping away distractions and breaking work into smaller portions.
- **Revision techniques**. Ask about what the school says about these, and suggest possible others – flashcards, acronyms, visualising notes, doing practice tests on the computer.

> *A well-tried revision technique is the so-called PQRST:*
>
> - *Preview – you think about what you're going to be doing and scan your materials*
> - *Question – you ask yourself questions about what you're trying to learn, or remember*
> - *Read – you read your materials with these questions in mind*
> - *Summarise – you summarise what you've read, by notes, underlinings, writing down key words*
> - *Test – you test yourself on what you've learned.*

Offer to test her, if it would help. Collaborate on setting rules about things like mobile phones. And make sure that any music being played is a help not a hindrance – decibel level is a good clue. Praise her when she's working well, and prompt her to notice how much better it feels to have got down and got on with some work, rather than procrastinating and doing nothing.

Cramming furiously is a common policy just before exams, but the brain needs time to assimilate knowledge and anyway overload can quickly set in. Don't let her sit up all night doing this in the days before an exam. On the other hand, a quick review of topics she's not sure of before going into an exam can work wonders, and some learning experts also recommend doing this just before bed, so that the brain can assimilate the last thing it has seen at night.

Exam techniques

Again, this is something good schools teach, but there is no harm in reinforcing their teaching at home. Talk to your child about:

- reading instructions carefully
- scanning an exam paper to decide which questions to do (if there is a choice)
- doing the easy questions first and returning to the harder ones
- taking time to plan an essay or story, before launching into writing it
- making a guess at questions if you really don't know the answer – no one gets marks for an empty space.

Apart from anything else, running through such things helps a child to visualise what is coming, and therefore to be less daunted when the actual day comes round.

Exam stress and nerves

Many, many children get freaked out by exams. 'They have headaches,' said one primary school teacher, of her seven-year-olds, 'they get tummy aches, they can't sleep, they get nervous twitches . . .' And the stakes get relentlessly higher. Perhaps it is not surprising that the charity ChildLine gets 800 calls a year specifically relating to exam stress.

But there are well tried and tested ways of dealing with it that you can teach your child. They include:

- **breathing** – teach her how to breathe deeply and evenly, down into her stomach, when she feels any panicky feelings coming on. There are loads of different ways of doing this, but a simple one is to count to four breathing in, four holding your breath and four breathing out

- **time out** – two minutes of deep relaxation can do wonders. Teach her how to sit comfortably and let all her muscles go, from the top of her head to her toes. If she finds this hard, get her to squeeze each bit tightly in turn – calves, thighs, tummy etc. – then let it go. Teach her how to let her mind go, by visualising a happy, calm place that she likes to be in. Tropical beaches are often popular. Teach her she can do this any time she feels stressed
- **letting go** – teach her a trick or two about letting go. At the end of a revision session, for example, get her to do something simple like drink a class or water, or bend down and touch her toes, and to tell herself that, as she does that, she's drawing a line under what she has been doing, and is now moving on to do something to relax
- **visualisation** – this is a powerful tool both for relaxation and preparation. For relaxation, get her to shut her eyes, relax and slowly take herself on an imaginary journey through somewhere beautiful and calm. Maybe it will be a garden, or a path that she can imagine through the rainforest. The more she imagines the sights, smells, sounds and feel of this, the more powerful it will be. If she doesn't want to listen to you, buy her a tape. For preparation, get her to think ahead to the test or exam she will be taking. Get her to imagine herself going into the room feeling prepared and alert, sitting

down, looking at her paper and starting to write her answers. Get her to imagine some good questions, and others that are more difficult, but get her to imagine tackling the difficult ones calmly and sensibly, and coming out knowing that whatever happens she has done her best. Just as top tennis players often visualise a sizzling serve before they do it, this kind of run-through prepares the brain for what lies ahead and helps lay down the pattern for success.

Special help

If your child is dyslexic, or has other difficulties, she may be eligible for extra time, or other help, when it comes to exams. To get this, you will need to have a professional validation of her condition. For more details see Chapter 19.

On the day itself

Whether your child is seven, or seventeen, on exam or test day itself there are things you can do to help her set off in good spirits:

- make sure she is up early enough not to be rushing around late and in a panic
- make sure she has breakfast – ideally one that includes some good brain food like an egg, or porridge oats with nuts and fruit
- make sure that she has a bottle of water to take into the exam with her (if they are allowed – they ought to be)
- give her an apple or other snack for afterwards – using your brain uses up a lot of calories

- wish her luck and send her off in good heart
- be there for her, if you can, when she comes home. If not, ask her how it went as soon as you get home. If you take her exams seriously – but, of course, also calmly and tactfully – then so will she.

Move on, move on

If it hasn't gone well, or if results are disappointing, teach her how to review any mistakes, see what lessons can be learned – and then move on. In fact this is probably the most important lesson any parent can teach their child in this area. After all, nothing, during a child's schooldays, should ever be so disastrous, that she can't recover from it quickly and bounce back.

Teach her:

- that doing not so well this time doesn't inevitably mean she will do the same the next
- how to look at what might have gone wrong – could she have done more revision, read the paper more carefully, asked for help if she felt she wasn't being taught well in the subject
- how to learn from this and think about what she will do next time to do things better
- how everyone makes mistakes and has setbacks, but the only real failure is not to try and learn from them
- to move on. Yesterday's test is history. Tomorrow is full of possibilities. Help her to move towards them with both hands open to grasp them.

CHAPTER FOURTEEN

Out-of-school learning

'I have never let schooling interfere with my education.'
– MARK TWAIN

CHILDREN SPEND ONLY about 15 per cent of their waking time in school, so it is easy to see that they do most of their learning outside the school gates.

And learning, remember, is something that never stops. Every car journey you make, every trip to the shops, every conversation, every television programme and change in the weather floods a young brain with new sights, sounds, experiences and lessons. The truly wise parent tries to hold this in mind, and act accordingly.

A mother remembers asking a friend if she and her two children would like to come with her and her children to visit a butterfly house in west London. 'I felt pretty pleased with myself that I had arranged a holiday expedition that I thought would be both fun and educational. I told the kids about where we were going, and we got out a book on butterflies and packed it so we could look up things when we got there, but once we had battled our way on to the train all I wanted to do was to give the children a juice box each and hope they would leave me in peace for a bit. Not my friend. All the time she was pointing things out to them, answering their questions, asking them what they thought about things, just talking to them, really, and it struck me what a huge amount more they were learning from her, than from me. Even about little things like how trains are made up of carriages linked together, and how much people's back gardens vary from each other. "It's all so new to them," she said. "Mine have only been on a train twice before." And it struck me like a thunderbolt that I'd been thinking of the educational part of the day as being butterflies and nothing else, but she knew it was everything.'

But there are also hundreds of more structured learning opportunities for children outside school. For one thing, schools themselves are increasingly throwing open their doors for Saturday, holiday and after-school learning as more and more people come to realise that it is a crime to have these beautifully-equipped buildings standing idle for most of the time. Tens of millions of pounds of Lottery money, distributed through the New Opportunities Fund, have helped extend such programmes in recent years.

For another, private courses abound. From baby gymnastics to theatre groups to exam revision courses, the really keen parent can cram their whole child's life with activities specifically designed to broaden and extend his education, if that is what they choose to do.

But is more learning always better? Will your child miss out if he doesn't go to extra classes? And how do you judge what is worth doing, or not?

The main principles

All children are different, and so are the opportunities available to them. Ask yourself:

- What sort of child do I have? Does he have bags of energy, and love spending time with other children, or does he need and prefer time by himself? Is he up for any new experience, or particularly passionate about one kind of activity?
- What is actually available? A city child might be spoiled for choice, while a child living deep in the countryside might have more limited opportunities open to him.
- How will I judge whether something is right for him? Remember standards can and do vary. One of my children was keen on ballet when she was little, and went to three different classes in three different towns as we moved around. One was fabulous. It had an enthusiastic teacher who really put over her love of music and movement to her students. The other two, frankly, were little more than opportunities for my daughter to put on a pink leotard and prance around with her friends. You need to find out all you can about an activity before signing up.

When making a judgement, keep the following things in mind:

- You don't have to do things because everyone else is. And this isn't school. You don't have to stick at them, if you feel they are really not working out (although you will, of course, want to encourage your child to at least give a reasonable try to something he's started).
- All children need a balance between being busy and stimulated, and having down-time to decompress, assimilate, play and find their own amusements. The balance will vary from child to child, but no child benefits either from either being perpetually parked in front of the television, or from being rushed from one activity to the next, with no time to catch breath.
- Quiz yourself about why you want your child to do a particular activity. Is it to taste and experience something new, to extend an existing interest or to make up school work that you feel he is not getting in the classroom? And how important are other things, too, like building confidence, or making new friends?
- Does it feel like the right age to start something? If your child can barely hold a racquet yet, he is too young for tennis; if his concentration span is still minimal, he might resent having to learn a musical instrument. On the other hand, a thirteen-year-old girl whose passion is street dance will feel very disaffected in a ballet class of eight-year-olds. Catching the right moment is important. If in doubt, take advice from teachers and coaches in the field.
- Always run a full cost–benefit check on anything you are thinking of doing. Will it really be worth getting up

at dawn on Saturday morning and driving for miles to those swimming lessons everyone says are so fantastic? You'll lose your weekend lie-in, your child might object to getting up when he doesn't have to, it'll mean a lot of time in the car and you'll lose a great chunk of useful chore time. Well, it might be. Swimming is a vital safety skill, after all, and isn't taught as much as it should be in schools any more. It's a compulsory part of the curriculum, but standards are often low. So if there is someone around who is really skilled at getting young children to feel confident in the water, you might decide you need to seize the moment. But what about that karate class after school on a Friday? You have a gut feeling that your child is only asking to go because his friend goes, and because he likes the look of his friend's white suit. You know that he's always shattered by the end of the week, that the class is expensive, that it'll be a battle to drive there through the Friday-evening traffic and that you'll also have to drag his younger brother along because there won't be anyone at home to leave him with. If you decide it's just not worth it, say so, explain your reasons to him and stand your ground. After all, if he is really passionate about learning karate, you'll still be hearing about it in twelve months' time, and you can always change your mind later.

School clubs

Most schools now offer some extension activities, and many parents find them a godsend. They extend their children's learning, but in a safe and known environment, with their friends, and most probably with a teacher they already know, and without any need for them to be taken to a different place after school. Classes tend to be relatively inexpensive (or even free), and standards are usually OK.

At first, when your child starts schools you'll almost certainly find that school, and school alone, is pretty much all he can cope with, but as he gets older, and his appetite for new experiences grow, make sure you check out all the opportunities the school has to offer. Find out:

- what clubs and classes are available
- who goes (an eight-year-old might feel out of place if it's all ten- and eleven-year-olds)
- when you need to put your child's name down
- how much they cost.

If you're curious or uncertain about an activity, ask if you can step in and watch for a time to see what goes on and whether it would suit your child. Or ask if he can do a taster session before signing up.

Breakfast clubs

Lots of children go to school with no breakfast at all, and many more make do with a Coke and a packet of crisps from the corner shop. This obviously makes for listless and inattentive children in class. Also, many working parents have an early start to their day, so schools find that more and more children are hanging around the playground for up to an hour or more before school.

The outcome has been breakfast clubs where, for a small fee, children get breakfast, plus the chance to do other things – homework, games, reading – designed to put them in the right frame of mind for school.

Good ones are warm and welcoming. Others can be mediocre. If you are wondering about yours, ask to see a morning session and check out the following:

- **the menu** – are there good foods on offer, or is it all just white toast and sugary cereals? (A recent survey found many were serving a hair-raising diet of pop tarts and hot dogs.)
- **the atmosphere** – is it calm and purposeful? Are children chatting happily with the helpers and each other, or rushing around and being shouted at? If music is being played, is it brain-friendly Mozart or thought-jangling pop radio?
- **the activities** – is there help with homework? Is there a good assortment of books they can read and games they can play?

Lunchtime and after-school clubs at primary school

These might be anything from story-writing sessions, to netball training, to after-school Latin classes. And they might be run by teachers in the school, or outside experts who come in to use the school premises.

There is no one single pattern, and at primary school level, particularly, they can reflect the particular passion of the head. One school where the head is a former dancer offers a whole range of dance and movement classes. Another head might be equally keen on stretching pupils' intellectual capacities with chess or philosophy clubs. Most schools are likely to offer a mixture of things, with some sports sessions and some quieter activities such as computer or cooking clubs.

If your children's school has none of these, ask why not. And if you'd like to see them get off the ground, work with your PTA to see what might be possible. Many schools have successfully tapped into the expertise of their parents to get aerobics, drama, writing and model-making clubs off the ground. And many parents, in turn, have discovered just how rewarding it can be to share their enthusiasm with a small group of well-motivated youngsters. The charity ContinYou has helpful information about out-of-school learning (www.educationextra.org).

Holiday courses and Saturday learning

Weekend and holiday projects are available in some areas. They might be run by energetic organisations such as the Children's University, or the University of the First Age, in conjunction with schools and local education authorities, or else, in cities, through government projects designed to boost educational standards by encouraging both in- and out-of-school learning. Or they might be run by individual schools, or by your local education authority. Keep your eye out for what's on, and ears open for what people have to say about them. The word quickly gets around when something is really good.

> *I once visited a stately old grammar school in Birmingham. It was a Saturday morning, and the building should have been locked and quiet, but instead the classroom and laboratories were*

heaving with enthusiastic primary school children learning all kinds of things from human biology, to Japanese, to creative writing. Their teachers were either secondary school specialists, or outside experts, and while the classes were informal, the children's enjoyment of them was palpable. They were part of the Children's University, a project that started in Birmingham, but which has now spread to many parts of the UK, and is a big success story in out-of-school learning. One teacher told me of a young girl he had taught some years back. Although she came from a modest background, where university wasn't really thought of, her ambition had been so fired up by her Saturday science classes that she had ended up studying it at Oxford.

In the summer . . .

Summer camps are an American idea that has taken hold in the UK in recent years. Some are highly specialised residential courses for musical children, or for gifted and talented ones. Some are programmes of sports and other activities run by local authorities. Some take the form of family activity weeks on boarding school campuses. Many are commercial ventures run by private companies, either on their own sites, or in premises such as prep schools or sports centres.

Summer camps can give children a huge amount of fun,

challenge and camaraderie, but they need careful checking out. All have to conform to health and safety standards, but what they offer varies enormously. A camp leader at one commercially-run camp told me, 'We're told to do "art" on a Tuesday afternoon, but we're not given any projects to do, and there are hardly any materials. We just have to wing it, but we haven't a clue what we're doing. It's a crime people are paying for this.'

Check out:

- the company's reputation and how long it has been in the summer camp business
- the age and experience of the staff it employs
- how many staff there are
- the kind of children who go on it
- the cost
- the size of groups
- the timetable it offers.

And think hard about why you are interested. Are you looking for:

- a few diverting activities to fill up the holiday weeks
- some summer-time childminding
- a genuinely worthwhile experience for your child.

If it's the latter, many may disappoint you, and you might want to limit how long you book your child in for. I know from listening to children talk, that a half-hearted round of face-painting, football and mask-making, does very little for them. I also know that they feel it keenly when they know they have been 'parked' in a programme simply for their parents' convenience. Don't assume because a camp advertises a programme of 'summer fun!' that that's automatically how your child is going to see it.

Clubs at secondary school

Most secondary schools offer clubs and activities, and there can be exciting opportunities to try completely new things, like photography or car mechanics. As a parent, encourage your child to find out about them, and to get involved as soon as they feel ready. The reasons are as follows. A child who is involved is going to:

- get more out of school
- have a wider circle of friends
- get to know teachers in a different way
- develop his skills and abilities
- feel more part of the school than a student who does nothing.

And he is less likely to:

- develop the teenage attitude that learning is uncool
- spend his free time hanging around the streets or the shops
- come under the undiluted influence of a bad peer group
- be a quiet little mouse who is overlooked and unmemorable in his big new school.

However, pressure won't work on a reluctant joiner. Do your best to encourage him to try things – 'Just give it a go!' – and even be a little devious if necessary. One parent got together with another to cook up a joint story that, 'X wants to go to jazz dance, but she only will if you will' to get their reluctant fourteen-year-olds involved. But be realistic, too, and recognise that it is his life, and that if you insist it could lead to other problems.

Science and library clubs

There are some great clubs run for children in venues such as local libraries and museums. Read the local newspaper and watch out for fliers home from school about them.

I once visited a science club in a library in south London where children from six to eleven were doing a whole bunch of exciting things. One group was sending an e-mail to the Mars mission control, asking for their names to be included on a list that was to be taken into space, others were asking the librarian where they could find a book that would explain what the term 'event horizon' meant, and others were building volcanoes.

'We do get to do things like this at school,' one boy explained, as he carefully added baking soda to his fizzing volcano, 'But we never get to finish them. They're always saying, "Right, come on now, pack up, it's time for music."'

At another library in the East Midlands, a ten-year-old explained shyly why coming to her reading group was the best part of her week. 'It's because everyone likes books in the same way that I do, and when someone talks, we all listen. In my class most people don't read. They only laugh and muck about.'

Sports activities

Yes, yes and yes again!

PE and other physical activities have become shockingly constrained in schools by, among other things, the demands of an overloaded curriculum. In addition, many pupils are driven to and from the school gate, and spend long hours in front of the television. So much so that school inspectors are now warning of a 'vicious circle' of physical deterioration among our young people.

If you are worried about whether your child is getting enough physical activity, you are almost certainly right to, and you should move heaven and earth to find a sports team, dance centre, self-defence class, riding school or swimming session where he will get to move around energetically at least once a week. And stick to your mission. If he says he doesn't like basketball, try football. If he hates the water, try skateboarding, or ice-skating. Some parents I know got a roller-hockey club up and running at a local sports centre because it was a sport their son was passionate about – and were then inundated with kids who wanted to learn it. Even if there are tears and tantrums on the way, the reward if you manage to get him moving will be a fit and alert child, with a more positive attitude to life, better social skills, more friends, and one who is likely to do better in his academic work than his couch-potato friends.

Music activities

Learning an instrument, singing in a choir, joining a band . . . children can get incredible pleasure plus a whole array of other things – improved concentration, memory, self-confidence, dexterity – out of developing their musical talents. But they are more likely to do this out of school than in. School music has been starved of time and money for decades now, and although £270 million has been invested in it over the past five years, only about one-in-ten primary school children gets the chance to learn an instrument at school. So you may well have to find your own teacher – your local authority music service should be able to help – and hire or buy your own instrument. To support your child as he learns, music teachers say:

- praise and encourage him
- listen to him practise and note improvements
- encourage him to listen to a wide variety of music
- keep in close touch with the teacher
- find ways for him to join a band or orchestra as he gets more proficient.

Other clubs

- **Churches.** These often have children's groups, which may well reinforce your family's values and offer an additional social framework to school. For older children, church youth clubs can be a useful way of negotiating the transition from childhood to adolescence in a group of familiar friends where you are likely to know the other parents, and you will also know that outings and weekend trips will be supervised.

- **Uniformed groups**. These include the Beavers, Cubs and Brownies, Scouts and Guides, and the Boys' Brigade, offer varied programmes of talks, activities, games and badges, and provide exactly the kind of adventures, camaraderie and challenges that modern children can be woefully short of. 'Juliet adored Brownies,' says one mother. 'She liked everything about it, from meeting up with her friends to walk down to the church hall, to getting her badges and going camping. I sometimes think she learned more there, than she ever did at school.' For more information: www.guides.org.uk; www.scouts.org.uk; www.boys-brigade.org.uk.
- **Drama clubs and classes.** These are widely available, teach children valuable communication and projection skills, and can be great confidence-boosters for those who are shy or timid – especially if they lead on to performances in front of proud parents, or getting involved in something like the local panto. Stagecoach Schools offer weekend drama classes across the UK: www.stagecoachtheatrearts.com.

Revision courses

What about out-of-school learning that consciously reinforces school work? Is getting extra help a good idea, or can it be counter-productive?

Sometimes Easter revision courses are available to help children prepare for the end of Key Stage 2 tests that they take at the end of primary school. Some schools make them available to all pupils; others target only those who need extra help. Although they sound horribly like cramming, many pupils get a surprising amount of enjoyment out of them. They like going to school in their own clothes, and talking to their teachers in a more relaxed atmosphere, and as one boy told me, 'I don't do anything in the holidays anyway, so it's cool to come to school.'

Sometimes summer courses are available for children transferring to secondary school to give them some re-inforcement in subjects like English, maths and science, before starting at their new schools. Although research figures seem to show that these courses don't do much to boost achievement, if they are offered to your child, it is worth considering whether they might help him gain some useful confidence and practise his basic skills.

Extra help and tutoring

These days, tutoring is widespread – more widespread than it probably should be. You won't have your child in school long before you start to hear of this child who is going to so-and-so for maths, and that one who is going to so-and-so for English. Even Prime Minister Tony Blair, has resorted to tutors for his children, despite the fact that the head of his eldest child's school publicly expressed unease about the extra pressure such tutoring puts on children, as well as about whether the high fees charged by some tutors are worth it.

Never rush into extra formal work for your child, especially at the early stages of school, when children are coming to things at very different paces. If your child isn't taking to reading like a fish to water, for example, wait and see if he really needs that extra hand, and talk to his teacher about your worries and what you might do about them, before doing anything else.

Talk to his teacher, too, if you have made your mind up to get extra help, as it will help you tell a tutor precisely what areas your child needs to work on – although it's worth being aware that, while some teachers might welcome and support this, others may be prickly about it, and may tell you are wrong to do it. Listen to the reasoning, and be quietly purposeful in setting out the situation as you see it. At the end of the day, it's your child, and your decision – and of course you wouldn't be foolish enough to want to push and pressurise your child unnecessarily. Would you?

Sometimes a grandparent or friend will offer some help, but it is important that whoever is teaching your child out-of-school knows the modern school curriculum, and today's ways of doing things, otherwise confusion can take hold. When my children came back from the US they were thrown into a complete spin over how to do long division – were they borrowing, or trading, and, whatever it was they were doing, which was the right way to do it? Conflicting language and methods of teaching can be a real problem. Avoid such confusion at all costs, as it can create a lifelong stumbling block about something that could have been very simply sorted out.

To find a good tutor, use word-of-mouth, or reputable national or regional tutoring agencies, which you can find on the Internet or in the telephone book – their age and size should give some indication of their standing, and you can also quiz them about their standards and ask to see references. It is possible to find terrific tutors via less formal avenues like advertisements in local papers, but it is absolutely vital you check out any would-be tutor's credentials and background before leaving your child with them. Ask for the phone numbers of some families they have worked with, and check out what they say, and have a tutor come to your home, or stick around at theirs (outside, in the car, if need be), until you are completely positive the situation is OK. In addition, always agree with a new tutor that you will try them out for a couple of sessions before making any longer commitment. Never continue with a tutor you have doubts over, or whom your child dislikes – you will simply be wasting your money.

Commercial maths and English courses

Currently the main provider of commercial maths and English courses in the UK is the company Kumon, which offers individualised work, once or twice a week, for children of all ages and all abilities, with lots of practice sheets to reinforce the basics. The system started out in Japan, arrived here in 1995, and now has hundreds of centres up and down the country.

It is the kind of highly structured system guaranteed to gladden a worried parent's heart – lots of practice in the basics – and claims many success stories. Children work at a level where they can complete worksheets quickly and get great marks, so they gain confidence as they move up the levels. Some children benefit hugely from this kind of rigorous reinforcement; others don't respond as well. Every parent has to work out for themselves what they hope their child will get out of it, whether the system will suit him, and whether the not inconsiderable cost will be worth it. For more information: www.kumon.co.uk.

A warning

Never stubbornly pursue something that really isn't working for your child. Children have to go to school; they don't have to be taught, tutored and coached outside of school hours. If they are, it should be to enhance their lives, not to make them miserable. And your child won't learn anything from a tutor he hates, or a summer camp that suits you but not him – except perhaps to resent you for forcing him to do it.

Of course, you have to give things a proper try; you'll do your child no favours by allowing him to pick things up and drop them almost instantly, but if something really isn't coming right, don't force it. Always ask yourself: who am I doing this for, him or me? And, if it's him, what, exactly, do I feel he is getting out of it? If the answer is a zero, or even a negative, stop it right now.

When my son was eight he joined a demanding after-school karate class. Other mothers told me how wonderful the teacher was, and how much their boys loved his strict discipline and the high demands he made of them. Mine, on the other hand, came out from his first session in tears. Much to my mortification, he continued to do so every time I took him back over the next few weeks. But I kept insisting. I told myself it was for his own good. That he would get used to it, and it would make him stronger. What I really meant was: it would be good for me. Because then I'd have a son who looked as tough and brave as all the other kids on the block. With hindsight, I hated myself for doing that and knew I had been wrong. And to this day he remembers the torture of those weeks, and has never wanted anything to do with any kind of martial arts since.

And finally . . .

Today's children do an awful lot of their learning via the Internet and television. Some will be good, and some not so great, so keep an eye on what they're absorbing, and talk to them about it. Make time for simple things like going to the library, or the park, together. And never underestimate the learning opportunities of everyday life. The celebrity cook Nigella Lawson says she learned her trade simply from watching her mother: 'She didn't teach it as such, we just picked it up.'

And leave plenty of time for staring into space, and being bored. Children learn more than we can imagine when they are simply idling around, doing nothing very much, but simply being themselves, with their thoughts drifting and their eye being engaged by whatever it falls on. Or perhaps we can imagine. After all, we've all been there and done it – and can probably remember, to this day, some of those personal, private learning experiences of childhood.

CHAPTER FIFTEEN

Money and possessions

'The best things in life aren't things.' – ART BUCHWALD

OUR CHILDREN LIVE in a materialistic world. A very materialistic world. Like it or not, 'stuff' is going to form a central part of their school days, shaping their learning and helping to dictate what kind of people they will grow up into.

Toys, sweets, magazines, clothes, money, CDs, television, computers, mobile phones, video games, DVDs . . . our children are going to have to learn to deal with all of these, and we as parents have the most incredibly important job to do here. Because with our careful help they can learn how to be masters of their stuff, to keep it under control and make it work for them. But without our help, they will be mastered by it – with serious implications for their schooldays and beyond.

But learning how to deal with 'stuff' can be tough – it's an area where almost all families admit to rows and problems. So to give yourself strength, bear in mind that, in learning to deal with money and possessions, children learn an awful lot of other important life lessons too. They:

- learn hard facts about economics and budgeting

- develop personal skills such as time-management and self-discipline
- come face-to-face with dilemmas about issues of fairness, honesty and sharing
- have to start sorting out what matters most to them.

Basic values

As soon as your child is at school, she is out in the world where attitudes towards possessions and money may be very different from the ones she's used to. You may be astonished by the amounts of money some children have to spend, or their extensive wardrobes, or their pocketfuls of sweets – many parents are. Or you may be brought up short by coming across children who don't have nearly as much money or as many possessions as your own child does. What are your values here, and which ones do you most want your child to grow up with? And, having sorted that out, how will you set about helping her acquire them?

Ask yourself what really matters to you. Is it more important, for example, that your child always looks clean and well turned-out, or that she learns that clothes cost money, and should last? Would you prefer to help her be happy and fit in easily with her friends by buying her whatever everyone else has, or to teach her the hard lesson that sometimes people have to wait for what they want? Do you want to keep her on a tight financial rein, with only a little bit of pocket money to call her own, so she learns the value of money and how to spend it carefully, or do you want her to grow up sufficiently free of the daily grind of worrying about every last penny to develop into an open-handed person who feels easily able to share what she has with others?

These are all supremely difficult issues, with no absolute rights or wrongs. Everyone sees them differently, and the point where we decide to place ourselves on the spectrum between everything and nothing will be very much a question of our own resources, upbringing, background and expectations. The important thing is to be aware that there are choices, and that the choices we make will have a powerful impact on our children.

Many parents have found out – often the hard way – that there are some important guidelines.

- Always talk honestly and openly with your child about issues of money and possessions. Explain that the family income is limited, and that choices have to be made – one mother used a packet of chocolate biscuits to show her child how the family income was divided up. And whenever you say 'yes' or 'no' to something, explain your reasons. Explain, too, that different families have different incomes, and attitudes to possessions. The more you treat your child like an adult in this respect – in fact, in any respect – the more mature will be her responses.
- Make sure she understands the difference between want and need. It is truly alarming how many young children no longer seem able to differentiate between the two.
- Help your child come to see that money and possessions aren't always the route to happiness. Discuss how she feels about different things. Which makes her happier – lots of sweets or having good friends? What

are things that make her feel good about herself – looking after her pet or being the child who's got the latest gadget?

- Help her see that everything has to be earned, by someone, in some way or another – a concept, incidentally, which many children understand instinctively. When even quite young children are interviewed about pocket money, the majority have strong views about what children should do around the house to 'earn' it. This lesson, of course, also extends, as your child gets older, to things like who pays for lights left burning all night and the phone bill.
- Talk to her from the beginning about how advertisements are there to make us want things, and how we don't have to be manipulated by them.
- Show her the ways in which you shop around to get the best price for things and talk to her about concepts like buying things on credit. If you lend her money for something, expect her to pay you back.
- Don't, as a general rule, use money as a bribe for good behaviour, or exam performance. Children don't get paid for such things in later life, so it is not a particularly helpful relationship to establish.
- Allow for circumstances. No rules have to be totally inflexible, and special occasions demand special responses.

Taking things to school

When your child first goes to school, she may well be encouraged to bring in a cuddly toy to make her feel safe or something interesting to talk about for show and tell.

However, it quickly gets more complicated than that, which is why most schools lay down rules for what children can or can't bring to school. There are several good reasons for this:

- to cut down on theft, blame and recrimination – all schools, even the best, have some problems with thefts
- to cut down on envy and social divisions – not all children will have parents who can afford to buy them lots of things
- to minimise classroom distractions and upsets. 'How my heart sinks if I see a child carrying in a complicated Lego model,' said one primary school teacher. 'I just think of the trouble ahead when it gets knocked off the window ledge, and pieces go missing, and everyone starts scrabbling round under the desks to look for them.'
- to concentrate children's minds on the true business of school – learning through lessons and play, rather than through gadgets and toys.

So know the rules, and respect them. Don't think that because your own child won't be parted from her brand-new watch or robot, school rules somehow don't really apply to you.

Mobile phones

If you have a young child, you might think you don't need to know about this yet, but it is increasingly common for children as young as five to have them. Parents like the idea that they can get in touch with their child at any time and feel it helps keep children safe. However, if you are wondering about getting your young child a mobile, think about the following points first.

- The jury is still out on the full picture of their health effects, but it is already proven that the radio-wave action of phones causes subtle differences to brain chemistry – and children's skulls are thin, and their heads and nervous systems are still growing.
- Owning a mobile makes children vulnerable to crime – they are five times more likely to be mugged for their phone than adults.
- Almost one-in-five children say they have been bullied or threatened via their mobile.
- Texting and speaking on a phone can block out other activities, important for learning, such as face-to-face talking and playing. The parenting advice service Childalert reports £100,000 a day is now being spent by under-eighteens on text messaging, and that feelings of self-worth are becoming increasingly bound up with having lots of messages and phone calls – very worrying, especially for vulnerable children.
- Do they really help with safety? If your child is still young, shouldn't you know exactly where she is and who is looking after her, anyway? A phone call from you, miles away, won't keep her safe.
- Many schools ban them, and all schools ban them in lessons.

Obviously, as children get older, the case for having a mobile increases. When she does finally get one – often this is around the start of the teen years – make sure she knows to:

- always consider specific absorption rate (SAR) values when choosing a phone, to try and minimise the effects of radio waves
- keep phone calls short, and preferably only for emergencies
- use it unobtrusively and be aware of who is around her
- keep her phone hidden when not in use
- security mark it and the battery, and register her phone with the operator so the SIM card can, hopefully, be blocked if it is stolen.

Also, teach her basic politeness. Phones should be switched off at times when they might annoy other people. Phones definitely shouldn't come to the table at mealtimes, and calls shouldn't be taken, or text messages read or sent, in the middle of face-to-face conversations. Sounds like common sense? It is amazing how often children don't have a clue about such things. But these kind of basic social skills will be a vital part of their armoury as they go on in life.

Television

Ten-year-olds in England have poorer attitudes to reading and read less for fun than their peers in many other developed countries. Is it coincidence that they also watch more television and play computer games more frequently than these peers? Or is it, as Roald Dahl put it: 'What do you get from a glut of TV? A pain in the neck, and an IQ of three.'?

There is a mighty body of research about children and television, not all of it crystal clear in its conclusions. Broadly, it seems to show that:

- too much television can stunt the language development of young children (a scary finding considering the average three-year-old now watches two hours and forty minutes of television a day, and 42 per cent have a television in their bedroom)
- watching a lot of violence on television may either desensitise children to violence, or make them more aggressive or fearful
- children do poorer homework while watching it
- long hours in front of it wreaks havoc with health and fitness.

As parents, we don't need researchers to tell us these things. We can see that too much time in front of the box turns our children into passive zombies with who-knows-what going on in their brains.

Yet do we act on it? Increasingly not. The pressures against limiting viewing hours are huge, and according to research published by the Broadcasting Standards Commission and the Independent Television Commission, many children now see television as another member of the family, a constant background to their lives and simply can't imagine it being turned off. Most do their homework in front of it, and most parents let them. Research also shows that one-in-five children say they watch television after the 9 p.m. 'watershed' – although many primary school teachers say that in their experience it is far more than this.

What can we do? An awful lot, if we are brave and strong enough to try. And to give ourselves that strength we need to remind ourselves that the habits and patterns we help shape in our children when they are young will stand them in terrific stead right through their school years and beyond.

A study of the effects of television arriving on the remote South Atlantic island of St Helena showed that children who watched television with their parents were much less likely to commit anti-social acts than those who watched alone. Researchers concluded they absorbed their values and attitudes from what their parents chose to watch, and how they talked about it.

Here are some basic guidelines for sensible television watching.

- Don't let your child have a television in her room. Instead, stay aware of what she is watching, and watch with her.
- Never let your child do her homework in front of the television – she'll be looking up at the screen something like two-and-a-half times every minute, and her concentration will be shot to pieces.
- Talk to her about the effects of what she – and we – are seeing. How do we feel when advertisements make us want things we can't afford? Does watching violent and nasty things upset us? Does watching a lot of television put people in a kind of trance, so they don't want to get up and do anything else?
- Be aware that the more channels you have, the narrower

the range of what your child watches is likely to be. Cartoons and music TV can come to dominate the viewing schedule. Make her sometimes watch a programme that you want to see – it's surprising how interested children can get in a history programme or nature documentary when forced to watch it.

- Discuss the limits you intend to place on her viewing, and why. Children, on average, watch about two-and-a-half hours of TV a day, almost double what the average adult watches, and many watch far, far more. Instead, find alternatives that will help her develop her physical fitness, language skills and creativity.
- Be old-fashioned. Set limits on what she can see. Don't let young children watch adult films and television programmes – but also be aware that, even if you are rigorous about this, they are almost certainly going to see them at friends' houses, so also make sure you talk to them about switching off, or walking away from, things that make them uneasy, about telling adults about anything that worries them and about ways in which they can remind themselves that what they see on the television screen is not real life.
- Do something radical – ban all TV for a weekend, or send it out of the house for a week. Talk about how it feels, and what changes it made in the family. Alternatively, just try to break the TV habit a little. One mother was astonished at the difference to their family's morning routine when they turned off both the television and radio. 'Everyone immediately calmed down and there somehow even seemed more time to do things.'

It is possible to get gadgets which block the amount of time your children can watch television, and they can have their uses. But, by and large, it is much better to teach children how to manage things for themselves, rather than rely on policing equipment to limit their access.

Computers

Once at school, computers will be an important and growing part of your child's learning – there are already primary schools where all the pupils have a laptop and do all their work on it. The overwhelming majority of children also have a computer at home, and almost three-quarters of children have Internet access. Children use computers for homework, research, chatting and playing games. If you haven't got one, it isn't the end of the world – all children can use them at school, and as they get older that access increases – but, if you can afford it, it is definitely a worthwhile investment. Or you may be interested in investing in a separate computer for your child – especially since something like a quarter of all computer-owning families have reported their computer crashing from the games and programmes loaded on it by the children.

If this sounds like you, it is worth:

- thinking carefully about what, exactly, she is going to use it for
- talking to whoever is in charge of computers at her school, to see whether what you buy should tie in with the ones she uses there
- comparing prices via reputable retailers and consumer magazines

- thinking about what support and back-up you can get – children's capacity to generate computer chaos is legendary (although, as they get older, their capacity to sort out problems can also be impressive).

One experienced IT teacher suggests looking at computers that are just under the top of the range. They are cheaper than the whizz-bang new ones, he argues, and have had time to have any glitches ironed out. Also, you don't need the very latest technology for what children do.

Once you have a computer, limit your child's time on it. (In fact you could take one family's tip and set a daily limit on 'screen time' in general, wrapping computers, console games, TV and videos into a single package, and teaching your child how to make hard choices.) This is for two good reasons. First, computers are addictive, and can come to block out other activities. Second, it is really easy to waste time on them. When it comes to homework research, help your child know which websites or pieces of educational software are most useful, and make sure she understands how to collect the right amount of useful information for whatever project she is doing. More does not always mean better. As one leading neuroscientist has pointed out – computers give you facts, but not context. To build a sense of context, young children need to be out walking and talking, playing and exploring. Living, in short.

A good starting point for parents wanting to know more about computers and education is www.parentsonline.gov.uk.

Internet safety

Ninety five per cent of parents of school-age children are worried about paedophilia on the net, and lurid newspaper stories do nothing to calm our fears. We obviously need to talk about this issue with our children, and advise them to be careful on the Internet. But there are other Internet worries to which we should pay at least as much attention. You can limit what your child has access to by buying filtering software, or using the facilities of some browsers to block sites – blocking technology has more of a role here than with television, as what children can get access to on the Internet is arguably much more hair-raising. But since a quarter of children over ten who have access to the net at home say they have seen potentially harmful things, you do also need to give your child the tools to deal with this. As with television, the more interest you show the better. So:

- put the computer somewhere central and visible – not the child's bedroom
- take time to sit with her and explore useful sites and browsers
- check which websites and chat rooms she is using, and steer her towards suitable ones
- make sure she understands about the disturbing things she might come across on the Internet, and teach her Internet safety.

Here are the basic Internet safety rules that every child should know:

- *never give out personal details to anyone you talk to on the net, or arrange to meet them alone*
- *if you come across things like violence, racism or pornography, leave the site and tell an adult*
- *stick to sites agreed with your parents*
- *don't open e-mails and attachments sent to you by someone you don't know – they may have a virus that will damage your computer*
- *don't fill out any forms that ask for personal details without consulting your parents*
- *be aware that no company should ask for details from a child under twelve without getting parental approval*
- *never buy things over the net without your parents' approval*
- *in chat rooms, don't pretend to be another person from who you are, even for fun*
- *be aware, on the other hand, that the people you are chatting to may not be who they say they are*
- *don't let anyone be rude or abusive to you, just go away; and never be rude or abusive to anyone else.*

Computer games

As with television, research into the effects of computer games is confusing. Some seems to show that they help hand–eye coordination and quick responses, and that they, along with television and computers, are actually helping raise children's IQ levels. Other research variously indicates that violent games cause aggressive behaviour, or that, on the contrary, they are a useful channel for diffusing such behaviour. There certainly seems to be a worry that they can encourage vulnerable children to withdraw into their own company, and from the real world, so follow your instincts:

- limit time on them if you feel they are taking over
- limit it further if you don't like the effects that games seem to have on your child
- limit time on them if you don't like the effects they are having on you – your jangled nerves matter just as much as their fun
- don't buy violent games if you don't want to, and talk to your child about what you think of any particular game's contents.

Music

Music will surround your child as she grows up. And most of it will be pop music of some sort. Even nursery-age children know which songs are in the charts, and by the end of primary school both boys and girls can bump and grind their hips like the raunchiest lap dancer. Older children plug themselves into earphones, or shut their bedroom doors and turn up the decibels. Is any of this a worry? Yes if, as with television and computers, you feel it is becoming addictive or starting to warp your child's values. To keep things in balance:

- Take an interest. Music matters a lot to many children. If you simply mock their heroes, or denigrate the music they like, they will feel demeaned, embarrassed and resentful.
- Talk about things in the music culture, such as how songs are promoted, what makes someone a celebrity, and the values being promoted in different lyrics.
- Insist music takes a back seat to people. You should never have to shout over a CD or minidisc player to talk to your child.

Clothes, school uniforms and sports kit

There is huge pressure on parents these days to buy expensive brands of clothes and shoes, and to buy lots of them. There are also huge pressures on children to look and act older than their years. Only you can decide how far down this road you want to go, but if you want to try and resist these pressures, here are some useful tips.

- Make sure your child understands that the fashion road is one with no end to it. Such are the pressures of advertising and marketing that she will never, ever feel she has enough of the right, up-to-the-minute stuff to be happy.
- Keep trips to the shopping centre to a minimum. It is both expensive and brain-sapping if a young child

comes to believe that the biggest treat in life is going shopping and buying things.

- Discuss with your child which clothes you will buy, and which ones you think are excessive or too expensive. Help her learn that she will have to contribute her own money for things you aren't willing to pay for.

> *'Shoes are definitely the worst,' says one mother. 'It started when my daughter was eight and went downhill every year after that. I remember the start of one school year, standing in the middle of Clark's shoe shop having a complete screaming match with her because she was insisting that a 2½ inch heel was what the school called "flat". She wasn't normally like that, but she seemed to be completely terrified of being seen in "sad" shoes.' The daughter, admits the mother, got her way. And, to her, the mother's, annoyance she also turned out to be right. The school never mentioned the heels.*

School uniforms help relieve some of this pressure to follow fashion and, interestingly, surveys show that children understand this and are glad of it. But do not be surprised if, as they get older, they customise it in fairly in-your-face ways by shortening their ties and skirts, or doing outrageous things with make-up or hair dye. All kids do, and all schools wage a war of attrition against it. It is part of growing up.

One of the rationales for school uniform is that it saves parents money, but some schools, particularly some private ones, have astonishing lists of the uniform and kit they expect parents to buy. The total can be hundreds of pounds. Never be shy of haunting the second-hand shop, or of questioning whether the more arcane items are really necessary. Other parents will be feeling exactly the same as you, and anyway the last thing your child will want is squeaky-clean uniform that shouts out 'new girl!'

But don't stint on safety items. Mouthguards are vital if children are playing sports like hockey, and although the ones specially moulded to your child's mouth are more expensive, they are also better than the off-the-peg ones. Remember, the alternative could be years of expensive, remedial orthodontist treatment.

Piercing and tattoos

These are just as much a part of children's lives, these days, as clothes and fashion – at least once they hit the early teen years. Ears, tongues, cheeks and eyebrows are all seen as fair game by young fashionistas. You may feel OK about this; you may hate it. Your children's school will certainly have strong views about it, which you ought to be aware of. (Your children's teachers, too, being only human, may well not be able to see past the studs and piercings of your child if she turns up in front of them looking like someone you wouldn't want to meet on a dark night.) Whatever the situation, make sure your child understands your opinions – and why you hold them. Extol the virtues of temporary tattoos, rather than real ones. And make sure she understands the health risks of children stabbing holes into each other's bodies. An unclean tattoo salon, or a friend with a safety pin, can lead to big problems with infections and scarring.

Pocket money and allowances

The majority of children get regular pocket money from their parents, and at present average amounts come out at about £2 to £3 a week for children aged seven to ten, rising to about £7 a week for children aged eleven to fourteen. Most families who give pocket money start between the ages of five and seven, and increase the amount steadily – usually annually – as children get older. During the teen years it becomes increasingly common for children to have a monthly allowance, out of which they usually have to buy things they need, such as toiletries and bus fares, as well as spending it on their own pleasures.

What children and young people buy with their own money is: sweets, toys, magazines, computer games, music CDs, mobile phone cards, clothes and make-up, and visits to the cinema and shops.

And about one-in-four older children has a paper round or a shop job to supplement their income.

All of which sounds very modest and reasonable, until you discover that, in addition to regular pocket money, parents also cough up an additional £57m a year when asked – more than £250 a child – over and above regular pocket money. And that a staggering quarter of parents say they will buy their child anything they say they want.

But these parents are being cruel, not kind. Research shows that children who don't have to budget grow up into adults who are bad with money, while those who are taught to budget and save continue those habits all their lives.

So it makes sense to:

- set pocket money rates and stick to them
- have broad and clear guidelines about what that money is for, and what you will pay for, and sit down together and hammer out any conflicts that arise
- help your child learn about hard choices and compromises – if her heart is set on that expensive pair of trainers, suggest that you pay what you would pay for a reasonable pair, and that she pays the rest via pocket money, or money earned around the house
- talk to her openly about how different families manage their money, and how, while some children do have a lot of money, not 'everyone' has the things that she herself can't have. Explain to her that she is always going to come across people who seem to have more than her, and that it is her choice whether this is going to make her feel miserable and envious – or not
- help her to save and budget – open a bank account for her, and encourage her to use it and to see how savings add up and earn interest (some parents, who can afford it, put their weekly child benefit into such an account)
- encourage her to earn her own money by doing jobs around the house – cleaning the car, hoovering or babysitting, paid at an agreed rate. If she babysits outside the family, make sure she is being paid fairly (hourly rates tend to be between £2 and £5, depending on circumstances). Make sure she knows how to deal with an emergency and encourage her to take a first-aid course if one is available locally. There is no minimum

age for babysitting, but most sitters start at about thirteen or older.

- encourage her to be generous and think of others – 90 per cent of seven- to eleven-year-olds say they have given pocket money to charity. If your child is not one of those, help her to notice how helping others can feel as good, or better, than just buying more stuff for herself.

Teaching about money at school

It sometimes seems daft that we spend so much time teaching our children about the Battle of Agincourt, or tectonic plates, and so little about crucial life skills like money management. Especially when our youngsters are going to grow up to face lives of such terrifiying financial complexity. They will have to manage student loans and top-up fees, dodge consumer fraud, switch jobs frequently, hack their way through a jungle of competing financial services and amass their own pension.

> *'If I had my way,' says a youth worker, 'no child would ever leave school without having done a compulsory two-hour course on debt and credit. The finance companies make it so easy for them these days to borrow whatever they want, and then, before they know it, they've got these enormous debts hanging round their necks. And then they've probably got them for life. Because once you've got them, it's really hard to get rid of them.'*

Increasing numbers of schools are now trying to address this, by weaving money issues into regular lessons, as well as specifically teaching children about things like savings, currency exchange rates and how the stock market works – often under the curriculum umbrellas of citizenship and personal, health and social education. Primary-age children might play games with toy coins, or work out the costs of a technology project they are undertaking. Older ones may assemble budgets for hypothetical families, or play simulation games that illustrate the instability of international trade. 'I've learned a lot about how money can go up and down,' said one chastened Norfolk eleven-year-old. 'I didn't know it could do that. Now if Dad now says we can't afford something, I think I'll be a lot more sympathetic. Before I just took money for granted.'

If your child's school does nothing in this field, it might be worth finding out why not, and whether it could think of doing so. You can get information and ideas to show to them from the Personal Finance Education Group, www.pfeg.org. If it won't, or can't, then think about what you as a parent could do to introduce these topics to your child. Schools, after all, will never have the time to do everything that adds up to a good, twenty-first century education for our children – we, as parents, have to play our part.

The organisation of things

A perennial source of family friction is things being lost, stolen or mislaid. It leads to rows in the mornings – and children going off to school jangled and in no good state to learn – and causes rifts between children and parents.

There is probably no way of avoiding this altogether. Agendas are different. Parents, having paid for things with money earned by their own hard work, care more about them than their children, whose minds are on a dozen other things and can't see what the fuss is about. But problems may be minimised if you can:

- make sure you label or mark all your child's uniform and kit, and give her a good bag to keep it in
- don't let her go to school with lots of money, or expensive toys
- encourage her to develop a reasonable level of tidiness and organisation
- tell the school about any items that go missing, possibly stolen
- help your child learn to check she has everything she needs for school each morning
- help her learn to keep her cash and, when older, cards in a safe place
- Also, encourage her to think carefully about lending – and borrowing – things. This can be a huge problem between families, and it helps to talk through the issues. Help her to understand that things she borrows must be looked after and given back, and that she has every right to expect her friends to do the same. Explain that she doesn't have to lend things she doesn't want to – some children can be very persuasive at getting others to give them precious things – and that you can't buy friends by giving them things. If you have to deal with another parent over this kind of issue, be polite – but firm.

CHAPTER SIXTEEN

Your child and other children – siblings, friends, classmates

'The only way to have a friend is to be one.'
– RALPH WALDO EMERSON

OTHER CHILDREN MAKE up one of the most important parts of a child's school life. They can dictate how well they settle at school, how happy they are there and how successful they become in their school careers. Studies show that high-achieving children are bolstered by having high-achieving friends, while youngsters who veer off the rails into crime, truancy and drug-taking are also strongly influenced by their peers.

Because of this, and because children's friendships almost always have their ups and downs, they can be a great source of worry to parents. Many of us badly want our children to be happy and popular, and fret if there are any problems at all in this area.

And so, to some extent, do children. A recent annual 'school-gate' survey of children's attitudes showed that the biggest individual worry of seven- to nine-year-olds is bullying, while ten- to twelve-year-olds worry most about children who do drink and drugs.

On the other hand, some aspects of being part of the crowd don't seem to matter nearly as much as we parents tend to think. One survey found that while most parents of school-age children think that their children worry about being trendy and fashionable, in fact only 16 per cent of them say they worry about it. And by thirteen, just when parents might think their children would be most involved with their friends and peers, their biggest worry turns out to be 'doing well at school'.

Siblings – the first relationships

Brothers and sisters often form a child's first relationships with other children, and can be powerful forces for good or bad in their learning. When I look back on videos of my own children when they were tiny, I see something I was far too busy to notice at the time, and that is how our second child spent almost all her time as a baby watching her active and inquisitive brother zoom around the room. It is clear, in these videos, that she is soaking up everything he can teach her about the world, and that, as a result, she is getting a very different early education from the one he had, as the only child in a house of sedate adults.

Also, where in the family your child comes, will affect how they progress through school. First children tend to be more diligent, hard-working and anxious to please, than happy-go-lucky younger ones who are more likely to do things their own way – although these generalisations don't, of course, apply to everyone.

Sibling rivalry

Having more than one child can mean sibling rivalry, a wearing aspect of family life and one that can sometimes seriously undermine a child's progress in school. If a non-reading brother sneers at his sister for being a swot, or for sucking up to the teacher, she can quickly start to mask her desire to learn behind a veneer of not caring. Or if rivalrous brothers spend all their time fighting, wrestling and arguing, it will take large chunks of energy away from other, more productive parts of their lives.

Parenting experts point out that a lot of these arguments and fights are designed to get a parent's attention, and that it is best to ignore them, if you possibly can. Instead, they say:

- spend time separately with each of your children
- praise them for not squabbling
- listen to complaints, but don't get bound up in them
- make it clear that you expect each to consider the others' feelings.

And, remember, sibling rivalries can vanish in a flash, in the face of outside threats. 'I'll be all right at secondary school,' one shrimp-like ten-year-old boy once told me with absolute confidence. 'My brother's there. He's going to look out for me.'

Single children

Single children, in contrast, are dealt a different set of cards. On the one hand, they are likely to get plenty of undivided attention from the adults in their life. On the other hand, they may find it hard to share and be part of a group. If you are the parent of a single child, be very aware that these are skills they won't necessarily pick up at home, and consciously help your child develop friendships and come to understand the importance of sharing, cooperation and give-and-take. Help him understand, too, that quarrels aren't the end of the world, and how to make up after them.

Friends and school achievement

Friends and peers have a huge influence on a child's learning. This is something most parents know instinctively, and which most of us look at closely when choosing a school for our child. A big part of the appeal of good test scores, of course, is what they seem to say about a school's culture and the kind of kids who go there. And while thousands of pupils do brilliantly each year in schools where standards of behaviour and achievement are low, there is no doubt that these children have to work a hundred times harder for their success than pupils who are surrounded by others who want to do well.

This is worth bearing in mind if you find yourself in a situation where your child is happy in school, but you are unhappy about the overall standards of work and behaviour. In this case, you will certainly need to make very clear to him what you expect in terms of how hard he works and how he behaves – even if these expectations are different from those of his school, his teachers and his peers. You will also have to give him every help as he tries to live up to these standards. If the gulf is really huge, you may well decide he has to switch schools. This can be very hard for a child who feels happy where he is, but if the move is made carefully short-term pain should quickly lead to longer terms gains. For a smooth transition you will need to choose your alternative school thoughtfully, explain very clearly and honestly your reasons for moving him, and support him all you can during the first few weeks in his new class.

What friendships teach our children

But friendships and relationships with classmates are about much more than doing well in school. They are about:

- learning how to get on with people.
- developing important social skills
- discovering who you are, and how you want to relate to the world around you.

For most children, too, friendships are the source of a huge amount of pleasure and happiness, although they can also be a source of upset and hurt.

Our own attitudes

Watching our children learn to negotiate the often-choppy waters of friendship can be painful. Because we are older and wiser, we can often foresee how a particular friendship is going to go wrong, or when our child is heading for a hurt. And because we remember how it feels to be teased, or left out, or made to feel stupid or pathetic, our hearts are wrung out when the same thing happens to our children. Try and bear in mind that:

- all children sometimes have problems with their friends, this is perfectly normal, and learning to sort them out helps them learn how to deal with the world
- not all children are the same – some are natural loners, some like one or two close friends, others prefer a social whirl
- things change all the time – what seems like the end of the world on Monday may have vanished without trace by Tuesday
- you can do an awful lot to help your child learn how to have and keep good friendships.

Friendships at primary school

When children start school, their friendships tend to be casual and controlled by their parents. You get to say who is coming over to play. But this soon changes. By six and seven they have quite strong views about who their friends are, although these friends can change often, and fallings-out are routine. By nine and ten children are already getting into the pre-teen years, starting to think about their appearance and about who's cool or not. They tend to cluster with their own kind – boys with boys, and girls with girls – and can be very unkind to those not in their 'gang'. By the end of primary school, friends have often become almost more important than family, and start to have a similarly big influence on attitudes and behaviour.

What to do if your child is struggling to make friends at school

- Make sure he feels loved and secure at home.

- Make sure his teacher knows the problem – being included in groups in the classroom, being given an extra responsibility (flower monitor, for example), and words of praise and encouragement can make all the difference.
- Be proactive yourself – invite other children over to play, maybe under the pretence of asking their parents over for tea.

What you can do to help your child develop good relationships

- Do everything in your power to make him feel safe, loved and happy – it will be the bedrock of his feeling good about himself, which in turn will be the foundation of him getting on well with other people.
- Talk to him about friendship, how it works, its ups and downs, and why friends are important.
- Model good friendships to him – make sure he knows who your good friends are, let him see you with your friends, tell him why you like them, and talk to him about the kinds of ups and downs all friendships can go through.
- Make an effort to get to know other parents at school and their children – and do this, if possible, as soon as your child starts school, when these relationships form easily; it can get much harder later on. 'We moved to the West Country and my child had to switch primary schools in Year 5, and I never did make the same sort of connections that I had done in his other school,' says one parent, sadly. 'People had their own friends, and when they all reminisced about "That awful Miss Turner

they had in Year 1", I never knew what they were talking about.'

- Encourage your child to ask friends home, and to talk to you about his friends, and about the dynamics of who's who in his classroom.
- Help him to learn how to figure people out by asking questions: Why do you think Oliver's always saying things like that? Or, what do you think makes James lose his temper so often? Children are often quite emotionally sophisticated, and understand instinctively that, for example, a classmate might be playing up because of stressful things that are going on at home, but it helps to give them the language to express it.
- Encourage your child to get to know a wide circle of friends and acquaintances, and not cling to one best friend – it's an absolute disaster when that one friendship goes wrong!
- Help him learn how it feels to be part of a group – maybe by playing a sport or joining a club.
- Teach him a wide range of good social skills. These might include the importance of smiling and looking friendly; the kind of ways he could reach out to another child he wants to be friendly with; how to be assertive and stick to his own views, without being aggressive and rude; how bad habits like constant sniffing, or boasting, can be a big turn-off to other children; how, on the other hand, being cheerful and enthusiastic, and having good ideas about what to do and play can be appealing; how skills like negotiating, sharing and compromising are all important parts of friendship; and about how, if things do go wrong, it is good to try and learn some lessons from it and move on.

When things go wrong

Lots and lots of things go wrong with young children's friendships. They fall out. They fight. They sulk. They don't speak. They say bad things about each other. Sometimes, as a parent, you can't quite believe how horrible other children can be to your child. And sometimes – even worse – you have the horrible experience of learning just how awful your child can be to others. When the going gets tough:

- Be aware of the warning signs of trouble, like a child not sleeping, or not wanting to have a long-standing friend round.
- Try to get him to talk about what's wrong – but with cautious probing, not confrontational questions.
- If he does talk, do more listening than talking. Keep your own views to yourself, and don't lay the law down or speak badly of any friend. Condemn any behaviour you don't approve of, but not the child doing it. Try and encourage him to figure out, for himself, what he wants to do about the situation, and don't try to force anything.
- If you think it will help, pick up the phone and talk to the parents of the other children involved – but be calm and reasonable, not accusatory. Your child may not have told you the full story. Together you may be able to sort things out.
- If there is a bad situation in school, talk to his teacher about it and ask what can be done. Sometimes a simple move like changing a classroom seating pattern, or alerting a playground worker to keeping an eye on things at lunchtime, may help. But don't exaggerate a small problem, or expect miracles. Primary and prep

school teachers, to be honest, get heartily sick of parents coming to them fussing over what are often – to them – merely the minor ups and downs of childhood friendships.

- If he is old enough, help him to understand after the crisis has blown over that even really upsetting things can have a good side – they help us learn about ourselves, about other people, and about ways in which we can get over problems, and we are always stronger people as a result.

Friendships at secondary school

The pre-teen and early teen years are perilous times when it comes to friendships. It's when the worst fights can occur, the meanest girl gangs can grow up, and when the more precocious children start to flirt with drink, drugs and sex. Perhaps it's understandable that if you ask any class of eleven-year-olds what they are most worried about when it comes to moving up to secondary school, they will talk about hanging on to their old friends and making new ones.

It is at this stage that your earlier investment in your child's social development will pay off. If you have talked to him a lot about friendships and group dynamics, if you have supported him through the choppy waters of his primary school relationships, and if you have taken the time and effort to get to know his friends, and those friends' parents, the chances are that he will move smoothly into the social life of his new secondary school.

But it's worth remembering just what a minefield it can be. American teacher and author, Rosalind Wiseman, has written a whole book, *Queen Bees and Wannabes* (see Further reading), about the cliques, gossip, parties and pairings-off of young adolescent girls in the US, and it is eye-popping stuff about just how savage, complicated and unforgiving the world teenagers have to operate in is. This is yet another reason why being around for your child as he embarks on his career at 'big school' is as important as ever.

Getting in with a bad crowd

This is every parent's nightmare, but it happens quite often, and sometimes for reasons that are hard to predict. Because, while it is certainly true that vulnerable children are the most prone to getting into bad company, it can also happen to seemingly well-balanced ones. 'For some reason,' said one despairing parent, 'my daughter is always drawn to the bottom of the heap. It has an absolutely fatal attraction for her, and always has had, right since she started nursery.'

If this seems to be happening with your child:

- stay calm
- don't get too heavy – strong disapproval will only make the new friends seem more enticing
- make it clear what kind of attitudes and behaviour you respect in people, and which ones you don't approve of
- stick to your family rules about going out and curfews, no matter how hard the pressure is to change them
- try and keep other avenues open via long-standing family friendships, or new activities.

Even if your child is only just starting school as you read this, remember that the patterns you lay down now will be what will count for everything in later years. 'Everyone gets tempted to go along with the stupid stuff when they get to secondary school,' one school leaver once told me. 'And everyone does do some of it. But the main thing that stops you doing more is not getting caught, or being punished, or anything like that. It's not wanting that horrible feeling you get when you know you've done something really dumb that's going to make your parents disappointed in you, and broken their trust.'

How schools help children develop good relationships

Most schools spend a lot of time helping children learn how to get on with each other. One way is through circle time, which is when primary school children sit together in a circle and talk about issues to do with feelings and behaviour. There are usually clear rules about who can talk, when, and teachers use the time to develop children's listening and speaking skills, as well as to encourage them to think about their own and other people's actions and feelings. A topic might be, 'I feel upset when . . .' or 'The thing I most want to achieve is . . .' . Or the children might play a cooperative game or do a group activity.

Primary schools also teach a little about drugs and about sex education (see Chapter 18), and encourage children to work together through cooperative classroom learning, and through playing sports and games.

At secondary school, this kind of thing tends to be wrapped into PHSE – personal, health and social education – which covers a whole gamut of things from negotiation to a healthy diet. Sometimes, it has to be said, these lessons aren't always taken that seriously by students, who feel certain messages are being continually rammed down their throats – 'Oh, no, not peer pressure again!' – but the curriculum covers many useful areas. Children also have citizenship education at secondary school, which aims to teach them about how the country is governed and their responsibilities as voters, how to make good moral and social choices, and the value of community involvement.

A good secondary school may well also have things like peer listening schemes, where students are trained how to listen to and help other students, and anti-bullying committees to involve students in sorting out problems with social relationships. Some schools are also trying out restorative justice schemes where a trained mediator brings bullies, victims, parents and teachers together in a 'classroom court' to resolve problems.

For a closer look at the specific problem of bullying as it affects both primary and secondary school children, turn to Chapter 17.

CHAPTER SEVENTEEN

Bullying

'The only tyranny I accept in this world is the still voice within.'
– GANDHI

I APPROACH WHAT one teacher calls 'that horrible, horrible "b" word' with fear and dread, both because of what it is, and what it is not. Bullying is undoubtedly terrible, and affects at some time or other about a quarter of primary school children and a tenth of secondary school ones. It can also go on a long time – a year is not uncommon. Two of my own children were badly bullied when they were younger, and each time I felt wretched and helpless in the face of it. But the word bullying is also bandied around so freely these days that sometimes it seems in danger of losing its true meaning.

What is bullying?

Bullying is something deliberately designed to cause distress. It can be:

- physical violence, like punching and kicking
- verbal aggression, like name-calling, or nasty text messages, websites or chat room talk

- emotional violence, like excluding, or rude gestures
- extortion, like demanding money or sweets.

What bullying is not:

- an isolated flare-up or fight
- friends falling out
- the normal teasing of childhood
- the natural forming and re-forming of groups of friends as children grow up.

Who are the bullies?

Bullies are often children with problems in their own lives. They might be children who are being bullied at home themselves, or who are struggling to cope in school. They can be sharp-tongued or sarcastic teachers. But they can also be my child, and yours. Not all bullies are even aware of the full hurtfulness of their actions. We need to be very sure to teach our children to think about how name-calling, or excluding friends, or spreading rumours, actually feels to children on the receiving end.

Who gets bullied?

'Usually anyone who's different,' said one sixteen-year-old, looking back down his years of schooling. 'But, actually, anyone really – unless you make it clear you don't care. Then they just can't get to you.'

Occasionally some children seem to attract bullying like magnets, often because there is something vulnerable about them, which the bullies sniff out. But almost any child can fall victim to bullying, even the bullies themselves.

What if my child is being bullied?

If you fear your child is being bullied, watch closely to see if you can see a pattern. Has she become frightened of something like walking to school, or taking the bus? Is she sleeping badly? Has her school work gone off? Is her lunch box untouched? Does she have any suspicious scratches or bruises (although these are common on any child who is busy playing and fooling around – only worry if other things are making you suspicious)? Are any of her possessions or money missing? Does she cheer up at weekends and in the holidays?

If so, ask her what the problem is. If you think you know what it is, ask her if it is what you think it is. If she won't tell you, tell her that you can see she's upset about something, and that you are there for her any time she wants to talk.

If she does tell you, she may beg you not to tell the school about it. But explain to her that bullies love silence because it allows them to operate at will. Talk about the kind of things you might say to her teacher, and about how her being strong and open about this might help to save someone else from being bullied in the same way.

What you should expect from the school

Schools now have detailed anti-bullying policies, which will lay out what they deem to be bullying, and what will be done about it. Sometimes these are better on paper than they are in practice, but the fact that they exist, means that you can rightly expect a school to take effective action on bullying. Talk to your child's teacher about your worries and ask what can be done. If you think you will find this difficult, or if you feel very upset and angry, prepare beforehand. Write down what has happened, and when, and how your child is feeling about it. Ask the teacher if you can talk together again in a few days' time, to see if things are improving. And make it clear that you think tackling the problem is a joint effort – you will be doing all you can at home to help ease the problem, and you expect the teacher to be doing the same at school.

Sometimes parents have to be very persistent to get a school to see that bullying is going on. One parent went in to complain about the behaviour of a classmate who was making her daughter's life a misery, only to be told, about that classmate, 'Oh, but she's a lovely girl'. 'The clear implication being,' she says, 'that my daughter was a liar.' The only way she got the school to take the issue seriously was by unobtrusively following the girls as they walked home from school, noting the pushing, shoving and vicious teasing that went on, and then giving the school chapter and verse of what she had witnessed.

If you don't feel enough is being done, pursue the issue with the head and the governors. If you are certain that this is a persistent bullying problem, you must take it seriously. At its mildest, bullying can undermine a child's confidence and disrupt school work. At its most serious – well, every year about 20,000 children call the children's charity, ChildLine, crying out for help with bullying (it's been the biggest single reason for children calling for six years), and every year a few children take their own lives because bullies appear to have driven them to it.

Some other things you can do

There may be a practical step you can take – like driving your child to school – which defuses the immediate situation, but don't be tempted to avoid rather than deal with the problem. Instead, help your child:

- to understand it's not her fault
- to tackle, if she wants to, any immediate problems such as a 'sad' schoolbag or a bad haircut (although starting to buy clothes that break the bank just to fit in with the playground fashion police is obviously not the road to go down)
- to practise ways of acting so she doesn't look like a victim – by standing tall, speaking out confidently and assertively, and using humour to defuse bad situations
- to avoid difficult situations by staying in a group, by walking away from bullies and by avoiding places where bullying takes place
- to broaden her horizons by taking up new activities and developing new friendships
- to know that, however horrible things are at present, they won't stay like that for ever – one of my daughter's worst bullies later turned into one of her closest friends.

Playground techniques for beating the bullies include:

- *breathing deeply, standing tall and trying not to show fear*
- *staring the bullies in the eyes and saying 'Stop it' or 'I don't like what you're doing'*
- *walking away*
- *pretending not to hear*
- *speaking to members of a gang individually*
- *preparing clever or funny replies*
- *actively looking for new friends.*

Some things not to do

Do not:

- rush up to school, full of accusations, until you know the full story
- take out your anger on the school, the bullies or their parents – it won't help and may make things worse
- encourage your child to be violent (although, sometimes, the world being a less than perfect place, a quick thump has been known to resolve a problem)
- brush aside or belittle her problems.

What if my child is a bully?

Just as every child can be bullied, so every child can be a

bully – hard though it is for a parent to accept. If you are told your child is bullying:

- do nothing until you have found out as much about what has been going on as you can, from as many different sources as possible
- raise the issue with your child, telling her you have to know the full story
- make a distinction between her behaviour and her – you disapprove of the former, but still love, unwaveringly, the latter
- don't let her pass the buck to someone else, or blame others in a group – children have to learn to take responsibility for their own actions
- accept that she needs to feel bad about what she's done, even if it's uncomfortable for her, and make sure that she apologises in words or writing to the child she has bullied
- think about anything that might have caused her to behave like this, and whether there is anything you can do about it – is she upset about things at home, frustrated by things at school, feeling low about herself or being led astray by friends
- draw a line under the incident and move on.

Finding more sources of help

If you find yourself in a really difficult situation, don't suffer alone. There are many parents who have gone through this kind of thing before and are very ready to help. Even just sharing the story can sometimes show the way forward. Contact Bullying Online: www.bullying.co.uk.

Some steps schools can take to prevent bullying

There are many thing schools can do to cut down on bullying. Most now have Anti-Bullying Charters.

Some useful further steps schools can take are to:

- include children in anti-bullying initiatives. School inspectors have found that anti-bullying policies work best when the pupils are involved
- keep a close eye on behaviour as pupils arrive at school in the morning, and leave in the afternoon – when trouble can happen
- create a strong ethos of mutual respect through things such as assemblies and how teachers speak to pupils.
- organise playground activities at lunchtime, providing quiet areas for children to retreat to, making 'anxiety boxes' available for children to post their particular complaints safely and anonymously, and training older children as peer counsellors or helpers to watch out for bullying and to be a friendly ear for children with problems
- record and monitor all bullying incidents and look for patterns.

If your school has bullying problems, and none of these things are in place, press for them to be introduced.

Some measures, however, are not always entirely productive. One parent remembers a school that had a 'friendship stop' in the middle of the playground where children could stand if they had no one to play with. 'It was supposed to stop children being left out, but what it actually did was wave a banner over their heads that said, "Look, I'm a sad so-and-so without any friends".'

CHAPTER EIGHTEEN

Boys and girls

'The main difference between men and women is that men are lunatics and women are idiots.' – REBECCA WEST

BOYS AND GIRLS ARE different. Very different. Their brains are different, they grow up differently, their bodies mature at different times and different rates, their responses to the world are different – so naturally the way they respond to school, and the way that school responds to them, also differs.

But our understanding of what these differences mean for the individual boy or girl is still unfolding. As a reporter on *The Times Educational Supplement* in the 1980s, I became one of the first journalists to write regularly about gender differences in education there was almost no general awareness that school could be a different experience for girls than for boys. But within days I was digging out piles of research, which showed how boys dominated school playgrounds, and grabbed all the teacher's attention in class. Since then girls have come on in leaps and bounds, and in recent years the focus has switched to looking at why boys are increasingly lagging behind girls in school, and what can be done to boost their achievements. This, in turn, has led some commentators to start pushing the pendulum back the other way by protesting that we mustn't forget that girls still have many problems, too . . .

The only important thing for any parent to remember is that whether their child is a boy or girl will affect how he or she goes through school, and that the kind of encouragement and support that they need to give, as a parent, may well differ accordingly.

But . . . a few words of caution before we begin.

- When we look at gender differences we are only ever talking about broad patterns. Girls tend to do this . . . Boys tend to be like that . . . Obviously, not all girls spend their playtimes hanging around the school railings whispering with their best friend, any more than all boys spend them kicking a ball and head-wrestling their buddies. As the mother of three children I can see clearly that my son and one of my daughters are very alike, while my two daughters, although they look like sisters and are often lumped together in people's minds as 'the girls', are as different from each another as chalk from cheese. However, whenever I read about the differences noted between boys and girls in schools, I can also see that for much of the time all three of my children fit fairly easily into the broad stereotypes described.
- It is important to remember that gender differences are relatively small. Other things, like when a child's birthday falls in the year, and whether they are therefore old or young in their year – see Chapter 5 – or what socio-economic background they come from, will have more effect on how they do at school than whether they are a boy or a girl.

- And differences, of course, mean only that. In no way are the tendencies of girls any better than those of boys, or vice versa.

Why boys' and girls' brains are different

All brains start out female, but quite early on in pregnancy along comes testosterone and turns some male. The male brain then develops more slowly from the female one because while oestrogen, the predominant hormone in girls' blood, stimulates brain cells to grow, testosterone, the main hormone in boys' blood, slows growth down. This slower development in turn leads to a different pattern of growth. While girls develop more connections between the left and right sides of their brains, boys grow a stronger mesh of internal connections within the right side of the brain – the side responsible for movement, feelings and an awareness of space. This seems to lead to boys, from the earliest age, being more drawn to how things work, while girls are more drawn to what makes people tick. There are also other differences between boys' and girls' brains, which researchers are still exploring.

We are still learning – and arguing about – what these mean. There is a new theory, for example, that autism might be an extreme form of the male brain, possibly caused by a testosterone surge in early pregnancy. But it certainly seems likely that the differences contribute to things like boys being better at maths than girls, and girls being more adept at using language. It may also contribute to that well-known fact that, while women easily juggle several balls in the air at once, men can only do one thing at a time!

However, so many other things come into play the very second that a baby boy or girl is born – how we nurture them, what we give them to play with, what we expect them to be like – it is likely that brain cells are only a small part of the story. And, remember, we now know that all brains get better at doing the things they practise (Chapter 9), so as parents, we should never be tempted to use these gender differences as an excuse to throw up our hands and say, 'Well, of course he's no good at writing. That's what boys are like.'

How boys and girls do at school

All around the world, girls do better in some areas of school work than boys. A study done by the Organisation for Economic Cooperation and Development (OECD) found that, at age fifteen, girls in forty-three countries were reading better than boys. However, the gap in England and Wales seems particularly large. The reading test scores for nine-year-olds in England and Wales show the gender gap to be more than twice that of either the US or Switzerland.

To put it bluntly, girls in England and Wales are outstripping boys by a mile in English, and are starting to outrun them in everything else, too.The latest figures for children hitting the expected levels of achievement are:

Seven-year-olds

Reading: 80 per cent of boys and 88 per cent of girls – a gap of 8 per cent

Writing: 76 per cent of boys and 87 per cent of girls – a gap of 11 per cent

Maths: 89 per cent of boys and 91 per cent of girls – a gap of 2 per cent

Eleven-year-olds

Reading: 78 per cent of boys and 84 per cent of girls – a gap of 6 per cent

Writing: 52 per cent of boys and 69 per cent of girls a gap of 17 per cent

[[Maths: 73 per cent of boys and 72 per cent of girls – a gap of 1 per cent in favour of boys]]

Science: 81 per cent of boys and 83 per cent of girls – a gap of 2 per cent

Fourteen-year-olds

Reading: 61 per cent of boys and 75 per cent of girls – a gap of 14 per cent

Writing: 59 per cent of boys and 72 per cent of girls – a gap of 13 per cent

Maths: 69 per cent of boys and 72 per cent of girls – a gap of 3 per cent

Science: 68 per cent of boys and 68 per cent of girls – no gap

This gender gap persists on through school – Bristol University researchers have shown it gets still wider between the ages of fourteen and sixteen – and although boys have traditionally got more of the highest grades at A level and at university, girls are now winning out here too. However, once out in the wider world, it is still young men who snaffle the better jobs and bigger salaries. Some things never change.

Why do boys do so badly?

Nobody knows for certain, but it's thought their performance could reflect:

- inherent differences between boys and girls
- how teachers treat boys
- the way that a lot of classroom work seems to suit girls better
- the fact that only about 13 per cent of primary school teachers are men
- peer group pressure not to work
- the messages boys get from society in general.

However, as parents, it is important for us to know that research from the US shows that one of the biggest predictors of children's achievements is the array of attitudes passed on to them by their parents. And we also need to know that, even in these days of equal opportunities, we parents are still too prone to stereotype our children. Studies show that if we have a girl who is good at arithmetic we will assume she does it by sheer effort, while, with a boy, we will believe it is by innate ability. And we will spend considerably more time reading to our daughters, than to our sons. We probably don't mean to, it's just that we've been gender-programmed along with everyone else. But if we really want our children to make the most of school we need to try and guard against passing on any of the kind of limiting beliefs that may have been fed to us when we ourselves were growing up.

Lads and dads

This might be the moment to say something about fathers. Many children go through school without one, either because biological Dad isn't around, or because he's working long hours and too busy to pay much attention.

But having father-type figures to look up to is very important for young children, especially boys. Oxford University researchers, who have followed 17,000 youngsters, born in 1958, through all the stages of their lives, have found that the child who has a strong father-figure around – that's someone who makes time to read and play with them, and gets involved in their education and daily life – will leave school with more qualifications, enjoy better mental health and be less likely to fall into anti-social behaviour than someone who doesn't. In fact it appears a father is central to a child's education – researchers say his level of involvement at seven directly predicts how well his child, boy or girl, will be doing in terms of educational attainment at twenty.

Compare and contrast this with the fact that most men spend less than fifteen minutes a day with their child and, according to a study by the British Market Research Bureau, only 12 per cent of fathers get involved with their children's education – two-thirds of them say work commitments get in the way.

It is hard. Our fragmented families and long-hours culture makes it really tough for men to find good ways of getting involved with their children. And those who try, or who by circumstances are forced to, sometimes find it embarrassing to be the only man at the school gate, or hard to carve out a place for themselves in mother-run family routines. But for men who want to give their children the best possible start in life, there's no way round it: they simply must. And mothers must help them and let them.

Fathers – or grandfathers, godfathers, stepfathers, uncles and friends – need to do things like:

- read to their children
- take them on outings
- cook and wash clothes for them, and share in the school run
- talk numbers with them at the supermarket or DIY store
- play games with them and cheer vigorously from the soccer sidelines
- play with them on the computer.

Mothers need to:

- ask their partner for help in looking after a child
- step back and allow them the space to get involved
- not criticise how they do it – ' Don't swing him around like that! You'll make him sick!'
- create opportunities for it to happen – 'I'm a bit busy. Could you go and ask Dad to do that?'.

How boys go through school

At the start of school, boys tend to lag behind girls in their mental development. They aren't yet very good at small, controlled movements – like holding a pencil – and they can find it torture to have to sit still at a desk when what they want and need to do is to get up and move around. This can make them start to switch off from learning at a very early age – good primary schools will always make sure their boys are making the best possible progress with the basics.

Going on through school boys continue to find language-based activities like reading, writing and talking more of a struggle than girls, although they may enjoy hands-on, trial-and-error, problem-solving activities. They tend to be active, and need a lot of physical exercise. Their friendship groups are fairly loose, and if they fall out with their friends, they will fall back in fairly quickly – this is known to have a physical basis, since adrenaline is quick to flood their responses, but dies back again equally fast. Sometimes, even quite early on in primary school, a 'gang' culture can develop among boys, which schools need to sit on hard before it takes hold. As they get older, boys are likely to become more competitive, peer group pressure will be strong, they need to feel macho, and they may find it humiliating to ask for, or accept, help with their schoolwork in front of their friends, either from a teacher or another pupil in class. They hide their emotions, would rather switch off than be 'second best', are turned off by mediocre teaching, and are more likely to suffer from learning and behavioural difficulties than girls. This, in part, explains why they are more likely to be disruptive in class, and much more likely to be in trouble – 83 per cent of permanent exclusions from school are boys. As puberty kicks in, around twelve or thirteen, growth spurts and hormone surges may well make boys disorganised, impulsive and moody. And if you think they play their music too loud – well boys are much more likely to have hearing problems than girls.

If you are still looking for a school for your boy, bear in mind that school inspectors say boys flourish when:

- *teachers are enthusiastic and imaginative*
- *there is a non-macho school culture*
- *there is a good sense of community*
- *clear expectations and boundaries are set*
- *success is celebrated*
- *lessons are clearly constructed*
- *short-term tasks are set for pupils in clear stages*
- *there is a variety of tasks, with real-life relevance*
- *there are plenty of clubs and activities*
- *there is an atmosphere of fun and competition.*

How to help your boy thrive at school

To give your boy the best possible support in school:

- Encourage him to feel safe and confident – by giving him lots of hugs and affection, and masses of praise and encouragement.

- Encourage his fine motor skills – by drawing, writing, cutting out, decorating cookies.
- Encourage his language skills – by talking, reading stories, explaining things, asking him to tell you about what he's playing on the computer or watching on TV, taking him to the library, and guiding him towards boy-friendly books – horror stories, ones about sport, or books of fascinating facts are often popular.
- Encourage him to get organised – by helping him sort his possessions, develop his own organisational systems, have a workable morning routine.
- Encourage him to control his behaviour – by laying down clear guidelines about respect, manners and the use of violence; by reasoning with him *after* any conflict or outburst, not during (and do this in private, not in front of other people, says family therapist and best-selling author on parenting boys Steve Biddulph, who notes how boys hate having to look people in the eye while they are being dressed down. Take him for a walk or allow him to doodle while you talk to him to get round this); by helping him to know and name his own emotions; by helping him understand how to make good choices by learning to think through options and strategies.
- Encourage his schoolwork – by giving him lots of praise; by helping him break down homework into small, clear, manageable tasks; by helping him to preview and review what he is doing (see Chapter 9); by having him checked out if he seems to have persistent problems with 'getting' school work, remembering it, or making sense as he speaks or writes. More boys have learning difficulties than girls.

- Encourage his sense of self – by making sure he has as many male role models in his life as possible, by raising it with his school if there are no male teachers around – it's hard for primary schools to recruit them, but not impossible. 'You just', as one primary school head-teacher said, proudly displaying her seven male members of staff, 'have to go out and find them.'
- Encourage his sense of responsibility by not doing too much for him, by expecting him to remember things for himself, by giving him appropriate task and chores to do at home and expecting him to do them.
- Encourage him to participate in school as much as possible – by getting him to join in clubs and activities, by taking up leadership opportunities in school, by joining enthusiastically in sport or PE.
- Get him one-to-one tutoring if he needs it – boys can flourish when they build a good personal relationship with a teacher, away from the jeering eyes of their peers.

Some teachers and parents have found the 'take five' approach, pioneered by consultant Geoff Hannan, an expert on gender differences in education, useful with boys, who tend to respond well to limited and structured pieces of work. Ask: what are five steps to doing this piece of writing? What are five things you want to have on your poster? What are five facts you can find out about photosynthesis? And so on, tailoring it to whatever piece of work is in hand.

How girls go through school

Girls are generally better behaved as they go through school than boys. Parents tend not to have to worry too much about their behaviour, or their work. But they may well have to worry about building their confidence, and making sure they develop all their talents.

The majority of girls in school sit quietly, pay attention, follow instructions and work hard. They find reading, writing and speaking easier than boys, and these days tend to take maths and science in their stride as well. High achievers will often strive for perfection. Middle and lower ones will do their best, and tend to be quiet rather than wayward in class – if they do get into trouble, it is more likely to be for talking, than for anything more physical. You'd think teachers would love them. But there are some funny old dynamics within schools. If I had a penny for every time a primary school teacher has told me how much more she enjoys teaching her naughty boys than her dutiful girls, I'd be lying on a beach in the Bahamas by now, enjoying my riches. What lies behind this? Teachers suggest a number of things that might affect how girls are seen in school.

- Girls can be secretive. They often go for a single best friend and exclude others. ('Girls' threesomes' says one primary teacher, rolling her eyes, 'an absolute disaster.') They love to whisper and gossip, and if there is any girls' bullying going on it will almost always be verbal and hidden, not the all-too-visible 'beatings up' of boyland.
- They can appear sullen. Girls tend to become masked and hidden when they have problems, not go for the

noisy acting-out favoured by boys. Even these days, when everyone is acutely aware of equal opportunities in schools, studies show that girls still command less of a teacher's time than boys. And the quiet, mousy girl is likely to disappear off the class radar altogether.

- They can be seen as too knowing. Girls watch human behaviour, and often have a very mature understanding of it. Teachers, being only human, don't always like being observed like this.
- They can be over-anxious to please. Girls tend to be acutely aware of what people want from them, and to strive for acceptance by giving them as much of it as possible. If a teacher asks for a two-page story, some girls will write twenty; they will spend hours writing up a science report with fancy underlinings and colour-shaded diagrams; and, in class, their hand may be up every time a question is asked, straining and straining to be picked to answer.
- Girls aren't always as obviously enthusiastic about new things as boys and may have to be cajoled into physical activities. And if things go wrong at school, they are more likely to stay away than boys – one reason, some people think, why boys get excluded more than girls. Girls exclude themselves.
- Girls grow up more quickly than boys, and become aware of their sexual power quite a long time ahead of them. It is not uncommon for puberty to get going as early as eight or nine, and with it comes the inevitable obsession with clothes, boys, pop songs and celebrities. Some primary schools are now having to ban things such as thong underwear and high heels. These interests can push school into the margins of life, while other

pressures also take their toll. More and more teenage and even pre-teen girls are smoking, drinking heavily, self-harming and falling prey to eating disorders.

How to help your girl in school

- Make it very clear to her that she is loved for who she is, not what she is achieving.
- Encourage her to keep marks and grades in perspective – by celebrating her good work, but never overemphasising test success; by making sure she knows there are lots of important things in life that can't be measured; by encouraging her to see that school marks are only 'snapshots' of what is going on at at any one moment, and that these pictures change all the time.
- Help her manage her friendships – by widening her circle, if you think a twosome is getting too intense; by helping her understand her feelings, and those of other people; by helping her learn how to get over hurts and fallings outs; by talking to her about how hurtful rumours and gossip can be.
- Help her be as familiar with numbers as with words – by playing games, talking about numbers, getting her to pay for things in shops and count the change.
- Help her be at ease in the practical world – by doing jigsaws, solving problems, sewing, making models.
- Help her to be bold and creative in her thinking – by telling her mistakes are a sign of learning; encouraging her to think of different ways to approach a piece of work, or solve a problem; prompting her to 'think big' in her ideas; never letting her belittle herself and her abilities.

- Help her reign in any desire-to-please – by encouraging her to think more about what she is doing, than how it looks; by discouraging too much rubbing out or starting over; by getting her to see that more is not always better; by helping her learn how to do effective, not just extensive, research; by encouraging her to plan a story or essay before starting to write; by making sure she understands that a teacher's view of her work is only one person's perspective, not a God-like judgement delivered from on high; by not laying too much emphasis on 'good' – i.e. meek, obedient, neat – behaviour at home.

> *The girls from a leading girls' public school were rightly proud of the award-winning piece of space technology they had built, when I helped judge a young engineers competition, and explained it with confidence and panache. When I asked them how they had come to embark on the project – most of the entries were from groups of boys – they had a simple answer: 'No one ever told us we couldn't do this,' said one. 'They always told us that we could.'*

Single-sex schools

Some parents believe that their children will do better in a single-sex school, without the distraction of the other sex. Others believe that, since the world is co-ed, their children need to learn to get on and deal with it. It is true that some of the most impressive exam results in the country come from single-sex – particularly girls' – schools. However, many of these schools are either fee-paying, or selective state schools, and therefore already have an advantage in the kind of pupils they take in. On the plus side, single-sex schools can:

- reduce distractions
- encourage self-confidence and aiming high
- provide good same-sex adult role models
- encourage pupils into subjects normally dominated by the other sex
- offer sports and other activities suited to pupils' needs.

Against that they can also:

- provide a less than normal atmosphere – girls and boys don't learn to live alongside each other
- foster problems with boys' bullying or girls' eating disorders
- engender hothouse levels of competition in sport and exams
- attract the kind of teachers who are in retreat from the co-ed world.

London University researchers reviewed twenty years' worth of studies on single-sex education and found no conclusive evidence that single-sex schools do better by children. In fact the most recent research, from the US, shows that the only children to clearly benefit academically from single-sex schooling are girls from poorer backgrounds. But exam results aren't everything, and girls' schools have been shown to improve girls' senses of who they are and what they can achieve.

With such a complicated equation, parents have to make up their own minds. 'We sent our daughter to a single-sex school, because we wanted her to get the kind of confidence and the fantastic exam results that that school got,' admits one London mother, 'but we sent our son to a coeducational school, because we found the atmosphere in the all-boys schools that we looked at too macho and aggressive. We wanted girls around to civilise him.'

Single-sex classes

A scattering of schools – mainly secondaries – have experimented with putting boys and girls in separate classes for maths, English and sciences. The idea is that the girls won't feel put down in maths, and the boys will feel more free to open up, and to enjoy boy-friendly literature, in English. These classes do seem to improve pupils' confidence, and lead to improvements in test scores. However, not all teachers are sold on the idea, and some people believe that test scores improve mainly because the question of boys' and girls' achievements is being given more attention. Some schools have tried it and given it up. So it remains one of those things in education that never quite takes off, or goes away. In a similar way, schools are increasingly experimenting with classroom seating patterns, mixing up the boys and the girls, in order to try and break down stereotyped attitudes to learning. How well it works tends to depend on how skilfully the school does it, and how well it fits in with other school policies – there are no simple fixes in education. It is always a question of building a good culture for learning.

Sex education

We parents are often very worried about sex at school. We worry that sex education starts too young. We worry that it will lead to early sexual experimentation, or that by being open about things such as homosexuality or oral sex teachers will be 'promoting' them. But maybe we need to take more of a cue from our children – most of whom seem to take lessons about sex and relationships completely in their stride, seeing them as just another part of school life.

All schools set their own sex education policies, in consultation with parents and the local community, and these policies must be kept up to date, in written form, and available to parents. Which means if you ask to see it, they must show it to you.

But schools also have to follow government guidelines, which say that, when learning about sex and relationships, children are not only learning the mechanics, but also learning about their physical, moral and emotional development, about the importance of developing stable and loving relationships, and about how marriage matters for family life. This, to be honest, can make life very tough for some teachers. 'Almost half of the nine-year-olds in my class come from single-parent households,' explained one. 'Am I supposed to give them a lesson saying their mums have got it all wrong?' Perhaps not surprisingly, many teachers prefer to emphasise the importance of developing steady, loving relationships without prescribing what these should be. Schools also need to take into account local religious and racial sensibilities, so what they teach will vary according to where they are. Primary school guidelines from school inspectors suggest:

- that by seven children should know the external differences between male and female bodies, be able to show their feelings, and resist pressure from strangers
- that by eleven they should be able to express opinions about relationships, understand their changing emotions, discuss moral questions, resist unwanted physical contact, understand the changes of puberty, and the safety steps necessary to stop the spread of HIV and other viruses.

In secondary schools, children learn more about all these things. They learn about types of contraception, sexually transmitted infections, aspects of sexual relationships and how to make mature sexual decisions. A lesson for early teens might include rolling a condom on to a plastic penis, or getting pupils to list all the reasons to have sex, and then all the reasons not to. And if this sort of thing seems too early for you, bear in mind the words of an experienced headmaster when he told parents, 'Whatever you fear your children are going to get up to, I'm afraid they probably will – and two years earlier than you expect.'

Most schools try to put their SRE – sex and relationship education – into a moral framework, and to dovetail it with other kinds of learning, like developing children's emotional intelligence, their sense of citizenship and their knowledge about how to stay safe. But obviously the quality of teaching varies. Not all teachers find this area easy to handle.

Parents do have the right to withdraw their child from

school sex education lessons (although not from compulsory science lessons where sex comes into things), but the overwhelming majority realise that this is not a very productive thing to do. It sets children up for teasing in school, wraps sex up as something mysterious and nasty, and is unlikely to go very far towards protecting a modern child's innocence, given what surrounds them on all sides out of school.

However, as a parent, you need to make very sure that your child knows what your values and attitudes are in this area:

- from early on, talk naturally about sex and relationships, and your attitudes towards them
- but don't rush them into adult areas too soon, or give them too much information too early. Take your cues from them and where they are at, and respond appropriately
- don't assume they 'know everything' from school. Even if they do they may want to hear it from you, as well. Talk to pre-teen children about how their bodies will develop in puberty, and give them opportunities to ask you questions. This is especially true when it comes to talking to girls about starting their periods, since they or their friends may well find this happening well before the end of primary school
- make sure they know that in sex, as in other things, no one should treat anyone else hurtfully or as an object
- be respectful of their feelings and emotions, and never mock them
- if you don't approve of something – your daughter's provocative outfit or the near-pornographic posters on

your son's bedroom wall – say so, but explain why
- discourage early sexual involvement as much as you can – it can be overwhelming for young adolescents to deal with, it raises the threat of pregnancy and infection, and studies have shown it can be linked to poor school performance.

In fact, how children manage to deal with this side of their lives is very important indeed for succeeding at school. As children go through the top end of primary school and into secondary school, sex becomes a huge preoccupation, especially since this is also stoked sky-high by our highly-sexualised society. If that interest is framed by a strong family, with balanced, healthy and open attitudes, children will be able to find ways of wrestling their adolescent hormones into line at least enough to have some thinking space left over for their geography homework. If not, these flooding hormones can, like a tidal wave, knock them so far off course that they can never get back on it.

Equal opportunities in school

All maintained schools are obliged by law to provide equal opportunities for all their pupils. This should include a careful monitoring of things like exam results and exclusions, and attempts to put right any inequalities that this throws up. It should also mean that policies in areas like uniforms, sport and discipline are even-handed.

If you feel that your child's school favours boys' sport over girls' sport, or has teachers who are passing on stereotyped attitudes about girls' and boys' abilities, you have a right to complain.

And when it comes to your child's class – any teacher worth their salt these days ought to be keenly aware of the learning differences between boys and girls, and know how to tailor their teaching to draw them all in. If you don't feel this is happening, or if you feel your child is in a class that distinctly favours one sex over another, you absolutely must marshal your evidence and raise your concerns – soberly, determinedly – with the school.

CHAPTER NINETEEN

What if you think there's a problem?

'No problem can withstand the assault of sustained thinking.'
– VOLTAIRE

THIS IS A chapter about the way forward when you think your child could have a problem with school. For more about specific problems, listed A–Z, see Chapter 20.

You are not alone

Your child might develop a problem at school. In fact, it is rare for any family to swan through the school years without any sort of hiccup or setback. However, most problems are small and temporary, although some may need nipping in the bud. Others, of course, may be more serious. But if you should find yourself dealing with something more major remember that, however great the difficulty your child is facing, other parents will have faced up to it before. Which means there will be plenty of information and experience out there to help you, once you start to look.

The problems of school-age children may be about behaviour, learning or health – or any combination of these – and can show themselves in many different ways.

What are the signs of a problem?

- **Physical**. Your child might have nightmares, wet the bed, lose her appetite, develop a rash, tummy aches, nervous tics, or unusual fears and phobias.
- **Emotional**. She might seem unusually worried, jumpy, clingy, aggressive, introverted, attention-seeking, volatile, evasive or depressed. Older children might steal things, self-harm, or get into drink and drugs.
- **School-related**. She might have problems with friendships, stop wanting to go to school, find schoolwork difficult, fail to make good progress, find it hard to concentrate and behave in class, come home depressed and despondent, or not want to join in with school activities.

If you think there's a problem

Don't panic, observe your child carefully and try and pin down exactly what it is that is bothering you. Is it something she's doing? Or saying? Or just how she seems? Is it all the time, and if not, when does it happen? If it seems to be a work problem, which particular things does she find difficult? Keep notes (this is for several good reasons, explained later) and try and work out any patterns. Also check with yourself that what you're worrying about is your child's problem, not your own – if she doesn't care about never being invited to classmates' birthday parties, how anxious should you be?

Tell your child that you can see that she is unhappy and that you want to help her. Ask her what the problem is, and what she thinks would make it better, and if she can't tell you face-to-face, suggest she write it down, or even draw it – one eleven-year-old got it out by sending her mother an e-mail. Or try a question-and-answer session where she nods or shakes her head in answer to your questions.

Tell her class teacher why you are worried. Ask her if she has noticed anything amiss and, if not, ask her to watch your child in class and arrange to go in and talk to her again in a few days. Again, keep a note of the conversation.

The teacher may well be able to shed some light on things in the classroom, and offer some practical help – moving her seat in class, making sure someone watches out for her at playtime or giving her extra praise, encouragement or support with learning.

'My six-year-old had a whole month of bad dreams and tummy aches and not wanting to go to school when he started in a new class,' says one mother. 'I thought it was his new teacher, but it turned out to be because he was terrified of the gerbils in the classroom. He hated how they rustled and scampered in a glass case, on a shelf, right next to his face where he sat, but he didn't want to tell anyone about it because he said all the other children loved them, and he felt so stupid.'

If the class teacher is, herself, the problem – and it does happen; there can be a personality clash, or sometimes a teacher takes against a particular child – either raise your child's feelings, tactfully, with her and ask what the two of you can do, together, to sort it out, or, if you feel that isn't possible, look for alternative help. Sometimes classroom assistants can be great allies. They have more time than a teacher to watch out for individual pupils, children usually feel comfortable with them and to a parent they can often seem more approachable than a busy teacher. However, an entrenched problem in this area should be taken to the head, and if necessary to a parent governor. And a really serious complaint can be taken to the local education authority (that's one reason why notes of problems and conversations are always good idea; if you have to make a complaint against a school you need good evidence).

And always remember – you know your child better than anyone else. So trust your instincts. If you sense there is a problem, there probably is, and you should not let people brush you aside as a neurotic parent.

Tackling behaviour problems

Behaviour problems come in many guises. A child might be isolated or withdrawn, or be behaving in a disturbed manner – unsettling physical ticks and habits, or drawings that are always angry and dark, are the kind of things that set alarm bells ringing among primary teachers. She might be disruptive in class, or unkind to other children. If bullying is the issue, turn back to Chapter 17 for help. If it is a question of more generalised bad behaviour, it is vital to work with the school to see what can be done.

All schools have policies to encourage good behaviour, and to mobilise help and support for children with problems. If your child is running into difficulties in this area, you should expect the school to be willing to talk to you about this, to make suggestions about what the school and you can do together about it, and to agree to review the situation with you. You might, for example, agree that she needs to be moved away from disruptive friends, or be checked for possible learning difficulties. And you might agree on a common approach to her behaviour problems. If, for example, she never listens, you and her teacher might both decide to adopt the same strategy whenever you need to get her full attention. Maybe you will say: 'Look at me . . . no, properly . . . that's right . . . now listen carefully, because I want to ask you to . . .', and agree to give her any instructions slowly and precisely, and reward her with praise when she listens and follows.

However, remember that, as a parent, behaviour is one area where you have the absolute prime duty to do the teaching. You owe it to your own child – and to her friends and classmates. Remember that children:

- need – and want – boundaries
- need to know what is expected of them
- look to their parents to tell them this
- need their parents to act like adults
- respond well to rules that they see as fair and consistent.

Hold in mind that, in a society where there are no clear rules any more, it is up to you to lay down what is and isn't acceptable. Bear in mind that the foundation of good behaviour is encouraging your child to respect herself and others, and that the best way you can do this is to set an example. And remember that most good behaviour policies work by emphasising and rewarding good behaviour, and ignoring the bad.

If you are struggling with this area, and feel you are getting nowhere, there is a wealth of top-quality, step-by-step parenting advice around to help you know which strategies work, and how to put them into practice. Books, websites and parenting courses can all be useful – some are listed at the back of the book.

Parents have the power to change even the most difficult behaviour if they take time to watch closely what is happening, when it is happening and why, and then work out ways of addressing the problem, say family therapists Jean Robb and Hilary Letts. They tell the story of Luke, who could never share anything, and was rude and aggressive whenever he didn't get his own way, even though he was repeatedly told not to behave like that. Luke, they say, needed to be specifically taught that he wasn't the only person who mattered, and that when he was with other people he had to behave as if he was in a group. To do this, his father started to ask him 'Who else is in the picture?', whenever there was a problem, until Luke gradually learned, quite literally, to see himself in relation to other people, and to think about how to behave when he was with them.

Tackling health problems

For the sake of your own child, and others, be sure to follow your school's policy on keeping children off when they are unwell or infectious. It's tempting to think that because you have an important work meeting, and she doesn't seem too poorly, she's fine to go to school, but you wouldn't like it if other parents spread their children's coughs, colds and flu to your household in the same way.

If your child seems to be ill more frequently than others – bearing in mind that young children, whose immune systems are not yet toughened up, do catch everything going – or is generally listless and under par, do all you can to make sure she is getting good food, drink, rest and exercise (see Chapters 10 and 11). See your doctor if such problems persist, or if you suspect a specific physical problem, such as a hearing or speech difficulty.

If your child has a condition such as asthma or epilepsy, communicate fully with the school about this, give them as much information as possible about her condition and how it shows itself, and be very clear about exactly who will be responsible for administering or supervising any medication.

If your child is going to be off school for a long time because of a health problem, go and see your school head to establish what, exactly, can be done to keep her up to speed – as much as possible – with what is going on in class, and to keep her connected, socially, with friends and classmates.

Tackling learning problems

Children grow up and acquire skills at different rates, and bump into different barriers to their learning, which makes it very hard for a parent to know when a child is simply making progress at her own rate, and when there is something more serious going on.

If a problem seems minor, you and the school together

ought to be able to come up with strategies to help your child through it. If she is finding that reading isn't coming easily, for example, ask for guidance on how you should read with her, and whether there are specific things – matching letters to their individual letter sounds; encouraging her to scan ahead in a sentence to get the sense of a word she can't read – that her teacher thinks would help her become more fluent. Don't worry if she is not learning as fast as her friends. Do worry if she seems frustrated, upset or you sense a widening gap between what you think are her abilities and what she is achieving.

There is always a danger in giving checklists that might indicate a specific learning diffculty, because so often the things listed could describe practically any child at some point in their journey through school. But, with that caveat, some things that might signal something is wrong are:

- if teachers constantly say she's lazy
- if her performance is uneven – she's good at maths, for example, but has a block in writing
- if she finds handwriting and copying difficult
- if she takes a long time to finish written work
- if she has problems remembering oral instructions or times tables
- if she has problems telling the time
- if she has speech and language difficulties.

Learning and behaviour difficulties are often lumped together into broad categories – dyslexia and attention deficit and hyperactivity disorder are two most of us know about, and there are others such as dyscalculia, dysgraphia, dyspraxia and specific reading and spelling disabilities –

although some child psychologists and other professionals believe there can be danger in such labels, leading to false distinctions, limited expectations and off-the-peg treatments that may not suit every child.

They want us to realise that every child's difficulties are unique, and that by paying very careful attention to the whole child, and by pursuing strategies, which address that child's very particular problems, most children can make great progress in overcoming, or working around, their learning challenges. Dr Mel Levine, professor of paediatrics at the University of North Carolina Medical School, is one, and any parent running into learning difficulties at school might like to read his book, *A Mind at a Time* (see Further reading), a fascinating and positive take on how children's brains really work – as opposed to how we tend to think they work, or how we want them to.

For hands-on, blow-by-blow, practical help in unlocking your child's potential, the series of books by family therapists Jean Robb and Hilary Letts are hard to beat, and some of their titles are listed at the end of the book.

If your child has special educational needs

Children who have problems or disabilities, that clearly make it harder for them to learn than most other children of their age, are deemed to have special educational needs, and will get a varying level of extra support, depending on the problem. This might range from a few hours of help from a teaching assistant for perhaps a term or two, right through to full-time, permanent support, or even a place in a special school or unit, if a child has very severe problems.

Children with special needs go on their school's Special

Needs Register, and stay there as long as they continue to need help. Each child on the register will have an individual plan for their education (an IEP), which will outline the help they are getting, the targets that have been set for them, how parents can help at home and when progress is to be checked up on, and these plans should be reviewed two or three times a year.

If you are worried that your child might have special needs of some sort – and these encompass all kinds of learning, behavioural, emotional, physical and medical difficulties – you must talk over your worries with the class teacher, the school's special needs coordinator (SENCO) or the head. And keep on pressing for answers if you feel the situation is not being taken seriously enough. Parents often know far better than schools when there is something wrong with their child. Go along to any meetings well prepared, by writing down the things that are worrying you, and also any questions you want to ask. You should expect to be included in all discussions about your child, and you must feel free to question anything you don't understand, or you don't agree with.

Guidelines for assessing special needs are set down in the SEN Code of Practice, (www.dfes.gov.gsl.uk/publications/guidanceonthelaw/dfeepub/jul00/020700) which every one must take account of when working with a child. This sets out the ascending steps by which special needs are defined, although children with serious difficulties may skip the earlier stages. They are:

- **School Action** – the teacher identifies that the child needs extra help in the classroom
- **School Action Plus** – the child may be assessed by an

outside specialist, who may advise on a new education plan; the child is offered extra help either in a group, or individually, and either by a teaching assistant or specialist teacher

- **Pre-statementing** – the support continues, but the child is seen as needing a statutory assessment for a possible Statement of Special Educational Needs
- **Statementing** – a statement is drawn up, setting out the child's special needs and detailing what help must be given, and where the child will go to school.

It is relatively rare for a child to be 'statemented'. Parents who are sure their child needs it often have to fight tooth and nail for it, since it inevitably leads to expensive extra education provision, which the bureaucrats resist. It can also be a very frustrating process. It should only take about six months from start to finish, but parents who have been through the process talk about watching the months roll by as meetings are cancelled, vital pieces of paper are lost, phone calls aren't made, nothing is progressed and meanwhile their child's needs go unmet. 'It is torture. Sometimes you think you're going mad,' says one mother, who spent years fighting for the right level of help for her autistic child. 'And often it feels as if you're the only one who cares.'

This is where any parent has to summon all their strength to fight effectively for their child by:

- finding out everything possible about the special needs process
- joining useful support groups
- keeping track – and detailed notes – of all meetings, deadlines and promises

- remaining calm and polite in meetings, however great the frustration level
- listening to what people have to say
- staying stubbornly insistent about their child's needs, and drumming up help from every quarter possible.

If you and your local education authority cannot agree about how your child's special needs will be met you have the right, in England and Wales, to appeal to your local Special Educational Needs and Disability Tribunal.

For more information about special educational needs, contact the Advisory Centre for Education. It also produces a useful introductory booklet, *Getting Extra Help*, priced at £1.50. To contact ACE, phone 020 7354 8318, or visit their website at www.ace-ed.org.uk.

CHAPTER TWENTY

An A–Z of school problems – great and small

'To solve any problem, here are three questions to ask yourself: first, what could I do? Second, what could I read? And third, who could I ask?' – JIM ROHN

THIS CHAPTER GIVES information about specific school problems in alphabetical order. For general advice on how to go about tackling a school-related problem, turn to Chapter 19.

ADD and ADHD: Attention deficit disorder (ADD) and attention deficit and hyperactivy disorder (ADHD) are the labels given to children who have serious problems with paying attention, curbing their impulsive behaviour or sitting still. Such children might also be clumsy, socially awkward, disorganised and moody. At the mild end of the spectrum problems shade into the kind of restless behaviour shown by lots of children, but at the other end, children can be so out-of-control and disruptive that they can seem, to their poor parents, to be half-demented.

The roots of these problems are not fully understood, and experts argue about how many children have 'true' ADHD, or not. Some people believe the label is being used too readily as an excuse for bad behaviour. Others say it is actually under-diagnosed, and that many more children are struggling with these problems than get treatment. Genetics and heredity are known to play a part, although the fact that growing numbers of children are exhibiting ADHD-like symptoms means that many people believe there must also be environmental reasons for them. One primary school cut attention problems markedly, for example, when it ruthlessly cut out all E numbers from school lunches, and encouraged parents to do the same with lunchboxes. Many other schools are now following down this road. They can see, from the surges in bad behaviour an hour or so after breakfast, and lunch, that there is a clear connection between these and what children eat.

If you are worried your child might have ADHD, watch and note what is worrying you, find out all you can about the condition, related treatments and sources of help, get your school's advice and guidance, and seek an expert evaluation. And, remember, many children seem to grow out of it by their teenage years.

ADHD is treated in a range of different ways, with specialised learning support and behaviour management programmes, as well as with newer approaches, which use biofeedback mechanisms to reprogramme the brain. Drugs may also be offered, the best known of which is Ritalin, a derivative of aphetamine, which damps down the symptoms of the condition. In 1999, 158,000 prescriptions were issued in the UK; in 2002 that number had leapt to over 200,000. In the US Ritalin and other prescriptions such as asthma inhalers are so commonplace that teachers taking pupils on school trips hold out open bin bags at the bus door and tell pupils to 'drop your medication here'. Advocates say there are no side-effects, that it can be life-transforming for some children, and that 'you have to reach a child to teach a child'. Opponents argue it is a 'chemical cosh', which only masks the symptoms, and doesn't treat them. They also point out that Ritalin is now starting to circulate in playgrounds as an illegal drug for children who want to get high. The situation is further complicated by social pressures. Parents can come under pressure from schools to get their children on Ritalin and calmed down. Doctors can come under pressure from parents, who believe, or have been told, their children desperately need it.

Most parents probably hate the thought of putting their child on daily doses of a cocaine-like medicine. However, parents without this problem know nothing of what it is like to live with a severely ADHD child, so everyone's decision has to be their own. With any treatments:

- be very sure of all your options, and the pluses and minuses of these – read, research and talk to as many people as possible
- go for an holistic approach – if you do decide to go for drugs, put behaviour and learning programmes in place as well
- make sensible lifestyle changes – provide a stable, loving routine for your child, and ensure a good diet with lots of fresh food, and as few additives, stimulants and preservatives as possible
- get support – there are hundreds of local groups, but be wary of any that seem to believe there is only one way to treat ADHD.

National ADD Information and Support Service: 020 8906 9068; www.addiss.co.uk.

ADHD Family Support Group: 01373 826 045

Thanet ADDers: www.adders.org.

Autism spectrum disorders: Autism, and its milder associated condition, Asperger's syndrome, are developmental disorders, which lead to difficulties with relationships, communication and imagination. At the mild end of the spectrum, children might simply be odd and awkward, but a severely autistic child will find it impossible to talk and relate to other people, and may show rigid patterns of repetitive behaviour. The first signs usually emerge in pre-school children, and the 'cut-offness' of the condition becomes more marked as children grow. About half-a-million people in England and Wales have some form of autism, but there are signs it is growing. Two-thirds of teachers in England and Wales think there are more autistic children in school now than five years ago, and three-quarters of teachers say there are more cases in primary schools than secondary.

Causes are thought to include both hereditary and environmental factors. Some people have suggested the tripple MMR vaccine might be responsible for the rise in cases, although the evidence is disputed. If your child is in a class with a child who has these difficulties, explain to your child why he – the majority of sufferers are boys – behaves the way he does. If you are worried about any symptoms your own child is displaying, contact the National Autistic Society: 0870 600 8585; autismshelpline@nas.org.uk.

Bullying: *see* Chapter 17.

Conjunctivitis: This is a highly contagious eye infection, also known as 'pink eye', caused by bacteria or viruses, which spreads easily among children. If your child's eyes are red, itchy and crusty go to your doctor for eye drops, tell the school, and reinforce hand-washing and other basic hygiene routines. For other contagious conditions, *see* Skin problems.

For information: National Health Service Direct: 0845 4647; www.nhsdirect.nhs.uk.

Discrimination: All maintained schools have to publish and monitor equality policies, so blatant acts of discrimination usually get jumped on, but subtle – and even unconscious – discrimination is more widespread. For example, one-in-five disabled students in mainstream schools have said that their schools have tried to dissuade them from aiming for GCSEs, while primary school pupils have commented to researchers about how much stricter teachers often seem to be with black boys, than the rest of the class. There are still teachers who think girls are no good at maths and Chinese students are useless at creative writing. Since one of the fundamental keys to school success is the expectations that adults have for children, it is important to act if you think your child could be being discriminated against in any way because of the child's race, sex or disability. Pursue it with the school, offering evidence, and to the governors, and even the local education authority if necessary. And if you think the problem is widespread, press for some teacher training on the issue, or for the area to be more strongly emphasised in the curriculum.

Commission for Racial Equality: 020 7939 0000; www.cre.gov.uk.

Disability Rights Commission: 08457 622 633; www.drc-gb.org.

Equal Opportunities Commission: 0845 601 5901; www.eoc.org.uk.

Divorce or separation: If you are going through a divorce or separation, there are two important things to think about concerning your children. First, you need to bear in mind the emotional impact of the break-up on the children (not always easy, when everyone is dealing with their own stress) and do all you can to reassure them. Not by hiding things, waving aside their worries, or piling on the trips to McDonald's to compensate for domestic upheaval. But by talking as openly and honestly as you can to them, and making sure that they understand that no matter what other changes are happening, nothing will change in the way you love and care for them. Second, you need to think about how you and your partner are going to deal with the school. All parents have a right to be involved in their child's education, so you will need to think about how the partner who is moving out will keep in touch with the school, receive school reports and take part in any decisions about choosing or changing schools. You also need to think about things like who is going to pay for school trips, and how you are going to go to events like parents' evenings – together, or separately. Then keep the school informed about what is happening. This is partly so your children's teachers know what they are going through and can keep an eye on them, and also for paperwork reasons – these days schools tear their hair out trying to keep track of which parents belong to what child. But be reassured that researchers have found that while children often suffer short-term distress at their parents' break-up, most quickly bounce back and few show signs of long-term problems, provided their parents haven't used them as one of the battlefields of their marital conflict.

Department for Constitutional Affairs: www.dca.gov.uk/family/divleaf.htm.

Divorce-Online: 01235 527382; www.ondivorce.co.uk.

Drink, drugs and smoking: If your child is young, you will probably feel this section is not for you, but these things come around more quickly than most of us would want – certainly before the end of primary school. A quarter of eleven-year-olds are now said to have an alcoholic drink once a week, and half have experimented with smoking. In some city areas, a third of primary school age children have been exposed to illegal drugs, and almost one-in-ten have been offered them. Schools weave education about substance abuse into their PHSE and citizenship teachings but parents need to:

- be aware your child may know much more about drink and drugs than you think she does
- talk to her from the earliest age about your values, what you feel about these things, and how you think they should, and shouldn't be used
- be clued up about what's around these days
- talk to her about your suspicions if you think she might be smoking or drinking. (If she seems weary or headache-ridden in the mornings, or has mood swings, memory loss or is acting strangely.) Read up

on advice from the experts. And talk to the school, if necessary

- be aware most children fall from grace at least once on their journey into adulthood, often in their early teens. Help them learn from their mistake and move on.

DrugScope: 0800 77 6600; www.drugscope.org.uk.
Wired for Health: www.mindbodysoul.gov.uk.
Alcohol Concern: 0207 928 7377; www.alcoholconcern.org.
Action on Smoking and Health: 020 7739 5902; www.ash.org.

Dyslexia: This is the learning difficulty label most widely known among parents, and broadly describes a bundle of difficulties children have with information processing, especially in the areas of reading, spelling and writing. There may also be problems with how fast children can deal with information, how well their memory works, how they see and hear things, how organised they are and their self-esteem. Dyslcalculia is the label, which describes problems with numbers, and dyspraxia, difficulties with physical coordination. Just under 5 per cent of the population have these difficulties and, according to the Dyslexia Institute, there are 375,000 identified dyslexic pupils in UK schools – although since it is now thought that dyslexia affects boys and girls equally, but three times as many boys as girls get additional teaching for it, there are those who believe there are many more school children out there who need specialist help than who are getting it. As parents we need to bear in mind that any problems our daughters may have in this area are less likely to be picked up by us, or their schools, than those of our more boisterous sons.

Dyslexia varies hugely. Some children have a mild problem with spelling, others have acute difficulties with everything to do with reading and writing and other things. A child might be labelled 'mildly dyslexic', but then have a few severe weaknesses, such as in short-term memory or in the speed at which she can absorb information.

Likewise, any therapy or remedial help likewise needs to be carefully tailored. In the above case, for example, lessons might go too fast for the child to absorb properly, so the teacher needs to know she might need help going over things, and she might also need to learn specific strategies which help her to take things in more easily.

The actress Susan Hampshire, past president of the Dyslexia Institute, says: 'It is a lonely existence to be a child with a disability which no one can see or understand, you exasperate your teachers, you disappoint your parents, and worst of all you know that you are not just stupid.'

If you think your child is dyslexic, talk first to your child's teacher, who may put you on to the school's SENCO, the teacher responsible for coordinating special educational needs. If your child's difficulties are mild, she will probably be assessed by the SENCO, in school, and offered some classroom learning support. If the difficulties are more severe, she may be offered specialist teaching either one-to-one or in a small group, or assessed by an educational psychologist, who will look at her general ability, thinking skills, organisation and planning, her use of words and patterns, vocabulary, reading, writing, spelling, memory and sound skills. A report will then recommend what areas she needs help in, and whether she needs extra time in exams.

If you feel you are not getting the help she needs from the school, you can ask the local education authority for an assessment by an educational psychologist, and they must give you a decision within six weeks. If they turn you down, you have the right to appeal to an independent Special Educational Needs Tribunal.

Alternatively, you can pay out several hundred pounds for a private assessment, which you will get more promptly, although you need to be aware that the findings and recommendations of these aren't invariably recognised by schools. You can find these by contacting a national dyslexia organisation.

One of the most useful things about getting a diagnosis is that you can explain to your child that it is not her fault she can't spell, or remember things – children with these difficulties all too quickly come to believe they are 'thick'. Tell her that it is a biological difference – her brain is simply wired a little differently than other people's – and that this doesn't say anything at all about her abilities. Many famous high-achievers – Albert Einstein, Winston Churchill – have been dyslexic. Tell her that dyslexia can go hand in hand with exceptional skills in other areas such as creative, visual and spatial thinking. Many top architects, for example, are dyslexic and struggle to explain their visions in words. Tell her, too, that although the kind of reading, writing and memory tasks she finds difficult can seem to matter a lot in school, in her adult life they will only play a very small part of all the different things she'll do.

There is endless information about dyslexia available in books and on the Internet. Clue yourself up on what it is, how it manifests itself and how it can be treated. You may be happy with what the school is offering. Or you may want to look into getting additional help. If so, use the national charities to find a tutor who is properly trained to work with dyslexic children, and then work closely with that tutor over anything you can do at home. Mainstream dyslexia teaching uses well-tried strategies to work on children's weaknesses. Good teaching will always try and use all a child's senses, and there are also worthwhile programmes available on CD-Rom.

There are also alternative therapies available, which use lights and computers, or physical exercises to stimulate the brain. Some names you might come across are BrightStar or DDAT.

Obviously, you need to approach with caution anything that trumpets 'a cure' for dyslexia, especially if it's taking lots of money off you in the process, but view them with an open mind. There is growing evidence that they can greatly help some dyslexic children. To weigh up a therapy ask the following questions:

- How long has it been going?
- How does it work?
- What is the research evidence that it works?
- What kinds of diffculty does it address?
- How will it work with my child's difficulties?
- What are the side effects?
- How will the effect on my child be measured?
- Will there be follow-ups?
- How long does it take and what does it cost?

Bear in mind, too, that everything that is going on in a child's life will affect how her brain works. If she is very stressed, or getting a poor diet, she will not be able to think and focus properly. Making sure that your dyslexic child feels secure and loved is common sense, as is making sure she is not eating too much junk, getting a wide variety of fresh food and whole grains, and also getting enough of the omega-3 and omega-6 acids needed for brain function (see Chapter 10).

Stay positive, be assured there are many ways forward and, whatever you do, don't allow either your child or yourself to fall into the habit of using dyslexia as an excuse for anything she finds hard or can't be bothered to do.

British Dyslexia Organisation: 0118 966 2677; www.bda-dyslexia.org.uk.

Dyslexia Institute: 01784 222300; www.dyslexia-inst.org.uk.

Eating disorders: Cases of anorexia, bulimia and binge eating are all on the increase and the age of girls – 90 per cent of cases are girls – appears to be dropping. Four or five out of every 100,000 young women in the UK are affected with anorexia, where severe weight loss can lead to hospitalisation and even death. About 2 per cent of young women have bulimia, where enforced vomiting can damage kidneys. If your child is coming up to her teens, know that she will be well aware of these problems – from friends, magazines, television – and take seriously any dramatic weight loss, ruses to avoid eating, mood swings or obsessions with calories, diets and exercise. Girls sometimes vie to be the 'most anorexic'. So watch out for times of stress, like exams, and also for hothouse female environments like single-sex schools or girls' boarding houses.

Eating Disorders Association: adult helpline 0845 634 1414 (youth helpline 0845 634 7650); www.edauk.com.

National Centre for Eating Disorders: 01372 469493; www.eating-disorders.org.uk.

Exclusion from school: Schools have the right to exclude pupils for fixed-term periods – up to a maximum of forty-five days a year – or permanently. Around 10,000 pupils are excluded in England a year. It is possible for a pupil to be permanently excluded for one very serious offence, such as violence against a teacher or pupil, or supplying illegal drugs, but more commonly, exclusion comes at the end of a string of other in-school sanctions, and support mechanisms, all of which have, in the school's view, failed to work. Pupils cannot be excluded for minor offences, poor academic performance, issues of appearance (unless very serious), pregnancy or to punish parents for their behaviour. If your child is excluded, the school must send you a letter setting out full details, including your right to appeal, and where you can get help with this. An appeal is made to the disciplinary committee – a sub-committee of the school's governing body. If it upholds the exclusion, you have a right to appeal to an independent appeal panel. If you feel your child is being discriminated against because of special educational needs or a disability, you have the right to go to the Special Educational Needs and Disability Tribunal.

The charity, the Advisory Centre for Education, advises on parents' legal rights in respect to education. It runs an exclusion helpline, and has an information pack for parents of excluded children: 020 7704 9822; www.ace-ed.org.uk.

Giftedness: Some children are exceptionally bright, or have other gifts and talents beyond their years. Schools are supposed to identify their gifted and talented children and give them work that stretches and challenges them. But it often doesn't happen. Also, because this is a fuzzy area, parents and schools don't always agree on what constitutes gifted. And some parents think their children are geniuses in spite of opposing evidence! But if gifted children don't have their needs met they risk being bullied or becoming bored. They might start to play up – or play dumb. If you think your child is gifted you can do the online questionnaire of the National Association for Gifted Children, which covers things like your child's level of questioning, her capacity for abstract thinking and her imagination. And you may need to be persistent in talking to her school in order to get them to acknowledge her needs and give her appropriate work to do.

The National Association for Gifted Children supports children and families in this area: www.nagcbritain.org.uk.

Head lice: No matter how often you read that head lice prefer shiny, clean hair, the first time your child gets them you will probably feel alarmed and disgusted. Forget it. Practically every child gets 'nits' at some point, and some unlucky children seem to get them all the time. Your job is to get proficient at dealing with it. The signs are usually your child scratching her head, or dandruff-life, pale specks sticking to hairs. Or a letter home from school will alert you to a case of lice in the class, and urge you to check your child's hair. Adult lice are smaller than a match-head and often hard to see. They stick their egg cases ('nits') to individual hair shafts, but these are often shiny and well camouflaged until empty. Even so, detecting lice in fair-haired children can be like looking for needles in haystacks. To check for lice, wash your child's hair and condition it well, then comb it carefully through with a fine toothcomb, checking the comb after each stroke. If you want to treat the infestation with chemicals, buy special lotion from the chemist, follow the instructions carefully, and be aware that there might be problems with asthma and allergies. Alternative methods include battery-operated nit combs, a 'bug-busting' routine of diligent washing and combing out the lice before they get mature enough to lay eggs, and a raft of alternative remedies such as tea tree oil. Don't feel you have to wash bedding and clothes – the Department of Health says lice that drop off the head are at the end of their natural life anyway. Do wash and comb your child's hair weekly, with lots of conditioner to make it slippery and easier to check for lice, and tell the school, and your friends with children, when you have lice in the house.

For more information: Lice Advisory Bureau: 020 7617 0817 www.headliceadvice.net.

Department of Health: www.dh.gov.uk/.

Bug Buster helpline 020 7686 4321; www.chc.org/bugbusting.

Hospitalisation: If your child cannot go to school for a significant amount of time because of illness or injury, she has a right to education provided by your local education authority. This may mean attending a school in hospital, or having a home tutor, but whatever the provision, the aim is to make sure her schooling is disrupted as little as possible, and the standard of education she is offered must meet government guidelines. If your child is going to be off school for more than three weeks, talk to the school about what alternative provision can be put in place. And keep talking, while your child is away. Let the school have news of how she is doing, pass on messages to classmates and ask her teacher if there is any work she can do at home. Both social and educational contact is invaluable to a child who can't go to school. Also, make sure her classmates know what is the matter with her, and how you want them to treat her when she returns. Children need, for example, to be prepared for the baldness of chemotherapy, or to understand if they need to be careful about not banging into a broken leg.

Department for Education and Skills: www.dfes.gov.uk/sickchildren.

Left-handedness: Unlike in some other countries, left-handers are almost invariably allowed by schools to do their own thing and not forced to write with their right hand. But your child might have problems with clumsiness, smudging and difficulty with things like tying shoelaces. Tell the class teacher about these, and make life easier for her with shoes with velcro fastenings, and left-handed scissors. Tips to help with writing include: holding the pen further from the tip so you can see the writing; using smudge-free biros or felt-tips; and slanting paper at a comfortable angle.

Anything Left-handed: 020 8770 3722; www.anythingleft-handed.com.

Lying and stealing: Younger children often lie, or take things, without fully realising what they are doing, but by eight or nine, children have fairly clear notions of truth and ownership. This does not seem to stop a lot of them from doing wrong – one-in-four children aged eleven to sixteen admitted committing a crime in the last year when questioned for a survey by the Youth Justice Board. In a world where temptations are huge, and the boundaries getting fuzzier – Is downloading music from the Internet or copying homework stealing? – parents need to make very clear to their children what they believe to be wrong, and why. Stealing and lying must be taken seriously. Explain to your child that no one will be able to trust them if they behave like this. If a lie or theft has involved someone or something at school, help your child to put it right, and consider punishments like earlier bedtime, or a week without pocket money. If your child is accused of stealing or lying, listen to her side of the story before taking any action. Persistent stealing or lying could indicate a hidden problem. Is your child seeking attention, having problems with her friendships, feeling angry about something or needing to show bravado? Try and get to the bottom of things – talking to her teacher, if need be.

Parentline Plus: 0808 800 2222; www.parentlineplus.org.uk.

Parents Education and Support Forum: 020 7284 8370; www.parenting-forum.org.uk.

National Family and Parenting Institute: 020 7424 3460; www.nfpi.org.

Major medical problems: If your child has a serious medical problem – asthma, migraine, eczema, epilepsy and diabetes are common ones – reassure her that there are many children in school who have to take medicines, or who are different in some way. Get in touch with the relevant support charity and follow their guidelines about liaising with the school. Ensure that arrangements for taking any essential medications in school hours are properly in place, or that your child is completely confident about when and how to medicate herself. Schools should have policies for supporting children with medical problems in place under their health and safety procedures, but it is a parent's duty, not a teacher's, to ensure medicines are taken properly. A teacher may volunteer to supervise this during the school day, but teaching unions advise their members against doing this unless they have proper training. Make very sure that all teachers are aware of her condition, and be persistent – even to the point of making yourself a nuisance – if you feel they are not getting the message and treating her appropriately. Offer to come in and give a short talk on the condition, if you feel there's a serious block, or get hold of an explanatory leaflet and circulate it to teachers and governors. If there is ever an incident where your child has felt excluded, humiliated, frightened or wrongly chastised because of her condition, take it up with the school immediately, remembering to be firm rather than aggressive, and being clear about how you want your child's condition to be dealt with.

School phobia: This is the term used when a child persistently refuses to go to school, usually citing vague symptoms like tummy aches, headaches, sickness, sore throats or dizziness. There may be a single reason behind it – bullying, or dread of some classroom activity – but it could have roots both at home and at school. Children with school phobia tend to be anxious about leaving home, and also lack self-confidence in the school setting. Talk to your child gently to probe her feelings, and try to arrange for her to spend more time playing out-of-school with her friends and classmates. Tell the school what is going on, but don't let her stay off school. Mornings may be hard, and you may feel cruel, but the best cure for school phobia is being in school. If problems persist, talk to the school, or your doctor, about her seeing an educational psychologist or counsellor.

Young Minds: 020 7336 8446; www.youngminds.org.uk.

School safety: Fewer accidents happen to children at school than at home, but parents often worry about safety at school, and on school trips. Nothing is without risks, and accidents do happen, but most schools are extremely conscientious about health and safety issues. National guidelines for running school trips have recently been updated, although some people believe there is still room for improvement. Another issue is safety on the school bus to and from school. There are calls to abolish the outdated regulation that allows three children to share two seats. Never hesitate to quiz your school on anything that is worrying you, and if something has happened that bothers you, report it to the head.

Royal Society for the Prevention of Accidents: 0121 248 2000; www.rospa.org.uk.

Department of Education: www.teachernet.gov.uk.
Safe Routes to Schools: www.saferoutestoschools.org.uk.

Self-harm: If you have any worries that your child might be hurting herself, take them seriously. Increasing numbers of school children are harming themselves, mostly by cutting, and sometimes by taking overdoses, and although this happens most commonly among teens, younger children are also at risk. Signs might be unexplained scars or wearing long-sleeved clothes even in hot weather. Figures from the Office of National Statistics show one-in-seventy-five under-tens self-harm, and hospitals report seeing children as young as six. Sufferers describe how they do it to release tension. Psychologists talk about the need for control in situations children don't feel they can control, and also the desire to make internal pain visible. Self-harm is often associated with family problems, anxiety and attention disorders, but health workers have also noted how there can sometimes be a 'fashion' for it in a school. See your GP if you think your child has a problem, so she can be referred for specialist help.

National Self-harm Network: www.nshn.co.uk.

Self-harm Alliance: 01242 578820; www.selfharmalliance.org.

Young People and Self-harm: www.selffharm.org.uk.

Skin problems: There are various skin conditions that children catch all too readily at school. Impetigo is a bacterial infection, which causes crusty red, spreading sores, usually around the mouth, although also elsewhere. It needs to be treated with antibiotics. Ringworm is not a worm, but a fungus infection, which usually shows itself as a raised red ridge, often in the armpit or groin. Treatment might be a lotion or oral medicine. Scabies is a mite that burrows under the skin and causes intense itching, often in the various folds of the body, or under watchstraps and bracelets, and is treated with creams.

Then there are other infectious and contagious diseases, which manifest themselves in skin problems. Slap cheek presents with a red rash on the cheeks – but only a week or so after the flu-like infectious stage is over. *Molluscum contagiosum* is a viral infection, which shows up as itchy, white, pearl-like bumps on the body, legs and arms, and is caught from other infected children.

Go to the doctor for all of these conditions – don't be embarrassed, they aren't caused by 'dirty' children – and be sure to tell the school so they can warn other parents to be on the watch. Conditions like these need stamping out, or they can go round and round.

For information on all of these: National Health Service Direct: 0845 4647; www.nhsdirect.nhs.uk.

Stress: It used to be thought that young children didn't show the same sort of mental health problems as adults, but now we know this is untrue. According to Young Minds, the children's mental health charity, as many as one-in-ten young people from five to fifteen are suffering from some sort of behavioural, emotional or hyperactivity disorder at any one time, and this might go as high as one-in-five, if less severe problems are included. Primary teachers are quite clear that many children in school are stressed by test pressures, and sometimes social pressures, such as the disruptive behaviour of wayward classmates.

Stress might show itself in depression, anxiety or more specific conditions such as obsessive compulsive disorder, where routines like hand-washing might be repeated many times. Problems tend to arise from a mixture of genetic predisposition coupled with other factors in a child's life – family break-up, or problems with friends or schoolwork.

If your child is generally ratty, shows unusual aggression, or changes in eating and sleeping, these might be signs of stress. Watch her carefully, talk and listen, and take any pressure off. This might mean making home a calmer, quieter place, cutting down on activities to give her time to 'veg out', and not putting the screws on over school-work. Make sure she eats a good diet and gets plenty of exercise. If there are upheavals going on in the family, don't shut her out of what's happening. Talk and listen to her about anything that's bothering her, and help her work her way towards her own solutions to problems.

Problems that persist for weeks, and that stop a child living her life to the full, need professional help. Your GP should be able to refer you to your local child and adolescent mental health service, which is staffed by specialist psychiatrists, psychologists, psychotherapists and social workers. Treatment may include cognitive therapy, which helps people think differently about their problems, and anti-depressant medication.

Young Minds: 020 7336 8445; www.youngminds.org.uk.

Truancy: Everyday about 50,000 UK children are missing from school, and 7.5 million days a year are missed due to unauthorised absences. Persistent truanting tends to be a teenage problem, and is often associated with other problems – crime, low school achievement, smoking, drinking and drugs – but any child can be tempted to join with friends in the risky delights of bunking off school. To minimise the temptation, make sure that from the outset you tell your child that school is a must. Don't allow days at home for vague 'tummy aches', and avoid being late in the morning – the message a child picks up from this is that school doesn't really matter. Above all, don't be tempted to keep your child off school for birthdays, shopping or for looking after someone at home. And only take a family holiday in term-time if there are overwhelming reasons why it is impossible to take it in the holidays. Remember that, as a parent, it is your responsibility to ensure your child attends school regularly and that new, tough anti-truancy laws mean you can face a fine of up to £2,500, or even three months in jail, if your child is a persistent truant. The government is also toying with the idea of on-the-spot fines of up to £100 for parents found out with their children on a school day. If your child does truant, talk to her about why. And work positively with the school, and with any education welfare staff it calls in, to see how the problem can be resolved.

Department of Education and Skills: www.dfes.gov.uk/behaviourandattendance.

Parentline Plus: 0808 800 2222; www.parentlineplus.org.uk.

Worms: These come several rungs above headlice in the 'ugh' stakes, but more than half of all children get thread-worms at least once, so most parents have to deal with them at some point. Warning signs are your child wriggling around a lot and having an itchy bottom. Sometimes you can see them, like little white cotton threads, around your child's anus at night when they come out to lay their eggs. Treatment is a pill, from the chemist, but be aware that everyone in the family needs to take one at the same time. You'll also need to wash all flannels and towels since worms are very contagious.

For information: National Health Service Direct: 0845 4647; www.nhsdirect.nhs.uk.

Further reading and useful websites

Further reading

Bean, Anita. *Kids' Food for Fitness*, A&C Black, 2002 – readable and sensible nutrition advice for children.

Biddulph, Steve. *Raising Boys*, Thorsons, 2003 – an international bestseller about rearing boys into happy and well-balanced men.

Biddulph, Steve. *The Secret of Happy Children*, Thorsons, 1998 – accessible bestseller about bringing up children well.

Bray, Wendy. *The Parentalk Guide to Primary School*, Hodder & Stoughton, 2003 – nuts and bolts parents' guide to primary school.

Buzan, Tony. *Mind Maps for Kids: The shortcut to success at school*, Thorsons – how to make the most of these, by the man who invented them.

Dryden, Gordon & Vos, Dr Jeannette. *The Learning Revolution*, Network Educational Press Ltd, 2001 – a mine of information about how our brains work and how we learn.

Figes, Kate. *The Terrible Teens. What every parent needs to know*, Penguin Books, 2002 – get prepared for adolescence!

Holford, Patrick. *Optimum Nutrition for the Mind*, Piatkus, 2003 – everything you need to know about what foods and drinks help to feed your child's mind.

Hunt, Candida, in consultation with Mountford, Annette. *The Parenting Puzzle: How to get the best out of family life*, Family Links, 2003 – worksheet-style manual on key issues such as discipline, family rules, self-esteem and communicating.

Levine, Dr Mel. *A Mind At A Time: How every child can succeed*, Simon & Schuster UK, 2003 – a heartening read about every child's individuality for any parents of a child with learning difficulties.

Liebeck, Pamela. *How Children Learn Mathematics: A guide for parents and teachers*, Penguin, 1990 – a useful maths primer.

Lucas, Bill & Smith, Alistair. *Help Your Child to Succeed: The essential guide for parents*, Network Educational Press Ltd, 2002 – terrific, short, user-friendly guide to helping your child learn and do well.

Neill-Hall, Juliet. *How to Help Your Child Succeed at School*, Hodder and Stoughton, 2003 – a teacher's explanation of how parents can develop primary skills.

Robb, Jean & Letts, Hilary. *Creating Kids Who Can*, Hodder & Stoughton, 2002 – a series of great, hands-on strategies for children of all kinds.

Robb, Jean & Letts, Hilary. *Creating Kids Who Can Concentrate*, Hodder & Stoughton, 2002 – for beating problems of attention and hyperactivity without drugs.

Robb, Jean & Letts, Hilary. *Creating Kids Who Can Pass Exams*, Hodder & Stoughton, 2002 – practical techniques for helping children succeed.

Robb, Jean & Letts, Hilary. *Creating Motivated Kids*, Hodder & Stoughton, 2003 – how to help children unlock their full potential.

Stanway, Dr Penny. *Good Food for Kids*, Hamlyn, 2000 – a mother and doctor's advice on a healthy diet for young children.

Winkley, David. *Handsworth Revolution: The odyssey of a school*, Giles de la Mare Publishers Ltd, 2002 – a great portrait of a primary school, plus thoughts on what a good education is all about.

Wiseman, Rosalind. *Queen Bees & Wannabes: Helping your daughter survive cliques, gossip, boyfriends and other realities of adolescence*, Piatkus, 2002 – an eye-opening account of the world of adolescent girls, and how parents can best guide and help them.

Useful websites

Advisory Centre for Education: www.ace-ed.org.uk – independent advice and support for children in state schools

Bullying Online: www.bullying.co.uk – help for all problems of bullying

Campaign for Learning: www.campaign-for-learning.org.uk – information about how we learn and learning opportunities

Childalert: www.childalert.co.uk – for child safety and well-being

Department of Education in Northern Ireland: www.deni.gov.uk – information on education in Northern Ireland

Education Otherwise: www.education-otherwise.org – help and advice about home schooling

Some homework websites:
www.bbc.co.uk/education/revision
www.homeworkhigh.co.uk
ww.homeworkelephant.co.uk

National Assembly for Wales: www.learning.wales.gov.uk – information on education in Wales

National Association of Gifted Children: www.nagcbritain.org.uk – support for families with gifted children

National Confederation of Parent Teacher Association:

www.ncpta.org.uk – for information and queries about school PTAs

National Governors' Council: www.ngc.org.uk – supports school governing bodies

OFSTED (Office for Standards in Education): www.ofsted.gov.uk – for school inspection reports and other school information

Parent Centre: www.parentcentre.gov.uk – school and curriculum information from the Department for Education and Skills

Parentalk: www.parentalk.co.uk – resources for parents

Parenting Education and Support Forum: www.parentingforum.org – support for parents, and their importance in child development

Parentline Plus: www.parentlineplus.org.uk – support for parents and parenting information

Parents Information Network (PIN): www.pin-parents.com – advice for parents about children and computers and the Internet

Scottish Executive Education Department: www.scotland.gov.uk – information on education in Scotland

Young Minds: www.youngminds.org.uk – help with children's mental health

Index

Optimum Nutrition for Babies and Young Children
Lucy Burney

Healthy children need healthy food. If you want to give your child the best possible start in life, good nourishment is vital. Top nutritionist Lucy Burney shows how easy it is to make quick, delicious, nutrient-rich meals that all your family will love.

- Includes over 150 tempting recipe ideas to ensure that your children grow strong, fit and bursting with health.
- Packed with important nutritional advice, including reassuring guidelines on breastfeeding and weaning, delicious meal plans for ultimate health, easy alternatives to processed foods
- Includes important information on allergies – and how to avoid them.

Lucy Burney is a qualified Nutrition Consultant who trained at the Institute for Optimum Nutrition, where she continues to practise as a third year tutor. She works at the Sayer clinic in Marble Arch and at the world-famous Hale Clinic as well as running her own busy practice in Wandsworth, South London and she writes a regular column for *Natural Parent* magazine.

ISBN: 0 7499 2028 9
Price: £10.99

Queen Bees and Wannabees
Rosalind Wiseman

The 'Gentler Sex'? Not so, according to Rosalind Wiseman. Girls can be cruel. In this compelling book, Rosalind Wiseman cracks the 'girl code' and explains how girls' friendships are the key to enduring adolescence – as well as the biggest threat to their happiness and well-being. She has spent a decade listening to girls talk about the powerful impact that girl cliques have on what they wear, how they respond to boys and how they feel about themselves.

- Understand the secret world of cliques
- Infiltrate 'Girl World' to analyse teasing and gossip; boys and sex; alcohol and drugs and more
- Help your daughter to take control of her situation – using the book's sample scripts, bulleted lists and easy to use advice.

Written in a down-to-earth style and packed with examples and tips, *Queen Bees and Wannabes* is an invaluable guide for parents to empower their daughters and themselves.

Rosalind Wiseman is a cofounder of the Empower Program, a non-profit organisation that works to empower adolescent girls and boys and stop violence. She is an adviser to Liz Claiborne's Women's Work program and has been featured on *The Oprah Winfrey Show* and CNN, and in publications such as *USA Today* and the *Washington Post*. She lives in Washington, D.C.

ISBN: 0 7499 2437 3
Price: £7.99

All Piatkus titles are available from:

Piatkus Books, c/o Bookpost, PO Box 29,
Douglas, Isle Of Man, IM99 1BQ

Telephone (+44) 01624 677237
Fax (+44) 01624 670923
Email; bookshop@enterprise.net
Free Postage and Packing in the United Kingdom
Credit Cards accepted. All Cheques payable to Bookpost

Prices and availability subject to change without prior notice.
Allow 14 days for delivery. When placing orders please state
if you do not wish to receive any additional information.